The McDonaldization of Society
Ninth Edition

With love to the newest member of the family, Mandela, and to his big sister, Marley, and his big brother, Bodhi.

The McDonaldization of Society

Into the Digital Age

Ninth Edition

George Ritzer

University of Maryland

Los Angeles | London | New Delhi
Singapore | Washington DC | Melbourne

FOR INFORMATION:

SAGE Publications, Inc.
2455 Teller Road
Thousand Oaks, California 91320
E-mail: order@sagepub.com

SAGE Publications Ltd.
1 Oliver's Yard
55 City Road
London, EC1Y 1SP
United Kingdom

SAGE Publications India Pvt. Ltd.
B 1/I 1 Mohan Cooperative Industrial Area
Mathura Road, New Delhi 110 044
India

SAGE Publications Asia-Pacific Pte. Ltd.
3 Church Street
#10-04 Samsung Hub
Singapore 049483

Printed in the United States of America

Library of Congress Cataloging-in-Publication Data

Names: Ritzer, George, author.

Title: The McDonaldization of society / George Ritzer, University of Maryland.

Description: Ninth edition. | Thousand Oaks, California : SAGE, [2019] | Includes bibliographical references and index.

Identifiers: LCCN 2017040207 | ISBN 9781506348551 (pbk. : alk. paper)

Subjects: LCSH: Social structure. | Social structure—United States. | United States—Social conditions—1980- | Management—Social aspects—United States. | Fast food restaurants—Social aspects—United States. | Rationalization (Psychology)

Classification: LCC HM706 .R58 2019 | DDC 306.0973/09048—dc23 LC record available at https://lccn.loc.gov/2017040207

This book is printed on acid-free paper.

MIX
Paper from responsible sources
FSC® C014174

Acquisitions Editor: Jeff Lasser
Editorial Assistant: Adeline Wilson
Marketing Manager: Jennifer Jones
Production Editor: Veronica Stapleton Hooper
Copy Editor: Gretchen Treadwell
Typesetter: Hurix Digital
Proofreader: Sally Jaskold
Indexer: Maria Sosnowski
Cover Designer: Janet Kiesel

18 19 20 21 22 10 9 8 7 6 5 4 3 2 1

BRIEF CONTENTS

DETAILED CONTENTS

Chapter 5 • Efficiency and Calculability: McJobs and Other McDonaldized Occupations 1

Chapter 6 • Predictability and Control: McJobs and Other McDonaldized Occupations 2

PREFACE

This ninth edition of *The McDonaldization of Society* is in many ways the most important and dramatic of all the revisions. While the process of McDonaldization is, if anything, stronger than ever, its center has shifted dramatically over the last several decades. That new reality is accorded a significant place in this analysis. For that reason—and others—a substantial reorientation of this book is needed.

From its inception in the early 1950s, and for several decades beyond that, the heart of the McDonaldization process lay in brick-and-mortar structures devoted to consumption (most notably, of course, the fast-food restaurant). However, its center has increasingly moved to the digital world, especially its consumption sites (most importantly, Amazon.com). While for the foreseeable future the vast majority of consumption will continue to take place in brick-and-mortar structures, an ever-increasing amount of it will occur online. However, there are limits to the online expansion of consumption. For example, we are a long way from being able to download hamburgers or pizza from the Internet.

While there are limits to consumption on the Internet, there is no limit to the McDonaldization of consumption—and virtually everything else—online. The digital nature of sites on the Internet has made it far easier to McDonaldize them than those in the brick-and-mortar world.

My first essay on McDonaldization appeared in 1983,[1] while the first edition of this book was published almost a decade later in 1992. The Internet was of little public importance in the decade or so between those two publications. The worldwide web accessible to the general public did not come into existence until late 1991. My original work on McDonaldization was done in the era of the hegemony of brick-and-mortar structures. While the vast majority of consumption continues to take place there, the height of McDonaldization is now to be found online.

However, it is important to note that a clear distinction between brick-and-mortar and digital sites, if it ever existed, is now eroding rapidly as they increasingly *augment* one another in a wide variety of ways. For example, the largely digital Amazon has recently purchased the Whole Foods chain of supermarkets and it has opened its own brick-and-mortar bookstores and convenience stores.

For its part, the mainly brick-and-mortar Wal-Mart is striving to become a more powerful force online. The digital world is important both on its own, as well as in the ways in which it interpenetrates with the material world. In other words, we now live in a world increasingly dominated by "bricks-and-clicks" (or, "atoms-and-bits").

As we move increasingly into the digital age, it is tempting to consider discarding the concept of McDonaldization because it has its roots, and is still so clearly embedded, in the brick-and-mortar world. However, the fact is that, as will be demonstrated throughout this book, the concept applies at least as well to the digital world. Arguably Amazon.com—as well as most other largely online sites—is far *more* McDonaldized than McDonald's itself. There is an even better fit between the concept of McDonaldization and the "bricks-and-clicks" world.

Take, for example, one of the key dimensions of McDonaldization, calculability, or an emphasis on that which can be quantified. While McDonald's clearly focuses on calculability in many ways (Big Macs, billions sold, value meals, etc.), it has clearly been outdone in emphasizing that which can be quantified by Internet sites (e.g., Amazon's many ratings and rankings), especially in their ability to collect and utilize "big data." We can be said to be living at the dawn of the era of "datafication"—the transformation of more and more information of all kinds into quantifiable data. More specifically and focusing on self-tracking devices such as Fitbit and Jawbone Up, Deborah Lupton argues that we have even been able to quantify the seemingly subjective self.[2] There is even a website—quantifiedself.com—whose motto is "self-knowledge through numbers." While brick-and-mortar businesses like McDonald's have also moved into the world of big data in many different ways, such data are not as central to it as they are in the largely digital world. In other words, big data plays a far bigger role in the functioning of Amazon.com (and much more of it is collected and accumulated there) than it does in McDonald's operations.

Big data is even more important to Amazon's new book shops, which are shaped by the big data from its website. In addition, the book shops are collecting data of their own that will augment, and improve, the online data.

While many other examples of the explosion of McDonaldization on the Internet (and in the integrated world of bricks-and-clicks) will be presented throughout this edition, one more example is offered here. From the beginning, I have argued that one of the reasons for McDonald's success, especially its far greater efficiency than its predecessors in the restaurant business, is in "putting its customers" to work in many different ways (serving as, in effect, their own waiters, bus persons, and disposers of trash). This idea has informed much of my work for the last decade on the "prosumer," or one who more or less simultaneously produces and consumes.[3] Clearly, McDonald's customers are prosumers, more specifically "working consumers," because they *both* produce and consume in the course of a visit to McDonald's.

In comparison to brick-and-mortar settings, the ability of digital settings to turn consumers into prosumers is almost unlimited. In most cases it is almost impossible *not* to be a prosumer in the digital world. While technology does a great deal of the online work for the prosumer, it is difficult, if not impossible, to get any help from human employees online. They are largely nonexistent or they have been purposely made difficult, if not impossible, to contact. As a result, consumers are largely on their own on the Internet to prosume—to "produce" that which they are interested in consuming. While this might well be seen as inefficient from the perspective of the consumer, it is highly efficient from the point of view of online sites, which are able to greatly reduce the number of paid employees and increase profits, as well as capital, for shareholders. After all, much of the work is done by unpaid prosumers rather than paid employees. Among other things, this means that these sites can do much more (e.g., sell more of virtually everything on Amazon.com) with far fewer paid employees. Amazon.com does far more business than McDonald's, but it does so with fewer employees. Wal-Mart, while still a largely brick-and-mortar business, dwarfs even Amazon in the amount of business done, but to do so it employs an infinitely greater number of workers.

It should already be clear from this that the "McDonaldization thesis,"[4] while still alive and well, needs to be updated in order to take into account the new realities of the digital world, as well as those that involve the augmentation of the brick-and-mortar and the digital in bricks-and-clicks.

Beyond a reorientation of the book in the direction described here, a number of other major changes have been made in order to return to its original focus, in part by shortening it significantly. As a result, most of the last two chapters of the previous edition have been jettisoned. While Chapter 8 of the previous edition dealt with ways of dealing with McDonaldization, there is only a brief discussion of that topic in this edition at the end of Chapter 7, which deals with the irrationality of rationality. One reason for this is that it is the irrationalities of McDonaldization that people and organizations most often seek to deal with.

More important, much of the material in Chapter 8 of the last edition now seems dated. For example, one hears little these days of the organizations dealt with in that context—bed-and-breakfasts (B&Bs), McLibel, Slow Food, Sprawl Busters, the movement for $15 an hour minimum wage, and so forth. One distressing conclusion is that they, like much else, have been overwhelmed by the increasing acceptance and pervasiveness of McDonaldization. As a result, the discussion of individual coping mechanisms has also been excised, largely because more and more people seem to embrace McDonaldization: to view it as a "velvet cage" rather than an "iron cage." Those in opposition to it are either smaller in number or less vociferous in their criticisms.

Much of the material in the last edition's Chapter 9 has also been cut. Some of that dealt with globalization in general, as well as my work on the globalization of nothing.[5] While McDonaldization is a globalizing process, and a prime example of the globalization of nothing, much of the discussion of globalization now seems to distract from the book's main theses (although McDonaldization is increasingly a global phenomenon). However, the concept of "nothing"—that which is centrally conceived, controlled, and lacking in distinctive content—will be deployed in Chapter 7 to help us better understand McDonaldized systems. Similarly distracting is the lengthy discussion of Starbuckization if for no other reason than the conclusion that it is but a variant on McDonaldization. Finally, rather than being relegated to an afterthought at the end of the final chapter of the last edition, the discussion of the Internet has not only been greatly expanded, but it has been built into the fabric of the book itself.

This edition will end up being much shorter than the previous edition. This will help sharpen its argument and message. It also will make it more useable for its primary purpose as a secondary reading in a wide range of courses in sociology, as well as in the many other disciplines in which the book is used.

I would like to thank Professor Samuel M. Claster, Edinboro University of Pennsylvania, for his insightful review of an earlier draft of this edition of the book. In addition, many thanks to many other reviewers (see below), as well as the people at SAGE Publications, especially my editor Jeff Lasser. Jeff has been there for me and for this book, as well as for all the other books that I have written for SAGE in recent years. He is a savvy publisher and more importantly a sweet and gentle person. As a result, he is a joy to work with. In the background is the vice president of SAGE, Michele Sordi. While I don't often have the need to ask for it, it is nice to know that her help and support are there whenever I might need it.

PUBLISHER'S ACKNOWLEDGMENTS

SAGE wishes to acknowledge the valuable contributions of the following reviewers.

Tennille Allen
Lewis University

Kristina Morris Baumli
University of the Arts

Jeremy L. Brunson
University of Northern Colorado

Patricia Campion
Saint Leo University

Samuel Claster
Edinboro University of Pennsylvania

Kerry Danner
Georgetown University

Alexa Dare
University of Portland

Rollie E. Dorsett
Austin Community College

Geoff Harkness
Morningside College

Jacqueline Olvera
Adelphi University

Ryan Orr
Millersville University

Michelle Oyakawa
The Ohio State University

Richard Stroiney
University of Hartford

Susan L. Wortmann
Nebraska Wesleyan University

INTRODUCTION

M cDonald's and Ray Kroc (1902–1984), the person most associated with it, were the subjects of the 2016 motion picture *The Founder*. However, Kroc was *not* the founder of McDonald's. Nor was he the source of the early innovations that were the basis of that restaurant chain's phenomenal success. Rather, it was the McDonald brothers—Richard and Maurice—who were the true founders of McDonald's in 1937 and its real innovators. Kroc *was* the ruthless force behind the franchising of McDonald's restaurants and the eventual creation of what is now a globe-straddling chain of tens of thousands of restaurants. But even Kroc could not have anticipated that McDonald's would become the basis of one of the most influential developments in contemporary society. Its reverberations extend far beyond its point of origin both in the United States and in the fast-food business. It has influenced a wide range of businesses and many other types of organizations. Most generally, it is a global force affecting the way of life of a significant portion of the world.[1] That impact continues and is likely to expand throughout the 21st century.[2] *

This chapter begins with a discussion of McDonaldization, the concept and process that defines this book. After summarizing the basic principles that lie at the base of McDonaldization, its advantages and disadvantages (its "irrationalities") are analyzed. We then turn to a discussion of McDonald's itself and its relationship to other "brick-and-mortar" consumption sites. The chapter concludes with a discussion of the broader influence (the "long arm") of McDonald's and the degree to which it has become a global cultural icon.

McDonald's has center stage in this analysis, at least initially, *because it is the major example of, and the paradigm for, the wide-ranging process of McDonaldization.*[3] Most of this chapter as well as of this book is about that process, as well as the many phenomena affected by it.

---

*Notes may be found at the back of the book, beginning on page 203.

1

McDonaldization is the process by which the principles of the fast-food restaurant are coming to dominate more and more sectors of American society as well as of the rest of the world.[4]

McDONALDIZATION: THE BASIC PRINCIPLES

Why has McDonald's proven to be so successful and powerful? Eating fast food at McDonald's has certainly become a "sign"[5] for many that, among other things, they are in tune with the contemporary lifestyle. There is also a kind of magic or enchantment associated with such food and its settings. The focus here is on the four principles—*efficiency, calculability, predictability,* and *control*[6]—that lie at the heart of the success of McDonald's and, more generally, of all McDonaldized systems. In short, McDonald's and other McDonaldized systems have succeeded because they offer consumers, workers, and managers the advantages of, and associated with, these principles. Chapters 3 through 6 will be devoted to these dimensions of McDonaldization, but they need to be introduced at this point.

Efficiency

One important element in the success of McDonaldized systems is their *efficiency*, or finding and using the optimum method for getting from one point to another.[7] For consumers, McDonald's (its drive-through is a particularly good example) offers the best available way to get from being hungry to being full. The fast-food model offers, or at least appears to offer, an efficient method for satisfying many other needs as well. Other businesses fashioned on the McDonald's model offer similar efficiency to their consumers in, for example, exercising, losing weight, lubricating cars, getting new glasses or contacts, completing income tax forms, making an online purchase, or using a ride-hailing service. Like their customers, workers in McDonaldized systems function efficiently by following the steps in a predesigned, often well-choreographed,[8] process.

Calculability

Calculability emphasizes the quantitative aspects of products sold (portion size, price) and services offered (the time it takes to get the product). In McDonaldized systems, quantity has become equivalent to quality; a lot of something, or the quick delivery of it, means it must be good. "As a culture, we tend to believe deeply that in general 'bigger is better.'"[9] People can quantify things and feel that they are getting a lot of food for what appears to be a nominal sum of money. This is best exemplified by the McDonald's "Dollar Menu"[10] and more recently by the $2 "McPick" (two sandwiches for $2). In a Denny's ad, a man says, "I'm going to eat too much, but I'm never going to pay too much."[11] This calculation does not take into account an important point, however: The profitability of fast-food chains indicates that the owners, not the consumers, get the better of the deal.

Consumers also calculate how much time it will take to drive to McDonald's, be served the food, eat it, and return home; they then compare that interval to the time required to prepare food at home. They often conclude, rightly or wrongly, that a trip to the fast-food restaurant will take less time than eating at home. This sort of calculation is especially important to home delivery franchises such as Domino's and Papa John's, as well as to other chains that emphasize saving time. A notable example of time savings in another sort of chain is LensCrafters, which has promised its customers "Glasses fast, glasses in one hour." H&M (and similar clothing chains) is known for its "fast fashion."

Some McDonaldized institutions combine the emphases on time and money. Domino's has promised pizza delivery in half an hour, or the pizza is free. Pizza Hut has claimed that it will serve a personal pan pizza in five minutes, or it, too, will be free.

Workers in McDonaldized systems also emphasize the quantitative rather than the qualitative aspects of their work. Because the quality of the work is allowed to vary little, workers focus on how quickly tasks can be accomplished. In a situation analogous to that of customers, workers are expected to do a lot of work, very quickly, for low pay.

As will be discussed in Chapter 3, calculability has become infinitely more important in the era of the computerized collection of massive amounts of data ("big data") and the automated mining and analysis of that data using applied mathematics, especially sophisticated algorithms, in order to uncover hidden patterns. These data are especially important with reference to digital sites (e.g., Facebook, Amazon), many of which are highly McDonaldized. Given the escalating importance of these sites and the big data associated with them, we can be said to live in an increasingly "computational culture."[12]

Predictability

McDonald's also offers *predictability,* the assurance that products and services will be much the same over time and in all locales. Egg McMuffins in New York will be virtually identical to those in Chicago and Los Angeles. Also, those eaten next week or next year will be about the same as those eaten today. Customers take great comfort in knowing that McDonald's offers no surprises. They know that the next Egg McMuffin they eat will not be awful, but it will not be exceptionally delicious, either. The success of the McDonald's model suggests that many people have come to prefer a world in which there are few surprises. "This is strange," notes a British observer, "considering [McDonald's is] the product of a culture which honours individualism above all."[13]

The workers in McDonaldized systems also behave in predictable ways. They follow corporate rules, the dictates of their managers, and the demands of the systems with which—and in which—they work (e.g., tending to automated French fry machines). In many cases, what they do, and even what they say (they are often scripted; see Chapter 4), is highly predictable.

Control

The fourth element in the success of McDonald's, *control*,[14] is exerted over the customers who enter McDonald's. Lines, limited menus, few options, and uncomfortable seats all lead diners to do what management wishes them to do— eat quickly and leave. Furthermore, the drive-through window invites diners to leave before they eat. In the Domino's model, customers increasingly never enter in the first place as they order online and await home delivery.

Those who work in McDonaldized organizations are also controlled to a high degree, and usually more blatantly and directly than customers. They are trained to do a limited number of tasks in precisely the way they are told to do them. This control is reinforced by the technologies used and the way the organization is set up to bolster this control. Managers and inspectors make sure that workers toe the line.

This discussion leads to the need to offer an expanded definition of McDonaldization incorporating the four dimensions discussed above:

McDonaldization is the process by which the principles of the fast-food restaurant—efficiency, calculability, predictability and control—are coming to dominate more and more sectors of American society as well as of the rest of the world.

THE ADVANTAGES OF McDONALDIZATION

McDonald's and other McDonaldized systems have succeeded so phenomenally for good, solid reasons. Most generally, McDonaldized systems offer the advantages associated with their basic principles—efficiency, calculability, predictability, and control.

Many knowledgeable people, such as the economic columnist Robert Samuelson, praise effusively this system as well as McDonald's business model (copied by many). Samuelson confesses to "openly worship[ing] McDonald's," and he thinks of it as "the greatest restaurant chain in history."[15] In addition, McDonald's offers many praiseworthy programs that benefit society, such as its Ronald McDonald Houses, which permit parents to stay with children undergoing treatment for serious medical problems; job-training programs for teenagers; programs to help keep its employees in school; efforts to hire and train the disabled; the McMasters program, aimed at hiring senior citizens; an enviable record of hiring and promoting minorities; and a social responsibility program with goals of improving the environment and animal welfare.[16]

The process of McDonaldization also moved ahead dramatically undoubtedly because it has led to positive changes.[17] Here are a few specific examples of such changes:

- A wider range of goods and services is available to a much larger proportion of the population than ever before.

- Availability of goods and services depends far less than before on time or geographic location; people can now do things that were impossible previously, such as text message, e-mail, arrange dates online, make online purchases, and participate in online social networks in the middle of the night with people halfway around the world.

- People are able to acquire what they want or need almost instantaneously and to get it far more conveniently.

- Goods and services are of far more uniform quality; many people even get better-quality goods and services than before McDonaldization.

- Far more economical alternatives to high-priced, customized goods and services are widely available; therefore, people can afford things (e.g., IKEA furniture rather than handmade furniture) they could not previously afford.

- Fast, efficient goods and services are available to a population that is working longer hours and has fewer hours to spare.

- In a rapidly changing, unfamiliar, and seemingly hostile world, the comparatively stable, familiar, and safe environment of a McDonaldized system offers comfort.

- Because of quantification, consumers can more easily compare competing products.

- Certain products (e.g., exercise and diet programs) are safer in a carefully regulated and controlled system.

- People are more likely to be treated similarly, no matter their race, sex, sexual orientation, or social class.

- Organizational and technological innovations are more quickly and easily diffused through networks of identical operators.

- One society's most popular products and services are more easily disseminated to others.

A CRITIQUE OF McDONALDIZATION: THE IRRATIONALITY OF RATIONALITY

McDonaldization clearly offers powerful advantages, but rational systems inevitably spawn irrationalities. The downside of McDonaldization will be dealt with most systematically under the heading of the irrationality of rationality; in fact, paradoxically, the irrationality of rationality can be thought of as the fifth dimension of McDonaldization. The major irrationalities of rationality will be discussed in Chapter 7. They are:

- inefficiency (rather than efficiency);

- high cost (even though McDonaldized goods and services are supposed to be inexpensive);

- its falseness, especially in the way employees relate to consumers;

- disenchantment;

- health and environmental dangers;

- homogenization;

- dehumanization.

Criticism can, in fact, be levelled at all of the specific elements of the McDonaldizing world. As just one example, at the opening of Euro Disney, a

French politician said that Disney will "bombard France with uprooted creations that are to culture what fast food is to gastronomy."[18] McDonald's and other purveyors of the fast-food model spend billions of dollars each year detailing the benefits of their system. Critics of the system, however, have few outlets for their ideas. For example, no one sponsors commercials between Saturday morning cartoons warning children of the dangers associated with fast-food restaurants.

Nonetheless, a legitimate question may be raised about this critique of McDonaldization: Is it animated by a romanticization of the past, an impossible desire to return to a world that no longer exists? Some critics do base their critiques on nostalgia for a time when life was slower and offered more surprises, when at least some people (those who were better off economically) were freer, and when one was more likely to deal with human beings than robots or computers.[19] Although they have a point, these critics have undoubtedly exaggerated the positive aspects of a world without McDonald's, and they have certainly tended to forget the liabilities associated with earlier eras. As an example of the latter, take the following anecdote about a visit to a pizzeria in Havana, Cuba, which in some respects is decades behind the United States:

> The pizza's not much to rave about—they scrimp on tomato sauce, and the dough is mushy.
>
> It was about 7:30 P.M., and as usual the place was standing-room-only, with people two deep jostling for a stool to come open and a waiting line spilling out onto the sidewalk.
>
> The menu is similarly Spartan. . . . To drink, there is tap water. That's it—no toppings, no soda, no beer, no coffee, no salt, no pepper. And no special orders.
>
> A very few people are eating. Most are waiting. . . . Fingers are drumming, flies are buzzing, the clock is ticking. The waiter wears a watch around his belt loop, but he hardly needs it; time is evidently not his chief concern. After a while, tempers begin to fray.
>
> But right now, it's 8:45 P.M. at the pizzeria, I've been waiting an hour and a quarter for two small pies.[20]

Few would prefer such a restaurant to the fast, friendly, more diverse offerings of, say, Pizza Hut. More important, however, critics who revere the past ignore the fact that we are not returning to such a world. In fact, fast-food restaurants have begun to appear even in Havana (and many more are likely).[21] The increase in the number of people crowding the planet, the acceleration of technological change, and the increasing pace of life make it impossible to go back to a world, if it ever existed, dominated by home-cooked meals, traditional restaurant dinners, high-quality foods, meals loaded with surprises, and restaurants run by chefs free to express their creativity.

It is more valid to critique McDonaldization from the perspective of a conceivable future.[22] Unfettered by the constraints of McDonaldized systems, but using the technological advances made possible by them, people could have the potential in the future to be far more thoughtful, skillful, creative, and well rounded. In short, if the world were less McDonaldized, people would be better able to live up to their human potential.

We must look at McDonaldization as both "enabling" and "constraining."[23] McDonaldized systems enable us to do many things we were not able to do in the past; however, these systems also keep us from doing things we otherwise could do. McDonaldization is a "double-edged" phenomenon.

McDONALD'S: CREATING THE "FAST-FOOD FACTORY"

As mentioned above, the basic McDonald's approach—and the basis of the McDonaldization process—was created by two brothers, Richard and Maurice McDonald, in their first restaurant in Pasadena, California, in 1937.[24] They based that restaurant on the principles of high speed, large volume, and low price. To avoid chaos, they offered customers a highly circumscribed menu. Instead of personalized service and traditional cooking techniques, the McDonald brothers used assembly-line procedures for cooking and serving food. In place of trained cooks, the brothers' "limited menu allowed them to break down food preparation into simple, repetitive tasks that could be learned quickly even by those stepping into a commercial kitchen for the first time."[25] They pioneered the use of specialized restaurant workers such as "grill men," "shake men," "fry men," and "dressers" (those who put the "extras" on burgers and who wrap them). They developed regulations dictating what workers should do and even what they should say. In these and other ways, the McDonald brothers took the lead in developing the rationalized "fast-food factory."[26]

Ray Kroc not only did not invent McDonald's basic principles, he also did not invent the franchise:

> Franchising is a system in which one large firm . . . grants or sells the right to distribute its products or use its trade name and processes to a number of smaller firms. . . . Franchise holders, although legally independent, must conform to detailed standards of operation designed and enforced by the parent company.[27]

Singer Sewing Company pioneered franchising after the Civil War, and automobile manufacturers and soft drink companies were franchising by the turn of the 20th century. By the 1930s, it had found its way into retail businesses such as Western Auto, Rexall pharmacies, and the IGA food markets.

There had been many efforts to franchise food service before Kroc arrived on the scene in the early 1950s. The first food service franchises, the A&W Root Beer stands, made their debut in 1924. Howard Johnson began franchising ice cream and other food in 1935. The first Dairy Queen opened in 1944; efforts to franchise it nationally led to a chain of about 2,500 outlets by 1948. Other well-known food franchises predated McDonald's. Big Boy started in the late 1930s, and Burger King (then Insta-Burger) and Kentucky Fried Chicken began in 1954. Thus, Kroc's first McDonald's, which opened on April 15, 1955, was a relative latecomer to franchising in general and to food franchising in particular.

In 1954, when Ray Kroc first visited it, McDonald's was a single drive-in hamburger stand in San Bernardino, California (ironically, the same city where Taco Bell was founded by Glen Bell).[28] The basic menu, the approach, and even some of the techniques for which McDonald's is famous had already been created by the McDonald brothers. Although it was a local sensation, the McDonald brothers were content to keep it that way. They were doing very well and had few grand ambitions despite a few tentative steps toward franchising. With plenty of ambition for all of them, Kroc became their franchising agent and went on to build the McDonald's franchise empire. At first, Kroc worked in partnership with the McDonald brothers, but after he bought them out in 1961 for $2.7 million, he was free to build the business as he wished.

Kroc took the specific products and techniques of the McDonald brothers and combined them with the principles of other franchises (food service and others), bureaucracies, scientific management, and the assembly-line (see Chapter 2). Kroc's genius was in bringing all these well-known ideas and techniques to bear on the fast-food business and adding his ambition to turn it, through franchising, into a national, then international, business phenomenon. McDonald's and McDonaldization, then, do not represent something new but, rather, represent the culmination of a series of rationalization processes that had been occurring throughout the 20th century.

Kroc was impressed, above all else, by the efficiency of the McDonald brothers' operation, as well as the enormous profit potential of such a system applied at a large number of restaurant sites. Here is how Kroc described his initial reactions to the McDonald's system: "I was fascinated by the simplicity and effectiveness of the system. . . . Each step in producing the limited menu was stripped down to its essence and accomplished with a minimum of effort. They sold hamburgers and cheeseburgers only. The burgers were all fried the same way."[29] But Kroc's obsession with streamlined processes predated his discovery of McDonald's. When he was selling blenders to restaurants, he was disturbed by the restaurants' lack of efficiency: "There was inefficiency, waste, and temperamental cooks, sloppy service and food whose [sic] quality was never consistent. What was needed was a simple product that moved from start to completion in a *streamlined* path" (italics added).[30] Kroc toyed with other alternatives for streamlining the restaurant meal before settling on the McDonald's hamburger as a model of efficiency:

> He had contemplated hot dogs, then rejected the idea. There were too many kinds of hot dogs . . . there were all sorts of different ways of cooking hot dogs . . . boiled, broiled, rotisseried, charcoaled. . . . Hamburgers . . . were simplicity itself. The condiments were added to the hamburger, not built in. And there was only one way to prepare the hamburger—to grill it.[31]

Kroc and his associates experimented with each component of the hamburger to increase the efficiency of producing and serving it. For example, they started with partially sliced buns that arrived in cardboard boxes. But the griddle workers had to spend time opening the boxes, separating the buns, slicing them in half, and discarding the leftover paper and cardboard. Eventually, McDonald's found that buns sliced completely in half, separated, and shipped in reusable boxes could be used more efficiently. The meat patty received similar attention. For example, the paper between the patties had to have just the right amount of wax so that the patties would readily slide off the paper and onto the grill. Kroc's goal in these innovations was greater efficiency:

> The purpose of all these refinements . . . was to make our griddle man's job easier to do quickly and well. And the other considerations of cost cutting,

inventory control, and so forth were important to be sure, but they were secondary to . . . what happened there at the smoking griddle. This was the vital passage of our *assembly-line,* and the product had to flow through it smoothly or the whole plant would falter."[32] (italics added)

To this day, efficiency remains the focus at McDonald's. For example, in at least one McDonald's, "the workers labored with an assembly-line efficiency."[33]

However, Kroc's major innovation lay in the way he franchised McDonald's. He did not permit regional franchises in which a single franchisee received control over all the outlets to be opened in a given area. Other franchisers had foundered because regional franchisees had grown too powerful and subverted the basic principles of the company. Kroc maximized central control, and thereby uniformity throughout the system, by granting franchises one at a time and rarely granting more than one franchise to a specific individual. Kroc also gained control over, and profited from, the franchisee's real estate.[34] Another of Kroc's innovations was to set the fee for a franchise at a rock-bottom $950. Other franchisers had set very high initial fees and made most of their money from the initial setup. As a result, they tended to lose interest in the continued viability of the franchisees. At McDonald's, profits did not come from high initial fees but from the 1.9% of store sales that headquarters demanded of its franchisees. The success of Kroc and his organization thus depended on the prosperity of the franchisees. This mutual interest was Kroc's greatest contribution to the franchise business and a key factor in the success of McDonald's and its franchisees, many of whom became multimillionaires.

Although Kroc imposed and enforced a uniform system, he encouraged the franchisees to come up with innovations that could enhance not only their operations but also those of the system as a whole. Take the case of product innovations. Kroc himself was not a great product innovator. One of his most notorious flops was the Hula Burger, a slice of grilled pineapple between two pieces of cheese wrapped in a toasted bun. Successful creations, such as the fish sandwich (the Filet-O-Fish), the Egg McMuffin, McDonald's breakfast meals, and even the Big Mac, came from franchisees. Thus, McDonald's achieved a balance between centralized control and the independence of franchisees.

Kroc spearheaded a series of developments that further rationalized the fast-food business.[35] For one thing, he (unwittingly) served as preacher and cheerleader for the principles of rationalization as he lectured "about uniformity, about a standardized menu, one size portions, same prices, same quality in every store."[36] This uniformity allowed McDonald's to differentiate itself from its competitors, whose food was typically inconsistent. McDonald's also led the field by imposing a limited menu (at first, 10 items), by creating tough standards for the fat content of its hamburgers, by converting to frozen hamburgers and French fries, by using inspectors to check on uniformity and conformity, and by forming in 1961 the first full-time training center in the business (called Hamburger University and offering a "degree" in "hamburgerology"). As of 2015, more than 275,000 people had graduated from Hamburger University located in a 130,000-square-foot, state-of-the-art facility on the McDonald's campus in Oak Brook, Illinois. Because of McDonald's international scope, translators and electronic equipment enable professors to teach and communicate in 28 languages at one time. McDonald's also manages several international training centers, including Hamburger Universities in Australia, Brazil, China, England, Germany, and Japan;[37] another center opened in 2015.[38] In 1958, McDonald's published an operations manual that detailed how to run a franchise.[39] This manual laid down many of the principles for operating a fast-food restaurant:

> It told operators *exactly* how to draw milk shakes, grill hamburgers, and fry potatoes. It specified *precise* cooking times for all products and temperature settings for all equipment. It fixed *standard* portions on every food item, down to the *quarter ounce* of onions placed on each hamburger patty and the *thirty-two slices per pound* of cheese. It specified that French fries be cut at *nine thirty-seconds of an inch* thick. And it defined quality *controls* that were unique to food service, including the disposal of meat and potato products that were held more than *ten minutes* in a serving bin.

> . . . Grill men . . . *were instructed* to put hamburgers down on the grill moving from left to right, creating *six rows of six* patties each. And because the first two rows were farthest from the heating element, they were instructed (and still are) to flip the third row first, then the fourth, fifth, and sixth before flipping the first two.[40] (italics added)

It is hard to imagine a more rational system.

McDonald's success and importance is readily apparent. By 1994 it had already sold 99 billion burgers;[41] it has now sold hundreds of billions of them. Its revenues peaked in 2013 at $28.1 billion (greater than the gross domestic product [GDP] of many countries, including Equador),[42] with a net income of $5.6 billion.[43] McDonald's revenue and net income have dropped slightly in recent years,[44] but it remains an economic superpower. It has well over 36,000 restaurants in 120 countries throughout the world, serving an average of nearly

70 million customers a day.[45, 46] A computer programmer compiled a visualization of all the McDonald's locations in the United States (just over 14,000 in 2016) and reported that it is impossible to get farther than 115 miles from a McDon-ald's. The "McFarthest Spot," as the programmer labeled it, lies in Nevada.[47] A British commentator archly notes, "There are McDonald's everywhere. There's one near you, and there's one being built right now even nearer to you. Soon, if McDonald's goes on expanding at its present rate, there might even be one in your house. You could find Ronald McDonald's boots under your bed. And maybe his red wig, too."[48]

McDONALD'S AND OTHER BRICK-AND-MORTAR CONSUMPTION SITES

When the first edition of this book was published in 1993, its focus was on "brick-and-mortar" consumption sites like your local McDonald's restaurant, and those of other chains of fast-food restaurants, as well as Wal-Mart, shopping malls, and so on. Before the advent of the consumption sites on the Internet, that's pretty much all there was (although the Sears mail order catalogue and that of others such as Montgomery Ward were exceptions; see below on IKEA's catalogue). Some brick-and-mortar sites (including McDonald's) have expanded enormously in the last two and a half decades, but many others have declined dramatically (department stores, big-box stores, some chain stores, shopping malls). Overall, but *not* in the fast-food business (among others), brick-and-mortar locales devoted to consumption are increasingly being supplanted in importance by the largely digital sites. *However, as we will see, a clear and unequivocal distinction between the brick-and-mortar and the digital is increasingly untenable; they are increasingly merging into one another.* For example, and as will be discussed further below, Domino's largely brick-and-mortar structures are increasingly doing business online and Amazon is opening brick-and-mortar bookstores and convenience stores.[49] More important, in mid-2017 Amazon bought the Whole Foods chain of 460 supermarkets for $13.4 billion.[50]

Largely brick-and-mortar franchises generated about $2.1 trillion in business in the United States in 2014. They employed over 8.5 million people.[51] Franchises are growing rapidly;[52] more than 80% of McDonald's restaurants are franchises (up from 57% in 2006). (Interestingly, another giant in the fast-food business—Starbucks—refuses to franchise its operations in the United States, but it does license them to independent owners. It has recently begun franchising in Europe and elsewhere.) In the words of the McDonald's 2008 report, "We believe locally-owned and operated restaurants are at the core of our competitive advantage, making us not just a global brand but also a locally relevant one."[53]

The McDonald's model has been adopted not only by other budget-minded hamburger franchises, such as Burger King and Wendy's, but also by a wide array of other low-priced fast-food businesses. In 2015, Yum! Brands, Inc., operated more than 42,000 restaurants in 130 countries and territories.[54] The best-known of its chains of restaurants are Pizza Hut, KFC, Taco Bell, as well as Wing-Street. Yum! Brands has more outlets than McDonald's, although its total sales (over $13 billion in 2015) and net income ($1.3 billion) are not nearly as high as McDonald's.[55] Subway (with almost 45,000 outlets in 106 countries; about 27,000 are in the United States)[56] is one of the fastest-growing fast-food businesses. It claims to be—and may actually be—the largest restaurant chain in the world.[57] The Cleveland, Ohio, market, to take one example, is so saturated with Subway restaurants that one opened *inside* the Jewish Community Center.[58] Among the innumerable other successful budget-oriented fast-food chains are Chipotle (now embattled because of a series of health scares), Chick-fil-A, Dunkin' Donuts, Firehouse Subs, Five Guys, Panera, and Jimmy John's.

In-N-Out Burger is a relatively small West Coast chain with over 300 restaurants. While Stacy Perman argues that In-N-Out Burger is "the antithesis of McDonald's,"[59] it is, in fact, in most ways highly McDonaldized. Another food chain is Pret A Manger, a British company (the name is French, meaning "ready to eat"). Founded in London in 1968, it remains based primarily in Great Britain. As of this writing, there are about 375 Pret A Manger restaurants in the world;[60] about 70 of them in the United States (New York, Washington, D.C., Chicago, and Boston), and more are promised.[61] Unlike In-N-Out and McDonald's, Pret A Manger does *not* sell hamburgers, but rather a variety of foods (salads, soups, wraps, desserts, etc.). Pret is best known for its high-quality sandwiches such as Balsamic Chicken & Avocado and Egg Salad & Arugula. Like In-N-Out, Pret avoids the use of preservatives and chemicals. Pret does not make its sandwiches to order, but it does have them made in the shops several times a day.

Even Halal Guys, the highly successful New York City purveyor of Middle Eastern street food, plans to have 200 brick-and-mortar storefronts in the United States, Canada, and Asia. Halal Guys's consultant says, "It's going to be the Chipotle of Middle Eastern food."[62]

The McDonald's model has been extended to more upscale, higher-priced, "fast casual," brick-and-mortar chain restaurants. Among the burger chains in this category are Shake Shack and its "ShackBurger."[63] Smashburger, currently the hottest new burger chain, is noted for its burgers made crispy by smashing them with a steel mold. However, the dominant higher-priced restaurant chains offer fuller menus. Major examples include Outback Steakhouse, Chili's, Olive Garden, Cheesecake Factory, and Red Lobster.

Morton's is an even more upscale, high-priced chain of steakhouses (Ruth's Chris is another) that has overtly modeled itself after McDonald's: "Despite the fawning service and the huge wine list, a meal at Morton's conforms to the same dictates of uniformity, cost control and portion regulation that have enabled American fast-food chains to rule the world."[64] In fact, the chief executive of Morton's was an owner of a number of Wendy's outlets and admits, "My experience with Wendy's has helped in Morton's venues."[65] To achieve uniformity, employees go "by the book": "an ingredient-by-ingredient illustrated binder describing the exact specifications of . . . Morton's kitchen items, sauces and garnishes. A row of color pictures in every Morton's kitchen displays the presentation for each dish."[66,67] Each Morton's also offers private boardrooms with standardized features, including "state-of-the-art, high-definition satellite television broadcast reception, large drop-down screens and theater-quality surround sound, Wi-Fi technology and Velocity broadcasting capabilities."

Other types of brick-and-mortar business are increasingly adapting the principles of the fast-food industry to their operational needs. Said the vice chair of Toys"R"Us, "We want to be thought of as a sort of McDonald's of toys."[68] (Interestingly, Toys"R"Us is now in decline because of its difficulty in competing with the even more massively McDonaldized Wal-Mart and its toy business.) The founder of Kidsports Fun and Fitness Club echoed this desire: "I want to be the McDonald's of the kids' fun and fitness business."[69] Other chains with similar ambitions include Gap, Jiffy Lube, AAMCO Transmissions, Midas Muffler & Brake Shops, Great Clips, H&R Block, Pearle Vision, Bally's, Kampgrounds of America (KOA) (called the "McDonald's of camping"),[70] KinderCare (dubbed "Kentucky Fried Children"),[71] Home Depot, PetSmart, Jenny Craig, and Curves (which claims to be the world's largest chain of women's fitness centers).[72] The European budget airline Ryanair has copied the McDonald's model in a process that has been called "Ryanization."[73]

McDonald's has been a resounding success in the international arena. The majority of McDonald's restaurants are now outside the United States (that was true of only about 25% of its restaurants in the mid-1980s).[74] Well over half of McDonald's revenue comes from its overseas operations.[75] McDonald's opened its first restaurant in Vietnam in Ho Chi Minh City in 2014[76]; now there are 14 of them there. As of 2016, the leader, by far, is Japan with almost 3,000 restaurants.[77] There are currently over 2,000 McDonald's restaurants in China.[78] (However, Yum! Brands operates more than 5,000 KFCs in China—the Chinese greatly prefer chicken to beef.[79] Yum! Brands is expanding faster in China than McDonald's.[80]) France, the bastion of fine food, has become the second most profitable market in the world (the United States is first) for McDonald's.[81] There were nearly 600 McDonald's in Russia in 2016.[82] In fact, many other fast-food restaurants are succeeding in Russia; Russians seem to love American fast food.[83] Although there have been recent setbacks for McDonald's in Great Britain, that nation remains the "fast-food capital of Europe."[84] Israel is described as "McDonaldized," with its shopping malls populated by "Ace Hardware, Toys'R'Us, Office Depot, and TCBY."[85]

Many highly McDonaldized, largely brick-and-mortar, firms outside the fast-food industry have also had success globally. Wal-Mart is the world's largest brick-and-mortar retailer with 2.3 million employees (over half of them in the United States) and almost $500 billion in sales in 2016. It opened its first international store (in Mexico) in 1991; over half of its 11,695 stores are now outside the United States, including in Argentina, Brazil, Canada, Chile, China, Costa Rica, El Salvador, Guatemala, Honduras, India, Japan, Mexico, Nicaragua, Puerto Rico, and the United Kingdom.[86] Although it is working hard to become a larger digital presence, Wal-Mart continues to be dominated by its brick-and-mortar sites.

Other nations have developed their own variants on the McDonald's chain. Canada has a chain of coffee shops called Tim Hortons (merged with Wendy's in 1995, purchased by Burger King in 2014, and now part of Restaurant Brands), with more than 4,500 brick-and-mortar outlets (about 700 in the United States) in 2016.[87] It is Canada's largest food service provider; much larger there than McDonald's. The chain dominates Canada's coffee business.[88] Paris, a city whose love for fine cuisine might lead one to think it would prove immune to fast food, has a large number of fast-food croissanteries. The revered French bread has also been McDonaldized,[89] although there is at least one effort to return to the production and sale of the classic French bread in traditional boulangeries.[90] An increasing number of French restaurants serve industrially produced food rather than food produced in their own kitchens. Overall, for the first time, in 2013 the French spent more money in fast-food restaurants than in traditional restaurants.[91] India has a chain of fast-food restaurants, Nirula's, that sells mutton burgers (about 80% of Indians are Hindus, who eat no beef) as well as local

Indian cuisine.[92] Mos Burger is a Japanese chain with more than 1,700 restaurants, including 6 in Australia.[93] In addition to the usual fare, Mos Burger sells Teriyaki chicken burgers, rice burgers, and "Oshiruko with brown rice cake."[94]

War-ravaged Beirut, Lebanon, once the most unlikely spot for an indigenous fast-food restaurant, witnessed the opening of Juicy Burger in 1984. It had a rainbow instead of golden arches and J. B. the Clown stood in for Ronald McDonald. Its owners hoped (in vain) that it would become the "McDonald's of the Arab world."[95] However, a new competitor for the most unlikely spot for a McDonald's clone is Teheran, Iran, which now has a "Mash Donald's." It joins "K.F.C. (Kabooki Fried Chicken), and clones of Pizza Hut (Pizza Hat) and Burger King (Burger House)."[96]

And now McDonaldization is coming full circle. Other countries with indigenous McDonaldized institutions have begun to export them to the United States. Great Britain's Pret A Manger has already been mentioned. Pollo Campero was founded in Guatemala in 1971 and by 2011 had over 350 restaurants in Latin America and several other countries, including the United States.[97] Jollibee, a Philippine chain, has over 3,000 stores, with a number of U.S. outlets.[98] In 2016 Jollibee purchased a 40% stake in Smashburger. Pollo Campero is a smaller presence in the United States than the American-owned Pollo Tropical chain (which has over 160 outlets, almost all in the United States, including Puerto Rico, as well as a smattering in Latin America).[99] However, Pollo Campero is more significant because it involves the invasion of the United States, the home of fast food, by a foreign (Guatemalen) chain. As exemplified by Jollibee's purchase of a large stake in Smashburger, even the hamburger business in the United States is not immune to an influx of foreign competition. BurgerFuel, a small, high-end, New Zealand burger chain with 88 outlets in six countries, plans to expand into the United States.[100]

While it is highly McDonaldized, IKEA, a Swedish-based (but Dutch-owned) home furnishings company, is a powerful force on its own. In fact, there is discussion of "IKEAization" independent of the process of McDonaldization. IKEA did about 35 billion euros of business in 2016, derived from the more than 684 million people visiting its nearly 400 brick-and-mortar superstores in 48 countries.[101] (Purchases were also made from the 212 million copies of its catalog printed in 62 editions and 29 languages.[102] In fact, that catalog is reputed to print annually the second largest number of copies in the world, just after the Bible.[103]) IKEA bridges the brick-and-mortar and digital worlds; its website reported 2.1 billion visitors in 2016.[104] IKEA is so popular in Europe that "it is said that one in ten Europeans is conceived on an IKEA bed."[105] Another significant franchise is H&M, an international chain of clothing stores. Founded in 1947, it now has more than 4,000 shops in 62 countries.[106] It currently employs more than 130,000 people and had almost $22 billion in sales in 2016.[107] Another leader in the global clothing business is Zara, which opened its first shop in 1975 and now has more than 2,000 of them in 90 countries. Zara is part of a large group of fashion retailers that make up the Spanish firm Inditex. Taken together, there are more than 7,200 Inditex shops in 93 countries operating under nine different brand names.[108] Inditex had total revenue of almost 21,000 billion euros in 2015.[109]

Much of the above emphasizes the geographic and spatial expansion of McDonald's and other McDonaldized brick-and-mortar businesses, but in addition they have all expanded temporally. McDonald's has shifted some of its attention from adding locations to adding hours to existing locales, thereby squeezing greater profits from each of them. For example, at first McDonald's did not offer breakfast, but now that meal has become the most important part of the business day; McDonald's dominates the fast-food breakfast market. There is also a trend toward remaining open on a 24/7 basis. While less than 1% of McDonald's restaurants in the United States operated nonstop in 2002, almost 40% were operating on that basis by 2009. Moreover, the vast majority of its U.S. locations are now open by 5 a.m.[110] Time, like space, is no barrier to the spread of McDonald's and McDonaldization.

THE LONG ARM OF McDONALD'S

Beyond the increasing influence of its business model (and of its impact on the larger culture; see below), McDonald's has striven to continually extend its reach within American society and beyond. As the company's chairperson said, "Our goal: to totally dominate the quick service restaurant industry worldwide. . . . I want McDonald's to dominate."[111]

McDonald's began as a phenomenon of suburbs and medium-sized towns, but later it began to build brick-and-mortar restaurants in smaller towns, which supposedly could not support such restaurants, and in many big cities where consumers were supposedly too sophisticated to eat in them.[112] Today, you can find many fast-food outlets in New York's Times Square. In Paris, McDonald's is not only on the Champs-Élysées, but there is even a branch *in* the Louvre.[113] Soon after it opened in 1992, the McDonald's in Moscow's Pushkin Square sold almost 30,000 hamburgers a day and employed a staff of 1,200 young people working two to a cash register.[114, 115] In early 1992, Beijing witnessed the opening of what still may be the world's largest McDonald's, with 700 seats, 29 cash registers, and nearly 1,000 employees. On its first day of business, it set a new one-day record for McDonald's by serving about 40,000 customers.[116] Among the more striking sites for a McDonald's restaurant are at the Grand Canyon; in what was once the world's tallest building, the Petronas Towers in Malaysia; as a ski-through on a slope in Sweden; and in a structure in Shrewsbury, England, that dates back to the 13th century.

McDonald's can even be found on the Guantanamo Bay U.S. Naval Base in Cuba and in the Pentagon. Small, satellite, express, or remote outlets, opened in areas that could not support full-scale fast-food restaurants, are also expanding rapidly. They are found in small storefronts in large cities and in nontraditional settings such as museums, department stores, service stations,[117] and even schools. These satellites typically offer only limited menus and may rely on larger outlets for food storage and preparation.[118] A flap arose over the placement of a McDonald's in the then-new federal courthouse in Boston.[119]

Not content to dominate the strips that surround many college campuses, fast-food restaurants have long since moved right onto many of those campuses. The first campus fast-food restaurant opened at the University of Cincinnati in 1973. Today, college cafeterias often look like shopping mall food courts (and it's no surprise, given that campus food service is a multibillion-dollar-a-year business).[120] In conjunction with a variety of "branded partners" (e.g., Pizza Hut and Subway), Marriott now supplies food to many colleges and universities.[121] The apparent approval of college administrations puts fast-food restaurants in a position to further influence the younger generation.

Fast food has long been available at many convenient rest stops along the road. After "refueling," we can proceed with our trip, which is likely to end in another community with about the same density and mix of fast-food restaurants as the locale we left behind. Fast food is ubiquitous in airports and is also increasingly available in hotels.[122]

In other sectors of society, the influence of fast-food restaurants has been subtler but no less profound. Food produced by McDonald's and other fast-food restaurants, or that strongly resembles such food, is now found in high schools and trade schools.[123] Said the director of nutrition for the American School Food Service Association, "Kids today live in a world where fast food has become a way of life. For us to get kids to eat, period, we have to provide some familiar items."[124] Few lower-grade schools as yet have in-house fast-food restaurants; however, many have had to alter school cafeteria menus and procedures to make fast food readily available.[125] Apples, yogurt, and milk may go straight into the trash can, but hamburgers, fries, and shakes are devoured. Fast-food restaurants also tend to cluster close to schools.[126] The attempt to hook school-age children on fast food reached something of a peak in Illinois, where McDonald's operated a program called "A for Cheeseburger." Students who received As on their report cards received a free cheeseburger, thereby linking success in school with McDonald's.[127] In Australia, toy versions of food featured by McDonald's have been marketed to children as young as three. The toys include "fake McDonald's fries, a self-assembling Big Mac, milkshake, Chicken McNuggets, baked apple pie and mini cookies."[128] Many fear that playing with such toy food will increase still further children's interest in eating the real thing.

The military has also been pressed to offer fast food on both bases and ships. Despite criticisms by physicians and nutritionists, fast-food outlets have turned up inside U.S. general hospitals and in children's hospitals.[129] While no private homes yet have a McDonald's of their own, meals at home often resemble those available in fast-food restaurants. Frozen, microwavable, and prepared foods, which bear a striking resemblance to meals available at fast-food restaurants, often find their way to the dinner table. There are even cookbooks—for example, *Secret Fast Food Recipes: The Fast Food Cookbook*—that allow one to prepare "genuine" fast food at home.[130] Then there is also home delivery of fast food, especially pizza, as revolutionized by Domino's.

The latest example of the influence of McDonald's is to be found in movie theaters and reflected in the following early 2017 newspaper headline: "To Woo Young Moviegoers, AMC Thinks Like McDonald's."[131] For example, building on McDonald's principle of calculability, especially large size (as best exemplified by the Big Mac), AMC theaters now offer "the Bavarian Beast," "a pound-and-a-half salted pretzel the size of a steering wheel."[132]

Another type of expansion involves what could be termed "vertical McDonaldization";[133] that is, the demands of the fast-food industry, as is well documented in Eric Schlosser's *Fast Food Nation,* have forced industries that service it to McDonaldize in order to satisfy its insatiable demands. Potato growing and processing, cattle ranching, chicken raising, and meat slaughtering and processing have all had to McDonaldize their operations, leading to dramatic increases in production. That growth has not come without costs, however.

As demonstrated in the movie *Food, Inc.* (2008), meat and poultry are now more likely to be disease ridden, small (often non-McDonaldized) producers and ranchers have been driven out of business, and millions of people have been forced to work in low-paying, demeaning, demanding, and sometimes outright dangerous jobs. For example, in the meatpacking industry, reasonably safe, unionized, secure, manageable, and relatively high-paying jobs in firms with once-household names such as Swift and Armour have been replaced with unsafe, nonunionized, insecure, unmanageable, and relatively low-paying positions with largely anonymous corporations. While some (largely owners, managers, and stockholders) have profited enormously from vertical McDonaldization, far more have been forced into a marginal economic existence.

McDonald's is such a powerful model that many businesses, as well as entities in many other domains, have acquired nicknames beginning with "Mc." Examples include "McDentists" and "McDoctors," meaning drive-in clinics designed to deal quickly and efficiently with minor dental and medical problems;[134] "McChild" care centers, meaning child care centers such as Kinder-Care; "McStables," designating the nationwide racehorse-training operation of D. Wayne Lukas; and "McPaper," describing the newspaper *USA TODAY*.[135] (Scholars have used the term "McSexy" to describe the McDonaldization of exotic dancing.)[136] McDonald's is not enamored, to put it mildly, of the proliferation of businesses using "Mc" as a prefix. Take the case of We Be Sushi, a San Francisco chain with a half-dozen outlets. A note appeared on the back of the menu explaining why the chain was not named "McSushi":

> The original name was McSushi. Our sign was up and we were ready to go. But before we could open our doors we received a very formal letter from the lawyers of, you guessed it, McDonald's. It seems that McDonald's has cornered the market on every McFood name possible from McBagle [*sic*] to McTaco. They explained that the use of the name McSushi would dilute the image of McDonald's.[137]

The derivatives of McDonald's have, in turn, exerted their own powerful influence. For example, the success of *USA TODAY* led many newspapers across the nation, as well as many other parts of the world, to adopt shorter stories and colorful weather maps. As one *USA TODAY* editor said, "The same newspaper editors who call us McPaper have been stealing our McNuggets."[138] Even serious journalistic enterprises such as the *New York Times* and *Washington Post* have changed (e.g., the use of color) as a result of the success of *USA TODAY*. The influence of *USA TODAY* is blatantly manifested in many local newspapers throughout the United States.[139] As in *USA TODAY*, stories usually start and finish on the same page. Many important details, much of a story's context, and much of what the principals have to say are cut back severely or omitted entirely. With its emphasis on light news and color graphics, the main function of such a newspaper seems to be entertainment.

Like virtually every other sector of society, sex has copied the McDonald's model.[140] In New York City, an official called a three-story pornographic center "the McDonald's of sex" because of its "cookie-cutter cleanliness and compliance with the law."[141] In the movie *Sleeper,* Woody Allen not only created a futuristic world in which McDonald's was an important and highly visible element, but he also envisioned a society in which people could enter a machine called an "orgasmatron" to experience an orgasm without going through the muss and fuss of sexual intercourse.

The porn site RedTube mimics the standardized interface of YouTube to provide various categories of adult content that users can view on the site or embed in their own web pages. The web is filled with video chat sites where users can request the performance of various sex acts. The Casual Encounters section on Craigslist.org provides people from every major city in the world with a centralized interface to find sexual partners. Tinder is a website usually used by people for the purpose of "hooking up," but more long-term relationships, even marriages, seem to be occurring as a result of initial contact via Tinder.[142] A variety of devices, termed "teledildonics" or cyberdildonics by the adult entertainment industry, enables users to stimulate one another through computer networks. 3Feel is a virtual 3-D environment where users can interact in real time and engage in sexual activity (with or without teledildonics).[143] As Woody Allen anticipated with his orgasmatron, "Participants can experience an orgasm without ever meeting or touching one another."[144]

> In a world where convenience is king, disembodied sex has its allure. You don't have to stir from your comfortable home. You pick up the phone, or log onto the computer and, if you're plugged in, a world of unheard of sexual splendor rolls out before your eyes.[145]

These examples suggest that no aspect of people's lives is immune to McDonaldization.

Various pharmaceuticals can be seen as McDonaldizing sex. Viagra (and similar drugs such as Cialis) do this by, for example, making more predictable the ability of males to have an erection. (There are not yet similar, effective, drugs for females, but research continues.) Such drugs also claim to work fast and to last for a long time. MDMA (ecstasy), an illicit drug, lasts for as much as eight hours and tends to increase the intensity of sensory information and feelings of social (including sexual) connectedness.

The preceding represents merely the tip of the iceberg as far as the long arm of McDonald's is concerned. Other areas affected by it (many of which will be discussed throughout this book) include the following:[146] outdoor recreation,[147] especially mountain climbing (e.g., reliance on guidebooks to climbing routes),[148] professional sports,[149] tourism,[150] the police,[151] the criminal justice system (profiling, "three strikes and you're out"),[152] family (books, TV shows devoted to quick fixes to family problems),[153] McSchools and the policies that serve to McDonaldize them,[154] McUniversities,[155] e-learning,[156] especially Massive Open Online Courses (MOOCs; see Chapter 7),[157] as well as entire academic fields such as kinesiology ("McKinesiology"),[158] the practice of medicine,[159] psychotherapy,[160] death and dying, including funeral practices in Islamic societies,[161] losing weight and the McDonaldization of the body,[162] farms and their supersizing,[163] religion and the McDonaldization of religious creeds[164] and spirituality,[165] banking,[166] McJobs (see Chapters 5 and 6),[167] politics ("cool" vs. "hot" politics; "drive-through democracy"),[168] and scientific research.

McDONALD'S AS AN AMERICAN AND A GLOBAL ICON

McDonald's has come to occupy a central place not just in the world of brick-and-mortar businesses, but also in American and global popular culture.[169] The opening of a new McDonald's in a small town can be an important social event. Said one Maryland high school student at such an opening, "Nothing this exciting ever happens in Dale City."[170] Even big-city, national, and global newspapers avidly cover developments in the fast-food business.

Fast-food restaurants also play symbolic roles on television programs and in the movies. They have been satirized on *Saturday Night Live* and played a prominent role in a number of movies including *Coming to America* (1988), *Falling Down* (1993), *Sleeper* (1973), *Tin Men* (1987), *Scotland, PA* (2001), *Fast Food Nation* (2006), the 2008 remake of the sci-fi classic *The Day the Earth Stood Still*, as well as *The Founder* (2016).

When plans were made to raze Ray Kroc's first McDonald's restaurant, hundreds of letters poured into company headquarters, including the following: "Please don't tear it down! . . . To destroy this major artifact of contemporary culture would, indeed, destroy part of the faith the people of the world have in your company."[171] In the end, the restaurant was rebuilt according to the original blueprints and turned into a museum.[172] A McDonald's executive explained the decision: "McDonald's . . . is really a part of Americana."

Americans aren't the only ones who feel this way. At the opening of the McDonald's in Moscow, one journalist described the franchise as the "ultimate icon of Americana."[173] When Pizza Hut opened in Moscow, a Russian student said, "It's a piece of America."[174] Reflecting on the growth of fast-food restaurants in Brazil, an executive associated with Pizza Hut of Brazil said that his nation "is experiencing a passion for things American."[175] On the popularity of KFC in Malaysia, the local owner said, "Anything Western, especially American, people here love. . . . They want to be associated with America."[176] One could go further and argue that at least culturally, McDonald's has become more important than the United States itself, at least in some people's eyes. Take the following news story about a former U.S. ambassador to Israel officiating at the opening of the first McDonald's in Jerusalem wearing a baseball cap with the McDonald's golden arches logo:

> An Israeli teen-ager walked up to him, carrying his own McDonald's hat, which he handed to Ambassador Indyk with a pen and asked: "Are you the Ambassador? Can I have your autograph?" Somewhat sheepishly, Ambassador Indyk replied: "Sure. I've never been asked for my autograph before."
>
> As the Ambassador prepared to sign his name, the Israeli teen-ager said to him, "Wow, what's it like to be the ambassador from McDonald's, going around the world opening McDonald's restaurants everywhere?"
>
> Ambassador Indyk looked at the Israeli youth and said, "No, no. I'm the American ambassador—not the ambassador from McDonald's!" Ambassador Indyk described what happened next: "I said to him, 'Does this mean you don't want my autograph?' And the kid said, 'No, I don't want your autograph,' and he took his hat back and walked away."[177]

Two other indices of the significance of McDonald's (and, implicitly, McDonaldization) are worth mentioning. The first is the annual "Big Mac index" (part of "burgernomics"), published, tongue-in-cheek, by a prestigious magazine, *The Economist*. It indicates the purchasing power of various currencies around the world based on the local price (in dollars) of the Big Mac. The Big Mac is used because it is a uniform commodity sold in many different nations. In the 2016 survey, a Big Mac in Switzerland cost $6.44, in the United States it cost an average of $4.93; in China, it was $2.68; and in Russia it was $1.53.[178] This measure indicates, at least roughly, where the cost of living is high or low, as well as which currencies are undervalued (China) and overvalued (Switzerland). Although *The Economist* is calculating the Big Mac index only half-seriously, the index represents the ubiquity and importance of McDonald's around the world.[179]

The second indicator of the global significance of McDonald's is the idea developed by Thomas Friedman that "no two countries that both have a McDonald's have ever fought a war since they each got McDonald's." Friedman calls this the "Golden Arches Theory of Conflict Prevention."[180] Another tongue-in-cheek idea, it implies that the path to world peace lies through the continued international expansion of McDonald's. Unfortunately, it was proved wrong by the NATO bombing of Serbia in 1999, which at the time had McDonald's.

To many people throughout the world, McDonald's has become a sacred institution.[181] At that opening of the McDonald's in Moscow, a worker spoke of it "as if it were the Cathedral in Chartres, . . . a place to experience 'celestial joy.'"[182] Kowinski argues that indoor shopping malls, which almost always encompass fast-food restaurants and other franchises and chains, are the modern "cathedrals of consumption" to which people go to practice their "consumer religion."[183] Similarly, a visit to another central element of McDonaldized society, Walt Disney World,[184] has been described as "the middle-class hajj, the compulsory visit to the sunbaked holy city."[185] McDonald's has achieved its exalted position because virtually all Americans, and many others, have passed through its golden arches (or by its drive-through windows) on innumerable occasions. Furthermore, most of us have been bombarded by commercials extolling the virtues of McDonald's, commercials tailored to a variety of audiences and that change as the chain introduces new foods, new contests, and new product tie-ins. These ever-present commercials, combined with the fact that people cannot drive or walk very far without having a McDonald's pop into view, have embedded McDonald's deep in popular consciousness. Some years ago a poll of school-age children showed that 96% of them could identify Ronald McDonald, second only to Santa Claus in name recognition.[186] Over the years, McDonald's has appealed to people in many ways. The restaurants themselves are depicted as spick-and-span, the food is said to be fresh and nutritious, the employees are shown to be young and eager, the managers appear gentle and caring, and the dining experience itself seems fun-filled. Through their purchases, people contribute, at least indirectly, to charities such as the Ronald McDonald Houses for sick children.

A LOOK AHEAD

Because this book is a work in the social sciences, I cannot merely assert that McDonaldization is spreading throughout society; evidence must be presented for that assertion. Numerous and diverse examples in each chapter demonstrate the degree to which McDonaldization has come to dominate, even define, society, and at an accelerating rate.

The focus throughout is on the impact of McDonaldized systems (e.g., fast-food restaurants, universities) on people, especially the people—consumers and workers—who are found in them. Following a discussion of the past and present of McDonaldization in Chapter 2, Chapters 3 and 4 concentrate on the consumers in McDonaldized settings. The focus is on the four basic principles of McDonaldization outlined in this chapter—efficiency, calculability, predictability, and control—and the ways in which they affect consumers. Chapters 5 and 6 shift the focus to the workers, the producers, in those settings and their McDonaldized occupations, especially their McJobs. As was the case with consumers, workers are discussed from the perspective of the four dimensions of McDonaldization. In Chapter 7, the fifth and paradoxical element of McDonaldization—the irrationality of rationality—is explored. While there is much that is positive about McDonald's and McDonaldization, including its basic principles, much of the book is a critique of McDonaldization. Chapter 7 presents that critique most clearly and directly, discussing a variety of irrationalities, the most important of which is dehumanization. Also discussed in this chapter are several perspectives on the issue of whether or not McDonaldization's irrationalities need to be dealt with and, if so, how.

McDONALDIZATION
PAST AND PRESENT

I n addition to defining and discussing McDonaldization, Chapter 1 dealt with
McDonald's itself and its influence on other important, largely brick-and-
mortar, sites of consumption. Chapter 2 begins with a discussion of a theoretical
perspective that is useful for analyzing not only these brick-and-mortar sites, but
also the increasingly important, largely digital, consumption sites, especially
Amazon. Second, we look back at some of McDonald's most important brick-
and-mortar predecessors. The principles of McDonaldization were, at least in
part, derived from those predecessors and those principles apply, at least to some
degree, to all of them. Third, we examine the state of McDonaldization today,
especially as it relates to our primary interest in consumption and the sites,
brick-and-mortar and digital, in which most consumption occurs. This leads to
a discussion and comparison of three of today's leading sites of consumption—
McDonald's, Wal-Mart, and Amazon. The conclusion derived from the discussion
of Amazon is that while the vast majority of consumption will continue to take
place in McDonaldized brick-and-mortar settings, digital settings are increasingly powerful alternatives to them. Some digital sites such Airbnb are seeking
to become more McDonaldized,[1] while others such as Amazon are even more
McDonaldized than the brick-and-mortar sites. However, the clear distinctions
between brick-and-mortar and digital worlds are eroding as those worlds increasingly interpenetrate. The resulting world of consumption, with brick-and-mortar
and digital sites augmenting one another, promises even more McDonaldization
in the future.

While some largely brick-and-mortar businesses such as McDonald's and
Wal-Mart are thriving, others are dead or dying. In spite of the demise of some

brick-and-mortar sites, the vast majority of consumption will continue to occur in those of them that survive. Nonetheless, much of it has begun to shift to the Internet where virtually everything (except hamburgers!, at least thus far) can be obtained from digital sites, most notably, Amazon. Wal-Mart, whose thousands of stores are powerful brick-and-mortar presences, is beginning to succeed in becoming a more important player in the digital world. Further obscuring the line between the brick-and-mortar and the digital is the fact that the digital giant Amazon (with 43% of e-commerce)[2] is in the early stages of an effort to become a more important force in the brick-and-mortar world. These trends demonstrate that not only are the differences between the brick-and-mortar and the digital eroding, but the brick-and-mortar and the digital are now increasingly augmenting one another in a "bricks-and-clicks" world and, in the process, creating much more powerful entities and forces. While the differences between the brick-and-mortar and the digital are declining, it is nonetheless important to keep that distinction in mind in order to better understand the McDonaldization of consumption—and of work—today.

THINKING ABOUT THE BRICK-AND-MORTAR "SOLIDS," DIGITAL "LIQUIDS," AND THE AUGMENTED REALITY OF "BRICKS-AND-CLICKS"

Both the distinction between the brick-and-mortar and the digital, as well as their relationship to one another, can be analyzed from the perspective of Zygmunt Bauman's work on solids and liquids.[3] Of specific concern here is the largely solid world of brick-and-mortar structures and the much more liquid realities as they exist, among other places, in the digital world. The fast-food restaurant is clearly one example of a solid structure. Among the others to be discussed in this chapter are such predecessors as the bureaucracy (discussed by Max Weber) and, more extremely, the Holocaust[4] and its concentration camps analyzed by, among others, Bauman (see below).[5] Just as Weber saw the bureaucracy as a solid rationalized structure and the fast-food restaurant has been described here in similar terms as being McDonaldized (a more contemporary term for rationalized), Bauman saw the concentration camp as yet another solid, highly rationalized structure. Solid structures are those that control movement of all kinds, including the movement of people and products. All of these solid structures (and others)—bureaucracies, fast-food restaurants, and especially concentration camps—can be thought of, in Weber's terms, as "iron cages."

However, Bauman argues that while solid structures, especially those involved in consumption, continue to exist, they are largely associated with a bygone era. We now live in an era increasingly characterized by liquidity rather than solidity. As he puts it, "Liquid life is consuming life."[6] This has a double meaning: Liquidity is encompassing more of life and, more specifically, consumption is increasingly synonymous with liquidity. Indeed, a recent article develops the idea of "liquid consumption."[7]

A good example of the shift from solidity to liquidity is to be found with changes in the way consumers possess movies and TV shows. In the not too distant past we witnessed a shift from possession of one solid form (VHS) to another (DVD). Now these solid forms have largely disappeared in the face of highly liquid forms available via cable, and streaming online from Hulu, Amazon, Netflix, and an increasing array of other providers. As a result of the increasing hegemony of these liquid systems, films, movies, and TV programs are less likely to be the solid physical property, or in the physical possession, of consumers.

Newer, more liquid, structures, especially in consumption, surround us, in Weber's terms, with little more than a "light cloak" rather than the bars of an iron cage. For example, with their drive-through, home delivery, and digital ordering systems, fast-food restaurants are lighter, more liquid, less constraining structures than they were in the past when customers had to drive to them, park their cars, physically enter the restaurants, and then return to their cars. However, it is the digital world which epitomizes that liquidity. We can, for example, quickly and easily go to Amazon and download an e-book in seconds or in a similar way access digital music on Spotify. Amazon has also moved strongly into the clothing business by offering through Prime Clothing the possibility of ordering 3 to 15 items of clothing without paying for them initially. Shipping is free as is the return of any unwanted items. To induce customers to keep items, Amazon offers discounts when they keep more than three items of clothing. Consumers pay for only the clothing they keep.[8] Not only are these Internet sites more liquid than their brick-and-mortar predecessors (book shops, record stores, clothing shops), but what they offer for sale is much more liquid than that which was available in many of their brick-and-mortar antecedents—hard- or paper-back books, vinyl records, and CDs.

Solid brick-and-mortar consumption sites (not only fast-food restaurants, but others such as supermarkets[9] and department stores) may be associated with an earlier stage in our history, but they are not going away any time soon. However, over time they will become increasingly less solid and more liquid. For example, many items for sale today in supermarkets—"cereal, canned soups, detergents, and Ziploc bags"[10]—will increasingly be purchased online. (However, there are inherent limits to the degree of liquidity of consumption settings like supermarkets. For example, most shoppers will still feel it necessary to physically go to a supermarket to buy products such as fruit, meat, and fish.) As a result, the future increasingly belongs to those domains, like the Internet, that are inherently more liquid and whose liquidity will only increase over time. The center of McDonaldization and of more and more consumption, among many other things, will move from brick-and-mortar structures to the digital world, especially the Internet.

Augmented Reality

While it is still possible to differentiate between the brick-and-mortar and the digital, it is better to think of them as creating a new *augmented reality* that now is different and separable from either the brick-and-mortar or the digital.[11]

Augmented reality has been in the news a great deal in recent years. In 2016, it was Pokemon Go's augmented reality in which digital images overlay the physical world; a digital creation could appear on a screen and seem as if it is in the viewer's physical location. Also in 2016, Snap introduced images that users can superimpose on their selfies to give themselves numerous appearances. In 2017 Facebook announced plans to introduce "the first mainstream augmented reality platform, a way for people to view and digitally manipulate the physical world around them through the lens of their smartphone camera."[12]

In terms of consumption, augmented reality today is highly liquid involving sites that in an increasingly seamless way blend "the digital and the physical allowing a shopper to shift seamlessly between the two realms. . . . Customers . . . tend to jump constantly between the two worlds without noticing."[13] These "bricks-and-clicks" businesses involve increasingly interconnected realities. For example, McDonaldized brick-and-mortar businesses are more and more likely to have digital components (online ordering; iPads to order food in restaurants) *and* their digital counterparts are increasingly likely to have material components. Wal-Mart has partnered with a Chinese online direct sales company to offer one-hour delivery from many of its stores in China.[14] More generally, it has begun to allow customers to pick up online purchases at one of its brick-and-mortar stores, with no charge for shipping. In 2017, Wal-Mart began offering a discount when online purchases are picked up at one of their stores. It has also begun to employ a "pick-up-tower," basically a huge vending machine, where customers can pick up online purchases without involving any of Wal-Mart's employees.[15] Wal-Mart, which has been dwarfed by Amazon in the online world, is becoming more competitive by increasing its digital presence thereby better augmenting its huge footprint and advantage in brick-and-mortar sites.

Domino's pizza, with over 12,000 brick-and-mortar shops around the world, offers another example of this new augmented, bricks-and-clicks, world. Domino's has remade itself since a low point in 2008 of declining sales and failing franchises. In doing so, it has not ignored its shops. In fact, in recent years it has invested heavily in dramatically redesigning them. In addition, its pizzas are still made in the same labor-intensive way in those redesigned shops. However, the really big change at Domino's has been the effort to maximize digital ordering and tracking of orders through various Internet sites. As a result, Domino's has increasing credibility as a high-tech business. Domino's share price has increased sixty-fold since 2008 and the company has grown exponentially.[16]

Domino's and Wal-Mart have moved in a more digital direction. Others were, and still are, largely digital businesses. One example (see below) is Stitch Fix, which, like Amazon's Prime clothing, sends buyers clothing based on things like size and stated preferences. Other, largely digital businesses, have sought to become greater physical, more solid, presences. For example, Bonobos (purchased by Wal-Mart in mid-2017 for $310 million)[17] is an online retailer of men's clothing that now has more than 30 brick-and-mortar shops throughout the United States. This allows customers to try on clothes before they purchase them online. They leave a Bonobos shop without the clothes they've purchased; the clothes are made in centralized production sites and shipped directly to their homes from a central warehouse.[18]

More important, Amazon, once almost totally digital, except for such aspects of its business as the warehousing and delivery of material products, has, as has already been mentioned, recently moved strongly into the brick-and-mortar world by opening solid physical bookstores (it already has about half of the consumer book market in the United States), convenience stores (Amazon Go), and, most significant, the purchase of the Whole Foods chain of supermarkets. This is a major example of the fact that the never hard-and-fast distinction between the material and the digital is fast disappearing. For example, as a result of its "grab-and-go" system Amazon Go consumers can physically go to the brick-and-mortar shop, select, pick up, and take home groceries, ready-to-eat meals, and even meal kits with all of the ingredients to create a meal at home in 30 minutes. Because of the integration of the digital in Amazon Go shops, it is not necessary for them to wait in line to physically pay for their purchases on checkout; Amazon Go offers checkout-free shopping. All shoppers need do is use the Amazon Go app on entering the store, take whatever automatically detected products they want to purchase, and leave the store.[19] Amazon Go's highly liquid "Just Walk Out Technology" is connected to the Internet and employs computer vision, sensors, and deep learning.[20] All of this serves to make shopping at Amazon Go far more McDonaldized (especially more efficient) than in any other brick-and-mortar convenience store or supermarket. (Uber has done much the same thing. Because rides are prepaid through an app, passengers can exit the Uber without the need to pay or tip.)

It remains to be seen what Amazon does with Whole Foods' brick-and-mortar supermarkets, but it will undoubtedly integrate them into its digital business. It might, for example, use the stores as distribution centers for digitally ordered products or launch pads for its nascent drone-delivery system.[21] In fact, Amazon is expanding in so many directions, and augmenting its online business in so many different ways, that it has raised fear of an emerging modern monopoly similar to the 19th-century railroads that led, in their day, to the development of anti-monopoly laws.[22]

We are clearly in the early stages of the development of these augmented businesses, which involve ever-closer integration of the digital and the material and the degree to which they augment one another. Among the possibilities being currently tested, on the horizon, or merely being imagined, are stores with

> fleets of gleaming robots . . . built-in facial recognition technology to adjust each sales pitch to a person's current mood or past spending preferences . . . voice-activated personal assistants, downloading the availability, color and fit of any and every garment to your smartphone . . . Three-D printing stations . . . floating, holographic product displays on the shop floor that change when a customer walks by . . . shoppers will make all their purchases from their own home, using virtual fitting rooms via virtual reality headsets. Drones will drop deliveries in the backyard or on the front steps.[23]

In spite of the eroding distinction between the brick-and-mortar and the digital, it is important to deploy it in this discussion if for no other reason than to make it clear that the McDonaldized world of the late 20th century, and the focus of early editions of this book, has changed dramatically in the early 21st century. Nevertheless, brick-and-mortar structures are likely to continue to be important.

Said the founder of the website Farfetch, "I am a huge believer in physical stores. They are not going to vanish and will stay at the center of the seismic retail revolution that is only just getting started."[24] One report predicted that 75% of all sales in 2025 will still be in brick-and-mortar sites. However, the shopping mall is among the major brick-and-mortar consumption sites in dramatic decline. Its food courts are the home of many fast-food chains and the mall itself is dominated by McDonaldized chain stores of one kind or another. The shopping mall is one of the predecessors of McDonaldization dealt with below.

The Changing Nature of Work

Much of the above focuses explicitly and implicitly on consumption and consumers, but workers are also profoundly affected by the changes just described. For example, the innovations at Amazon Go, as well as Amazon's acquisition of Whole Foods, are of huge importance not only for consumers, but also for workers.

About 10% of Americans now work in retail.[25] More specifically, approximately 3.5 million people in the United States are cashiers. In many ways, the goal of the deep learning and artificial intelligence (AI) behind, for example, Amazon Go, is to produce retail establishments that operate on their own with few, if any, visible employees. However, job loss associated with technological change, especially AI, will go far beyond cashiers to include "bank tellers, customer service representatives, telemarketers, stock and bond traders, even paralegals and radiologists . . . factory workers, construction workers, drivers, delivery workers, and many others"[26] In previous revolutions (industrial, computer) new jobs were created to replace those that were made obsolete, but in the AI revolution both low- and high-paying jobs will be decimated; it is possible that fewer new ones will be created.

While Whole Foods supermarkets require many workers, it seems likely that Amazon will seek to cut deeply into its workforce. The objective of its e-payment system is, at least in part, the elimination of human cashiers.[27] Once this step is taken, it is not a great leap from Amazon Go to imagining an automated store, even supermarket, of the future staffed by robots and where orders are delivered by drones. (Amazon.com is currently experimenting with drones.)

Of course, cashiers are not the only workers whose jobs are in increasing jeopardy because of automation and robotization. For example, many farm jobs have long been lost to mechanization. A new and imminent threat to the jobs of many migrant farm workers is the arrival of robotic fruit-picking machines to harvest crops that until now have been deemed too delicate to be harvested by machine. One member of a family that owns a large farming operation in Washington state said, in good McDonaldizing terms, "We are absolutely looking at ways we can increase our *efficiency*."[28]

Relatedly, the nature of work is changing dramatically. There is an increasing shift away from solid jobs in material settings (like the fast-food restaurant) to more liquid virtual work; to the "virtualization of work."[29] To put this slightly differently, an increasing number of people are being forced, or choosing voluntarily, to move to the "gig economy" from traditional, full-time jobs in large organizations for which they received W-2s, benefits (e.g., pensions), and so forth.[30] Those in the gig (or job) economy are part of an "on-demand" workforce.[31] In the gig economy, people regularly move from one short-term job, or gig, to another. The work is often deskilled and underpaid, micropaid, or unpaid.[32] It could be argued that these workers are exploited because the platforms through which they work are based on "value extraction from their workers."[33] The gig workers are often connected to those who need some work done through online platforms and apps on digital sites such as TaskRabbit (microwork involving a wide variety of short-term tasks), Clickworker (involving "penny tasks"), Hello Alfred (recurrent household tasks), Postmates (delivery), and Dogvacay (pet care). Like Uber drivers, those who have such gigs are generally paid automatically through the sites and the apps.

It is difficult for gig workers to survive economically solely on the basis of their gigs, and there is little security associated with such work. It is precarious; those who do it can be seen as part of the "precariat."[34] Furthermore, it can be a lonely existence with only brief, or even nonexistent, contact with those requesting the work. It is also likely that there is no contact with other "taskers." As one gig worker said, "The gig economy is such a lonely economy."[35]

However, there are good jobs ("venture labor" where gig workers are able to recruit others to work for them) in the gig economy such as highly skilled freelance work (e.g., software development) available on such sites as Upwork. Gig work, especially venture labor, also offers its satisfactions such as being empowering, offering autonomy (able to work on one's own in one's own way), having great flexibility in handling a wide variety of tasks, meeting—at least briefly—lots of new people, and being able to take time off when one wants. Whatever its problems or satisfactions, an increasing number of people will work in the gig economy.

Also profoundly affecting work in brick-and-mortar consumption sites is the fact that those involved will, in the future, even more than today, produce what they consume. At Amazon Go customers are on their own to pick up what they want and check out merely by passing themselves and their selections through an array of scanners. That is, customers will accomplish tasks, increasingly painlessly because of advanced technology, which are still performed in most other consumption settings by paid employees. In the not-too-distant future, this will cost many more of these employees (especially cashiers) their jobs,[36] while for others the nature of their jobs will change. For example, in the case of fast-food restaurants many employees will be shifted from behind the counter to working (e.g., cleaning up) in the dining area.[37]

However, it is important to note that, at least so far, the gains in new jobs in e-commerce—many of them gigs—have been much greater than job losses in the brick-and-mortar sector.[38] Full-time work in e-commerce often pays more than comparable brick-and-mortar jobs. However, those who are losing brick-and-mortar jobs are not necessarily those who are finding full-time jobs in the digital world. In fact, it is likely that those jobs are mainly going to a more educated and highly trained segment of the population much more familiar with, and skilled in, the digital world. While this change will have adverse effects on many workers, it will please most consumers by, for example, making online shopping far more McDonaldized than in extant brick-and-mortar convenience stores or supermarkets.

This excursion into thinking about solid and liquid consumption puts us in a better position to discuss and understand not only the most important predecessors to McDonald's and McDonaldization, but also other contemporary developments in consumption and McDonaldization, especially digital McDonaldization.

KEY PREDECESSORS

McDonald's and McDonaldization did not emerge in a vacuum; they were preceded by a series of social and economic developments that not only anticipated them but also gave them many of the basic characteristics touched on in Chapter 1.[39] This section will first examine the bureaucracy and Max Weber's theories about it and the larger process of rationalization. Next is a discussion of the Nazi Holocaust and its "solid" concentration camps, a method of mass killing that can be viewed as the logical extreme of Weber's fears about rationalization and bureaucratization. Then, several intertwined socioeconomic developments that were precursors of McDonaldization are discussed: scientific management as it was invented at the turn of the century by F. W. Taylor, Henry Ford's assembly-line, suburban developments such as Levittown, and the rise (and fall) of the shopping mall. These are not only of historical interest; most continue to be relevant to this day.

The Holocaust: The Concentration Camp and Mass-Produced Death

Max Weber wrote, often critically, about the iron cage of rationalization and bureaucratization. Almost a century later Zygmunt Bauman argued that Weber's worst fears about these processes were realized in the Nazi Holocaust, which began within a decade or two of Weber's death in 1920. Bauman contends that "the Holocaust may serve as a paradigm of modern bureaucratic rationality."[40] Like the bureaucracy, the Holocaust was a distinctive product of Western civilization. In fact, Bauman argued that the Holocaust was not an aberration but "in keeping with everything we know about our civilization, its guiding spirit, its priorities, its immanent vision of the world."[41] That is, the Holocaust required the rationality of the modern world. It could not have occurred in premodern, less rationalized societies.[42] In fact, the pogroms that had occurred in premodern societies were too inefficient to allow for the systematic murder of millions of people that occurred in the Holocaust.

The Holocaust can also be seen as an example of modern social engineering in which the goal was a perfectly rational society. To the Nazis, a perfect society was one free of Jews, as well as of gypsies, gays, lesbians, and the disabled. Hitler himself defined the Jews as a "virus," a disease that had to be eradicated from Nazi society.

The Holocaust had all the basic characteristics of rationalization (and therefore of McDonaldization). It was an effective mechanism for the destruction of massive numbers of human beings. For example, early experiments showed that bullets were inefficient; the Nazis eventually settled on gas as the most efficient means of destroying millions of people. The Nazis also found it efficient to use members of the Jewish community to perform a variety of tasks (for example, choosing the next group of victims) that the Nazis otherwise would have had to perform themselves.[43] These members of the Jewish community were, in a way, prosumers because they were helping to produce victims of the same gas chambers and ovens which would eventually kill (literally consume) them. Many Jews cooperated because it seemed like the "rational" thing to do (they might be able to save others or themselves) in such a rationalized system.

The Holocaust emphasized quantity, such as how many people could be killed in the shortest amount of time and at the lowest possible cost.[44] There was certainly little attention paid to the quality of the life, or even of the death, of the Jews as they marched inexorably to the gas chambers.

In another quantitative sense, the Holocaust has the dubious distinction of being seen as the most extreme of mass exterminations:

> Like everything else done in the modern—rational, planned, scientifically informed, expert, efficiently managed, coordinated—way, the Holocaust . . . put to shame all its alleged pre-modern equivalents, exposing them as primitive, wasteful and ineffective by comparison . . . the Holocaust . . . towers high above the past genocidal episodes.[45]

The Holocaust involved an effort to make mass murder routine. The whole process had an assembly-line quality about it. Trains snaked their way toward the concentration camps; victims lined up and followed a set series of steps. Once the process was complete, camp workers produced stacks of dead bodies for systematic disposal.

Finally, the victims of the Holocaust were managed by a huge nonhuman technology:

> [Auschwitz] was also a mundane extension of the modern factory system. Rather than producing goods, the raw material was human beings and the end-product was death, so many units per day marked carefully on the manager's production charts. The chimneys, the very symbol of the modern factory system, poured forth acrid smoke produced by burning human flesh. The brilliantly organized railroad grid of modern Europe carried a new kind of raw material to the factories. It did so in the same manner as with other cargo. . . . Engineers designed the crematoria; managers designed the system of bureaucracy that worked with a zest and efficiency.[46]

Needless to say, the Holocaust represented the ultimate in the irrationality of rationality. After all, what could be more dehumanizing than murdering millions of people in such a mechanical way? Furthermore, for the murders to have occurred in the first place, the victims had to be dehumanized—that is, "reduced to a set of quantitative measures."[47] Overall, "German bureaucratic machinery was put in the service of a goal incomprehensible in its irrationality."[48]

Discussing the Holocaust in the context of McDonaldization may seem extreme to some readers, perhaps unreasonable, even offensive. Clearly, the fast-food restaurant cannot be discussed in the same breath as the Holocaust. There has been no more heinous crime in the history of humankind. Yet there are strong reasons for presenting the Holocaust as a precursor of McDonaldization. First, the Holocaust was organized around the principles of formal rationality, relying extensively on the paradigm of that type of rationality—the bureaucracy. Second, the Holocaust was also linked to the factory system which, as we will soon discuss, is another precursor of McDonaldization. Third, the spread of formal rationality today, through the process of McDonaldization, supports Bauman's view that something like the Holocaust could happen again.

Scientific Management: Finding the One Best Way

A less dramatic but more broadly important precursor to McDonaldization was the development of scientific management. In fact, Weber at times mentioned scientific management in discussing the rationalization process.

Scientific management was created in the United States by Frederick W. Taylor in the late 19th and early 20th centuries. His ideas played a key role in shaping the work world throughout the 20th century and to this day.[49] Taylor developed a series of principles designed to rationalize work. He was hired by a number of large organizations (e.g., Bethlehem Steel) to implement those ideas, mostly in their factories.

Taylor was animated by the belief that the United States suffered from "inefficiency in almost all our daily acts" and that there was a need for "greater national efficiency." His followers came to be known as "efficiency experts." His "time-and-motion" studies were designed to replace what Taylor called the inefficient "rule-of-thumb" methods, which dominated work in his day, with what he thought of as the "one best way"—that is, the optimum means to the end of doing a job.[50] Taylor outlined a series of steps to be followed in time-and-motion studies. They included finding skilled workers; studying their elementary movements (as well as their tools and implements); timing each step carefully (calculability) with the aim of discovering the most efficient way of accomplishing each of them; eliminating "all false movements, slow movements, and useless movements"; and finally combining the most efficient movements (and tools) to create the "one best way" of doing a job.[51] Scientific management also placed great emphasis on predictability. Clearly, in delineating the one best way to do a job, Taylor sought an approach that each and every worker could use. Taylor also believed that allowing workers to choose their own tools and methods of doing a job led to low productivity and poor quality. Instead, he sought the complete standardization of tools and work processes. Taylor also favored clear and detailed standards that made sure all workers did a given type of job in the same way and would therefore consistently do what he considered good work and produce high-quality products.

Overall, scientific management produced a nonhuman technology that exerted great control over workers. When workers followed Taylor's methods, employers found that they worked much more efficiently, that everyone performed the same steps (that is, their work exhibited predictability), and that they produced a great deal more while their pay had to be increased only slightly (another instance of emphasizing calculability). Taylor's methods thus meant increased profits for those enterprises that employed them.

Like all rational systems, scientific management had its irrationalities. Above all, it was a dehumanizing system in which people were considered expendable and treated as such. Furthermore, because workers did only one or a few tasks, most of their skills and abilities remained unused.

Although one hears little these days of Taylor, efficiency experts, and time-and-motion studies, their impact is strongly felt in a McDonaldized society. For instance, hamburger chains strive to discover and implement the "one best way" to grill hamburgers, cook French fries, prepare shakes, process customers, and the rest. The most efficient ways of handling a variety of tasks have been codified in training manuals and taught to managers who, in turn, teach them to new employees. The design of the fast-food restaurant and its various technologies have been put in place to aid in the attainment of the most efficient means to the end of feeding large numbers of people. Here, again, McDonald's did not invent these ideas but, rather, brought them together with the principles of the bureaucracy and of the assembly-line, thus contributing to the creation of McDonaldization.

The Assembly-Line: Turning Workers Into Robots

Like the modern bureaucracy and scientific management, the assembly-line came into existence at the dawn of the 20th century. The assembly-line was pioneered in the automobile industry. The ideas associated with both bureaucratization and scientific management played a major role in shaping that industry. The automobile assembly-line was invented mainly because Henry Ford wanted to save time, energy, and money (that is, to be more efficient). Greater efficiency would lead to lower prices, increased sales, and greater profitability for the Ford Motor Company.[52]

Ford got the idea for the automobile assembly-line from the overhead trolley system used at the time by Chicago meatpackers to butcher cattle. As a steer carcass was propelled along on the trolley system, a line of highly specialized butchers performed specific tasks so that when it reached the end of the line, the carcass had been completely butchered. This system was clearly more efficient than having a single meat cutter, standing in one spot, handle all these tasks.

On the basis of this experience and his knowledge of the automobile business, Ford developed a set of principles for the construction of an automobile assembly-line, principles that to this day stand as models of efficiency, including reducing work-related movements to an absolute minimum, having parts needed in the assembly process travel the least possible distance, using mechanical (rather than human) means to move the car (and parts) from one step in the assembly process to the next, and eliminating complex sets of movements with the worker doing "as nearly as possible only one thing with one movement."[53]

The Japanese adopted American assembly-line technology after World War II and then made their own distinctive contributions to heightened efficiency. For example, the Japanese "just-in-time" system replaced the American "just-in-case" system. Both systems refer to the supply of needed parts to a manufacturing operation. In the American system, parts are stored in the plant until, or in case, they are needed. This system leads to inefficiencies such as the purchase and storage (at great cost) of parts not needed for quite some time. To counter these inefficiencies, the Japanese developed the just-in-time system: Needed parts arrived at the assembly-line just as they were to be placed in the car (or whatever object was being manufactured). In effect, all the Japanese company's suppliers became part of the assembly-line process.

In either system, the assembly-line permits the quantification of many elements of the production process and maximizes the number of cars or other goods produced. What each worker on the line does, such as putting a hubcap on each passing car, is highly predictable and leads to identical end products.

The assembly-line is also a nonhuman technology that permits maximum control over workers. It is immediately obvious when a worker fails to perform the required tasks. There would, for example, be a missing hubcap as the car moves down the line. The limited time allotted for each job allows little or no room for innovative ways of doing specific tasks. Thus, fewer, as well as less-skilled, workers are able to produce cars. Furthermore, the specialization of each task permits the replacement of human workers with robots. Today, mechanical robots handle more and more assembly-line tasks and some plants are nearly fully automated and robotized.[54]

As has been well detailed by many observers, there is much about the assembly-line that is irrational. For example, it can be a dehumanizing setting in which to work. Human beings, equipped with a wide array of skills and abilities, are asked to perform a limited number of highly simplified tasks repeatedly. Instead of expressing their human abilities on the job, people are forced to deny their humanity and to work like human robots.

Despite its flaws, the assembly-line represented a remarkable step forward in the rationalization of production and became widely used throughout manufacturing. Like bureaucracy and even the Holocaust and its camps, the automobile assembly-line is an excellent illustration of the basic elements of formal rationality.

The assembly-line also has had a profound influence on the development of the fast-food restaurant. "The people who pioneered fast food revered Ford's assembly-line methods."[55] The most obvious example of this mimicry is the conveyor belt Burger King used to cook its hamburgers (see Chapter 5). Less obvious is the fact that much of the work in a fast-food restaurant is performed in assembly-line fashion, with tasks broken down into their simplest components. For example, "making a hamburger" means grilling the burgers, putting them on the rolls, smearing on the "special sauce," laying on the lettuce and tomato, and wrapping the fully dressed burgers. Even customers face a kind of assembly-line, with a most obvious example being the three-step (order, pay, leave) drive-through window. As one observer notes, "The basic elements of the factory have obviously been introduced to the fast-food phenomenon . . . [with] the advent of the feeding machine."[56]

An interesting example of the assembly-line as a "feeding machine" is to be found in Yo! Sushi, a relatively small (over 90 restaurants), but global, chain of sushi restaurants. What distinguishes Yo! Sushi restaurants is a conveyor belt that runs around the counter. It is used to deliver food to consumers who make their selections as the food passes before them. It is, in a sense, an assembly-line designed to allow consumers (rather than the workers in, for example, Burger King) to create their own meal.[57]

An even more recent version of the assembly-line is to be found in Amazon's proposed digital, on-demand system for manufacturing apparel ordered online. The various pieces needed for, say, a jacket are cut to size automatically. They are then placed on a conveyor belt where they are stitched together by an automated sewing machine or human attendants.[58]

In addition to being a precursor, the automobile assembly-line laid the groundwork for McDonaldization in another way. Mass production gave many people ready access to affordable automobiles, which in turn led to the immense expansion of the highway system and of the tourist industry that grew up alongside it.[59] Restaurants, hotels, campgrounds, gas stations, and the like arose and served as the precursors to many of the franchises that today lie at the heart of the McDonaldized society.[60]

Levittown: Putting Up Houses—"Boom, Boom, Boom"

The availability of the mass-produced automobile also helped make suburbia possible, especially the communities characterized by similarly mass-produced suburban houses pioneered by Levitt & Sons. Between 1947 and 1951, this company built 17,447 homes on former New York potato fields, thereby creating Levittown, Long Island, and an instant community of 75,000 people.[61] The first houses in the second planned community of Levittown, Pennsylvania, went on sale in 1958. The two Levittowns provided the model for innumerable contemporary suburban developments. With their need for and access to automobiles, suburban dwellers were, and are, a natural constituency for the fast-food restaurant, especially its drive-through windows.

Levitt & Sons thought of their building sites as large factories using assembly-line technology: "What it amounted to was a reversal of the Detroit assembly-line. . . . There, the car moved while the workers stayed at their stations. In the case of our houses, it was the workers who moved, doing the same jobs at different locations."[62] The workers performed specialized tasks, much like their compatriots on the automobile assembly-line: "The same man does the same thing every day, despite the psychologists. It is boring; it is bad; but the reward of the green stuff seems to alleviate the boredom of the work."[63] The Levitts thus rationalized the work of the construction laborer much as Ford had done with the automobile worker, with much the same attitude toward the worker.

The housing site as well as the work was rationalized. In and around the building locale, the Levitts constructed warehouses, woodworking shops, plumbing shops, and a sand, gravel, and cement plant. Thus, instead of buying these services and their resulting products from others and then shipping them to the construction site, the products and services were onsite and controlled by the Levitts. Where possible, the Levitts also used prefabricated products. They deemed manufacturing an entirely prefabricated house less efficient, however, than making a partially prefabricated one.

The actual construction of each house followed a series of rigidly defined and rationalized steps. For example, in constructing the wall framework, the workers did no measuring or cutting; each piece had been cut to fit. The siding for a wall consisted of 73 large sheets of Colorbestos, replacing the former requirement of 570 small shingles. All houses were painted under high pressure, using the same two-tone scheme—green on ivory. As a result, "Once the groundwork is down, houses go up boom, boom, boom."[64] The result, of course, was a large number of nearly identical houses produced quickly at low cost.

The emphasis on quantitative factors went beyond the physical construction of the house. Advertisements for Levittown houses stressed "the size and value of the house."[65] In other words, Levittown, like its many successors in the march toward increased rationalization, tried to convince consumers that they were getting the most for the least amount of money.

These principles, once used exclusively in low-priced homes, have since been applied to high-priced homes, as well. "McMansions" are increasingly often little more than huge and luxuriously appointed, factory-made modular homes.[66]

Many have criticized life in identical houses in highly rationalized communities. One early critique renamed suburbia "Disturbia," describing the suburban home as a "split-level trap."[67] However, one can also look positively at suburban rationalization. For example, many residents of Levittown have customized their homes so that they no longer look as homogeneous as they once were.[68] Other observers have found much of merit in Levittown and suburbia. Herbert Gans, for example, concluded his study of a third Levittown built in New Jersey by arguing that "whatever its imperfections, Levittown is a good place to live."[69] Whether or not it is a "good" place to live, Levittown is certainly a rationalized place.

The Rise (and Fall) of Brick-and-Mortar Shopping Malls

Like the fast food restaurant, the development of fully enclosed shopping malls was fueled by the rise of automobiles and the growth of suburban housing.[70] However, the modern mall had precursors in arcades such as the Galleria Vittorio Emanuele in Milan, Italy (completed in 1877), and the first planned outdoor shopping center in the United States (built in 1916 in Lake Forest, Illinois). The original fully enclosed shopping mall was Southdale Center in Edina, Minnesota, which opened in 1956, not long after the opening of Ray Kroc's first McDonald's. Today, tens of thousands of malls in the United States are visited by hundreds of millions of shoppers each month. The biggest shopping mall in the United States

is the Mall of America, opened in 1992 down the road from Edina, in Bloomington, Minnesota. It includes three department stores, 520 specialty shops (many
of them parts of chains), 50 restaurants, and an amusement park, Nickelodeon
Universe, with 24 rides.[71] Enormous malls have become a global phenomenon.
In fact, 8 of the 10 largest mega-malls are found in Asia.[72] The largest, by far, is
the New South China Mall in Dongguan, China, which dwarfs the Canadian
and American mega-malls. It has 7.1 million square feet compared to the Mall of
America. However, few of the New South China Mall's 1,500 stores are open; it
is thought of as a "dead mall" (see below). While most of the world's largest mega-
malls are now in China, others can be found in the Philippines, Dubai, Turkey,
Kuala Lumpur, Colombia, Thailand, and Brazil. Found in these mega-malls are
themed zones, ski slopes (one in a mall in the desert of Dubai!), ice skating rinks,
walk-through aquariums, skyscraper hotels, and so on.

Shopping malls and McDonaldized chains have, at least in the past, complemented each other beautifully. This is especially true of fast food chains and the
malls' food courts. The malls provided a predictable, uniform, and profitable
venue for such chains. For their part, most malls would have much unrented
space and would not be able to exist had it not been for the chains. Simultaneous
products of the fast-moving automobile age, malls and chains fed off each other,
furthering McDonaldization.

Ironically, malls today have become a kind of community center for both young
and old. Many elderly people now use malls as places to both exercise and socialize.
Teens prowl the malls after school and on weekends, seeking social contact and
checking out the latest in fashions and mass entertainment. Because some parents also
take their children to malls to "play," malls are now offering play rooms (free ones as
well as profit-making outlets that charge an entry fee and offer things like free video
games and free movies).[73] Like many other contributors to the McDonaldization of
society, malls strive to engage customers from the cradle to the grave.

William Kowinski argues that the mall "was the culmination of all the
American dreams, both decent and demented; the fulfillment, the model of
the postwar paradise."[74] One could give priority to the mall, as Kowinski does,
and discuss the "malling of America." However, in my view, the fast-food restaurant is a far more powerful and influential force. Like the mall, however,
McDonaldization can be seen as both "decent and demented."

It is important to note that many malls today are in danger of closing, are in
the process of closing, and have already closed completely (such as the Randall
Park Mall outside Cleveland, Ohio; see the dead malls series of YouTube videos by Dan Bell,[75] as well as deadmalls.com for an extensive listing of shuttered
malls).[76] Most of the others have been plagued by an increasing number of empty

shops; they have become "zombie malls"—half-empty shells with few shops. Burlington Center in New Jersey once had over 100 tenants; it now has less than 20.[77] This is a devastating sight in malls that adversely affects the spectacle they are endeavoring to create in order to attract and retain customers.[78] Many of the mall-based shops that are going out of business, in bankruptcy, or retrenching are outlets of McDonaldized chains (e.g., Limited; Payless Shoesource). Because most malls have large food courts housing the major McDonaldized food chains, those chains are also threatened, although to a far lesser extent, by dead and zombie malls. Closed shops and restaurants mean less revenue to the mall owners and that makes it more difficult for them to survive.

While some malls are being bulldozed, or starting over from scratch and becoming something very different (full-fledged amusement parks, colleges, health centers), many others are struggling to redefine and to restructure themselves. They are seeking to retain shopping, but to go beyond it to "include more restaurants and entertainment, or health care and education."[79] These are the new anchors of shopping malls replacing traditional anchors such as Sears and Macy's.

Not only are malls on life-support, the same is true of many of the remaining brick-and-mortar department stores (others such as Gimbel's, Wanamaker's, and Hecht's are only distant memories). Among the surviving department stores, Macy's and J.C. Penney are closing stores and in 2017 the venerable Sears announced that there was "substantial doubt" that it would survive.[80] Furthermore, it also announced that it would close 109 of its K-Mart stores. Department stores have historically been the anchors of shopping malls, so their decline is intimately related, and contributes further, to the decline of malls.

In spite of the decline of malls and other brick-and-mortar consumption sites, much more consumption still takes place in them than in the rising online sites to be discussed below. In 2016, almost $102 billion was spent online, but this pales in comparison to the $1.24 trillion spent in brick-and-mortar sites. Spending online is less than 10% (8.3%) of the amount spent in those brick-and-mortar sites.[81] However, spending online is increasing rapidly, rising from an increase of $30 billion a year between 2010 and 2014 to an average projected annual increase of $40 billion in 2015–2017.[82]

McDONALDIZATION AND CONSUMPTION TODAY

The Internet in general, and Amazon (founded in 1994) in particular, was coming of age about the time the first edition of this book was published and long after I

wrote my first essay on the topic.[83] Without Internet sites such as Amazon to analyze from the perspective of McDonaldization, the focus was on all there was to
analyze—brick-and-mortar consumption sites such as McDonald's restaurants.
While, as we've seen, many brick-and-mortar sites (especially McDonald's) have
expanded dramatically in the intervening years, that growth has been dwarfed
by a wide and ever-increasing margin with the expansion and proliferation of
Internet sites devoted to consumption.

For example, Amazon, which started operations when McDonald's was
already a giant in the business world, has long since grown much larger than
McDonald's and its advantage will become ever-larger in the coming years. As
large and powerful as Amazon has become, Alibaba in China is an even bigger e-commerce site; also growing and of increasing importance is India-based
Flipkart. However, as discussed previously, when we look solely at retail business,
the brick-and-mortar realm retains a huge, but gradually diminishing, lead over
digital businesses.[84]

The concern here is not so much with amount of business, digital or otherwise, but with the process of McDonaldization and its impact on consumption. It
seems clear that although much more consumption continues, and will continue,
to occur in the brick-and-mortar world, the center of the McDonaldization of
consumption (and much, if not everything, else), as well as the most extreme
examples of it, are to be found not in the brick-and-mortar world, but rather in
the digital world. Consumption on digital sites tends to be much more *efficient,
predictable, calculable,* and *controlled* than consumption in brick-and-mortar sites.
This is certainly true for consumers, but in many ways it is even truer for the
"work" that gets done on those sites. As direct relationships with human workers
reduce to a minimum on digital sites, and in many cases are eliminated completely, that work is increasingly done by an array of nonhuman technologies
without direct human involvement. Because human beings are a, if not *the,* major
source of inefficiency, unpredictability, incalculability, and loss of control, digital
systems that minimize, or eliminate, their role are likely to approach a degree
of McDonaldization unimaginable in the brick-and-mortar world (although, of
course, in digital systems humans operate behind the scenes in creating, refining,
and maintaining those systems).

However, as we have seen, Amazon Go's new convenience store represents
an effort in the brick-and-mortar world to compete with online sites by limiting direct involvement with human workers and, in the process, to ratchet up
the level of McDonaldization. It does so by utilizing an array of technological
advances and by increasing the degree to which consumers become prosumers.

Nevertheless, *it is in the digital world, as well as the augmented world of bricks-and-clicks, that McDonaldization has reached new and unprecedented heights.* More generally, the worlds of online, offline, and integrated on- and offline consumption have grown far more McDonaldized and we are still in the early stages of this development, which is likely to accelerate at an ever-increasing pace.

Is "McDonaldization" Still the Best Label?

This leads to the issue of whether it makes sense to continue to use the term *McDonaldization* to describe the process of concern in this book. In discussing that issue, I will focus on three behemoths in the realm of consumption, as well as in its McDonaldization—McDonald's, Wal-Mart, and Amazon. The question then becomes whether either *Wal-Martization* or *Amazon.comization* would be better terms than *McDonaldization* for that process. These three corporations represent, in turn, (1) a business, McDonald's, that is dominated by brick-and-mortar sites (and likely to remain so); (2) another business, Wal-Mart, also dominated by such sites but in the process of becoming more of a digital presence (and competitor to Amazon); and (3) the almost totally digital Amazon that is ironically gaining a significant foothold in the brick-and-mortar world.

Among the things that these three examples demonstrate is, once again, that it is increasingly impossible (if it ever really was possible) to clearly distinguish between the material (brick-and-mortar) and the digital; as pointed out earlier they complement, and supplement, one another, creating augmented realities. Amazon is becoming more of a material reality in its bookstores, Amazon Go convenience stores, and its Whole Foods supermarkets, while Wal-Mart is desperate to become a bigger player in the digital world. The anomaly here is McDonald's. Because of what it sells—food—it is doomed to remain, at least for the foreseeable future, an almost totally brick-and-mortar phenomenon (McDonald's does now have digital kiosks for ordering food), at least until a way is found to transport food digitally, directly to consumers. Another brick-and-mortar mainstay, the hotel, has moved more in the digital direction by offering iPads with apps allowing guests to, for example, order food and call an Uber.[85] Other apps allow guests to book rooms, check in and out, and receive alerts when their rooms are ready and even unlock the rooms before they reach the door.

There are a variety of ironies in this comparison between McDonald's, Wal-Mart, and Amazon. First, although it is the paradigm for the process of McDonaldization, McDonald's is, in business terms, by far the least successful. It is the smallest in terms of total revenues and profits. Second, its future is bleak, at least in comparison to the other two. This is the case because, as largely a collection of brick-and-mortar entities in the business of selling only food, McDonald's is limited in the amount of business it can do. Its limitations are clear in comparison to the now quickly digitalizing Wal-Mart and the still almost fully digital Amazon and the incredibly large amount and number of diverse products that they both sell. Third, while its food and its general model have been globalized, it is far harder to globalize the food it sells than what Wal-Mart and Amazon sell (virtually everything). The latter can more easily alter what they sell in different world markets (adding and deleting as required from their inventories of products), but McDonald's can only offer its basic menu and a few foods adapted to different locales. Most of its famous menu (Big Mac, Egg McMuffin) is expected to, and must, remain intact. To successfully McDonaldize, McDonald's must keep its menu items limited in number. Consumers the world over know about, and expect to be offered, its signature menu items. Finally, it is far more difficult to McDonaldize largely brick-and-mortar businesses than it is largely digital businesses. Physical structures impose limitations on the process that do not exist in the more "liquid" digital world. Thus, for these and other reasons, McDonald's is in many ways the *least* McDonaldized of the three, and Amazon, because it is almost totally digital, encounters far fewer barriers to being ever more efficient, predictable, calculable, and controllable.

The following section compares these three giants of consumption with more detail in terms of both consumption and McDonaldization.

COMPARING McDONALD'S, WAL-MART, AND AMAZON

In Consumption

Wal-Mart is now by far the biggest player in the world of consumption. It did almost $500 billion in business in 2016; Amazon grossed $136 billion (and Amazon's founder, Jeff Bezos, became, at least briefly, the world's richest person in mid-2017[86]); McDonald's trailed badly doing *only* about $25 billion in business. Given the argument about the advantages of digitality, one would expect Amazon, founded in 1994, to lead the pack in terms of sales. However, Wal-Mart had a big head start since it was founded in 1962, long before Amazon. While this was almost a decade later than Kroc's McDonald's, it was almost three decades *before* Amazon. This head start, as well as Wal-Mart's aggressive global expansion, has given it a huge advantage over Amazon. However, as is the case with many online businesses, investors see a far brighter future for Amazon than Wal-Mart. In fact, Amazon's market capitalization is more than the combined valuation of Wal-Mart *and* that of Target, Costco, Macy's, and Kohl's.[87]

Conventional wisdom has been that Wal-Mart's advantage in sales is likely to decline, and even disappear, in the coming years unless it becomes a much more powerful digital player than it has been to this point. While its strength on the Internet has been growing, e-commerce accounts for less than 5% of Wal-Mart's total business. However, Wal-Mart experienced a dramatic increase (60%) in its digital sales in the first quarter of 2017. Part of this growth was a result of acquiring web retailer Jet.com in late 2016 for $3.2 billion (as well as the tiny Bonobos in 2017). However, Wal-Mart's CEO claimed that most of the growth in Internet business has been, and will in the future continue to be, organic. He also pointed to the augmentation involved in this growth in concert with the expansion of brick-and-mortar sales: "We can see that we're moving faster to combine our digital and physical assets to make shopping easier and more enjoyable for customers." [88] Wal-Mart is also improving its brick-and-mortar operations by, among other things, speeding up the checkout process and having customers use more apps. It is also becoming more of a digital enterprise by building up its online grocery business. While Wal-Mart and, to a lesser degree, Amazon, sell food, it constitutes a much smaller percentage of their business than McDonald's where food accounts for virtually all of its revenue.

Hampering McDonald's and, to a lesser degree, Wal-Mart in the future, as least in comparison to Amazon, is the fact they remain largely brick-and-mortar businesses. As we saw, Wal-Mart is making gains in its effort to compete better with Amazon online, but McDonald's is virtually a nonplayer in the digital world. Amazon continues to be much stronger in online consumption than Wal-Mart and it is difficult to envision a scenario where Wal-Mart rivals, let alone outdistances, Amazon in online sales. In spite of its efforts and resources, it will be very difficult for Wal-Mart to overtake Amazon online both because of the latter's huge lead in online sales *and* the fact that it continues to innovate and to explore new options. For example, Amazon has begun examining the possibility of entering the highly lucrative $300 billion a year pharmacy business.[89]

In Degree of McDonaldization

Because Wal-Mart's operations are highly rationalized, it remains much bigger than Amazon, and its business dwarfs that of McDonald's, so we might be tempted to think in terms of "Wal-Martization" rather than McDonaldization to describe the process of concern in this book. However, Wal-Mart continues to be dominated by its brick-and-mortar stores and that will limit its ability to rationalize, at least in comparison to the still almost totally digital, Amazon. Of course, McDonald's, as well as the fast-food industry, is even more trapped in the brick-and-mortar world. The irony is that given the realities of the restaurant business, McDonald's ability to McDonaldize as much as it did is quite remarkable. However, its ability to take that process much further is far more limited than Wal-Mart's and especially that of Amazon's.

At McDonald's, the reality of having raw, fresh ingredients delivered, and in stock, as well as of cooking and serving food, and then dealing with the debris when a diner is finished, are all complex, labor-intensive, processes in which much can go wrong. This is reflected, among other ways, in the health problems that have plagued a number of fast-food chains (e.g., Chipotle). Wal-Mart sells a lot of food, but most of it is taken home uncooked and prepared at home by consumers. Food is a relatively small component of Amazon's business.

Most of what both Wal-Mart and Amazon sell to customers flows through an admittedly highly complex transshipment process, but many products never leave the boxes in which the manufacturers package them. Both Wal-Mart and Amazon have McDonaldized this process to a high degree, but Amazon has the huge advantage of cutting out the cumbersome steps at Wal-Mart of shipping to the stores, stocking products, having customers trek to its stores, having salespeople on duty to answer questions and complete sales, having cashiers at checkout counters to receive payment, and then in many cases shipping the products to consumers' homes. While this is not as cumbersome as what transpires at McDonald's, it is far more cumbersome than the way similar transactions are handled online at Amazon.

These differences are reflected, among many other ways, by the number of people employed in these three corporations. Of the three corporations being discussed here, Wal-Mart, as is to be expected given the size of its global business and the fact that it is largely in the brick-and mortar world, employed 2.3 million people worldwide in 2016; 1.4 million of them were in the United States. McDonald's required 375,000 employees to do about $25 billion in business. Amazon did much more business than McDonald's and it did so with about 25,000 fewer employees (before the addition of Whole Food's workforce of over 90,000 employees). Wal-Mart did much more business than Amazon (and certainly McDonald's), but it required an enormous number of workers to do so. As has been pointed out several times before, people are not only costly, but they are the greatest impediments to the McDonaldization process, especially because the greatest irrationalities can be traced to them. For example, people are prone to inefficiency, unpredictability, and doing things that are difficult to quantify. In fact, the control dimension in the McDonaldization process is mainly about creating nonhuman technologies in order to control, not always successfully, human workers. Furthermore, the ultimate goal of these technologies is to replace humans with, among other things, automated technologies and robots.

Robotization is proceeding apace in many sectors of the economy. In many cases, human workers are teaching robots what they know so that someday, perhaps in the not-too-distant future, they will replace the humans who are doing the teaching.[90] Among the jobs, some surprising, that robots are being trained to handle are travel agents; lawyers who, among other things, search legal documents; customer service representatives; and software engineers. These robots serve to help to McDonaldize the work that goes on in their domains and, if they don't, they will be retaught and reprogrammed over and over until they do. In many, maybe most, cases, robots will be far less of a barrier to McDonaldization and, more likely, will serve to greatly expedite the expansion of the process.

Human consumers are also barriers to McDonaldization, but they are less easily dispensed with than human workers, at least until some point far into the future when more advanced technologies replace them with their avatars. However, the fact is that the consumption system cannot function, at least for the foreseeable future, without human consumers who are, at the minimum, animating their avatars. Aware that human consumers are barriers to McDonaldization, fast-food restaurants have tried, as much as possible, to keep them out of the restaurants themselves by routing them through drive-throughs or, like Domino's and other pizza chains, delivering food to them.

One of the obvious lessons here is that brick-and-mortar businesses require many more workers than digital businesses and that is a major factor in limiting the ability of the former to McDonaldize in comparison to the latter. This is related to the fact that it is much easier to transform consumers into prosumers (those who *both* produce and consume, sometimes simultaneously) online. Indeed, if Internet businesses and other digital sites are to operate successfully, *consumers must become prosumers*. While brick-and-mortar sites have long done this, most notably McDonald's efforts to get consumers to perform tasks traditionally performed by paid workers, this is accomplished much more easily and extensively on Internet sites where it is hard, if not impossible, for consumers to find workers to help them. In the main, if prosumers online want something done, they have little choice but to do it themselves.

Then there are all the material realities and impediments associated with brick-and-mortar sites. Consumers (and workers) must physically go to them in order to consume, goods must be delivered there, the goods must often be processed before they can be sold to consumers, consumers must transport their purchases to their homes, and so on. All of these steps are reduced in the online consumption of goods and they are almost entirely eliminated as far as digital products such as e-books and e-music are concerned.

Given the limitations of such brick-and-mortar sites as Wal-Mart's stores, and especially McDonald's restaurants, would we be justified in renaming the process of concern in this book "Amazon.comizaton"? A strong argument can be made in support of such a relabeling of the process of McDonaldization. However, as we saw, the basic principles of McDonaldization apply as well, or even better, to largely digital sites like Amazon.com than they do to brick-and-mortar sites like McDonald's. Amazon.com and many other successful digital sites are arguably *more* McDonaldized than brick-and-mortar sites; they are more *McDonaldized than McDonald's*. The present, and even more the future, belongs to the digital world in general, and Amazon.com in particular, but McDonald's is still the pioneer in the creation of the process of McDonaldization. As a result, we will continue to use that term for this process, even as it increasingly characterizes and is epitomized by the digital world.

Digital McDonaldization

While Amazon is the most important and powerful example of largely digital McDonaldization, there are many other important examples including Uber, Airbnb, and eBay. Among the many lesser-known of such digital, largely online, businesses are Farfetch (global marketplace for independent luxury boutiques), Hello Alfred (which, as mentioned above, dispatches contractors to do recurring household work), and Managed by Q (cleaning services and office maintenance). While these are largely digital, we must not forget that such digital businesses rely on an elaborate material infrastructure including computer hardware, fiber optic cable, and routing equipment, with all of it enabled by intertwined servers. This points, in a somewhat different way, to the lack of a clear dividing line between the material and the digital, as well as to the ways in which they augment one another.

All of these digital sites are part of what has been called "platform capitalism." Platforms are "digital infrastructures that enable two or more groups to interact."[91] That is, they offer digital platforms that bring together a variety of actors. Of greatest interest here are those that serve as intermediaries between users, especially buyers and sellers.[92] Amazon Go's platform, at least in the material world, goes even further in this, at least at the moment, by largely eliminating sellers and electronically bringing together shoppers and the products of interest to them. Uber's platform, as well as those of other transportation network companies (e.g., Lyfft, Didi Chuxing in China, among many others), matches up those who need transportation with those who have it to offer. In fact, Uber seeks to avoid transportation rules, especially, in Europe by seeking to be considered as a matching platform and *not* a transportation company. However, in a 2017 ruling by the European Court of Justice, Uber was found to be, most fundamentally, an organization involved in "a comprehensive system for on-demand urban transport."[93] Airbnb's platform links those looking for rentals with those offering them. TaskRabbit and Mechanical Turk are platforms that match those looking for work completing limited, discrete tasks with those offering such usually short-term, piece-rate work. Amazon is the most successful platform in this realm because it offers virtually everything to everyone. It even connects those not employed by Amazon (e.g., those with used books to sell) with those interested in making a purchase. Stitch Fix (see above) is a platform that matches largely female consumers with clothing of various types through use of proprietary algorithms.[94] It automatically sends consumers five pieces of (returnable) clothing selected by "stylists." This clearly constitutes a huge threat to chains of brick-and-mortar clothing shops.

In 2017, Amazon reached another milestone in surpassing brick-and-mortar Macy's as the largest seller of clothing in the United States.[95] This is another market that, like books and other products, may have reached a tipping point and may come to be increasingly dominated by online sales. To further expand its position in that market, it is also exploring the possibility of selling custom-fit clothing via the Internet. Amazon is working on a camera that would capture and upload customers' measurements.

Other web-based platforms such as Facebook and Google match people who want information with the sources of that information. While the latter sites—and many others—do not sell anything directly to users, all of their billions of users allow them to make huge profits from advertisers anxious to gain access to them and ultimately sell them goods and services.

Then there are the platforms—okCupid, Match.com, and Tinder—that are part of the "meet market" that allows people interested in dating—or just "hooking up"—to make contact with one another. The term *meet market* implies that in one way or another people are commodities to be "obtained" in that market.

Meet markets have done much to McDonaldize the process of meeting people for one reason or another.

While these platforms clearly have significant material components, they are also replacing other material realities such as taxicabs, hotels, and social clubs. As such, as these sites continue to morph from "transaction enablers" to "participation gatekeepers," they will greatly increase their ability to control the transactions that take place in their domains. Platforms provide the material substructure for a digital world that is revolutionizing capitalism and business as we have known them. They also make possible a level and degree of McDonaldization that is far beyond that which was ever possible in the brick-and-mortar world. There will be much more on this throughout the book, and many other digital examples will be discussed.

EFFICIENCY AND CALCULABILITY

Consumers 1

C hapter 2 dealt, in part, with the organizations and systems that were precursors to, as well as the earliest manifestations of, the process of McDonaldization. As we saw, the early forms include bureaucracies, industrial organizations, the assembly-line, and, of course, fast-food restaurants. Chapter 2 also dealt, in part, with a new largely online world—most notably on Amazon.com—where McDonaldization has reached new heights. Needless to say, people exist in and on these settings. It is the norm to distinguish between two types of people in, or on, these settings: consumers (or customers, clients) and producers (or workers). However, it is important to note that people as exclusively producers are of declining importance in material sites and virtually nonexistent on digital sites. In discussing the platform economy (see Chapter 2), which supports digital consumption sites, Herrman describes them as "employee-light."[1] For example, while Amazon.com employs about 14 workers for every $10 million in revenue generated, brick-and-mortar retailers require almost 50 workers to generate the same amount of revenue.[2] Uber and Airbnb do not employ drivers (Uber sees them as "independent contractors" lacking the rights of employees, e.g., for overtime) and homeowners; they are on their own in exchange for a percentage of the income derived from the services they offer. In Airbnb's case, homeowners get the lion's share of the income. They pay Airbnb a 3% fee, while guests pay the company a 6% to 12% fee. In the case of Uber, drivers usually get between 15% and 25% of the fare. However, these companies do employ people to manage these systems; Uber, with revenue of nearly $11 billion, has only about 7,000 employees.

These companies are also described as being "asset-light" and it is the "lightness" in both paid employees and assets that allows Internet sites to reach new heights of McDonaldization. For example, Uber owns no cars; those who drive for Uber own the cars and pay the expenses associated with buying (or leasing) and maintaining them. Similarly, Airbnb owns no properties; those who offer them for rent on the site do and they, too, are responsible for all of the expenses associated with them. With relatively few employees and minimal material assets, Internet sites are freed to maximize the process of McDonaldization. However, it is important to note that those who do the work in these systems—the drivers and homeowners—have little ability to McDonaldize most of what they do. In addition, as members of the "gig economy," they generally earn comparatively little and have no job security, in part because they do not have jobs in the conventional sense. This frees up Uber, Airbnb, and others to exploit them greatly.

We will adhere to the norm of differentiating between consumers and producers in the next four chapters. This chapter and the next will deal with consumers, while Chapters 5 and 6 will be devoted to producers. However, more and more scholars are rejecting the binary distinction between producers and consumers and thinking more in terms of "prosumers," or those who both produce and consume.[3] In fact, both are, in reality, prosumers because producers must consume at least to some degree and consumers must also produce in various ways. We will have more to say about prosumers at several points in this book, but for the time being we will set that concept aside and deal separately with consumers and producers.

This chapter deals with consumers in terms of two of the four basic dimensions of McDonaldization: efficiency and calculability. Chapter 4 does the same with the other two dimensions of McDonaldization: predictability and control. While the focus is on the consumer, workers—the producers—will inevitably be touched on in these chapters and discussions.

We will discuss a wide array of consumers in the next two chapters including tourists, students, campers, diners, patients, parents, mothers-to-be, shoppers (including cybershoppers), dieters, exercisers, and those looking for dates (or simply for sex).

EFFICIENCY: DRIVE-THROUGHS AND FINGER FOODS

Efficiency is perhaps the dimension of McDonaldization most often linked to the seeming increase in the pace of contemporary life. Increasing efficiency is behind just-in-time production, faster service, streamlined operations, and tight schedules everywhere—from the workplace, to Disney World, to the home, and most important, to consumption sites on the Internet.

Efficiency is generally a good thing. It is clearly advantageous to consumers, who are able to obtain what they need more quickly and with less effort. Similarly, efficient workers are able to perform their tasks more rapidly and easily. Managers and owners gain because more work gets done, more customers are served, and greater profits are earned. But as is the case with McDonaldization in general, and each of its dimensions, irrationalities such as surprising inefficiencies and the dehumanization of consumers and workers are associated with the drive for increased efficiency. Most extremely, the drive for efficiency in both brick-and-mortar and digital (e.g., websites) settings has the irrational consequence of the great reduction, if not near-total elimination, of human workers. Along with automated technologies, prosumers increasingly do the work, for no pay, those paid workers once did.

Efficiency means choosing (or having chosen for you by others) the optimum means to a given end. However, the truly optimum means to an end is rarely found. People and organizations rarely maximize because they are hampered by such factors as the constraints of history, financial circumstances, organizational realities, and the limitations of human nature.[4] Organizations continue to strive for maximization in the hope that they will at least increase their efficiency. Organizations are now coming closer to maximizing efficiency on the Internet, in brick-and-mortar settings where unpaid prosumers do more and more of the work, and in the world that augments the two.

In a McDonaldized society, consumers and workers rarely search for the best means to an end on their own; rather, they tend to rely on previously discovered and institutionalized means. Thus, when people start a new job, they are not expected to figure out for themselves how to do the work most efficiently. Instead, they undergo training designed to teach them what has been discovered over time to be the most efficient way of doing the work. Once on the job, people may discover little tricks that help them perform the task more efficiently, and these days, they are encouraged to pass this information on to management so that all workers performing that task can perform a bit more efficiently. In this way, over time, efficiency (and productivity) gradually increases. In fact, much of the economic boom in the late 20th and early 21st centuries was attributed to the dramatic increases in efficiency and productivity that permitted significant growth with little inflation. Even after the onset of the Great Recession beginning in late 2007, efficiency increased, but this time employers discovered ways of producing as much, or more, with fewer and fewer employees, more automated technology, and robots, as well as greater use of unpaid prosumers as "working consumers" (see Chapter 4).

For their part, consumers are generally interested in the most efficient ways to traverse a shopping mall, get through a fast-food restaurant, wend their way around a theme park or a cruise ship, and arrive at the right website and find what they want. To make this easier, all of these settings have created systems that direct, or even force, consumers in the most efficient direction. They have done so, at least in part, because it is in their interest to do so. Consumers who are able to get to desired locations and to obtain goods and services more expeditiously are then able to buy more of those goods and services. They are therefore able to spend more money creating greater profits for the owners of the locations. This has coincided with technological advances (automation, robotization, artificial intelligence, the boom in the Internet) that have served to further reduce the need for human workers. The ongoing and coming loss of jobs associated with these changes, especially robotization, has recently been termed a "robocalypse."[5] This loss of paying jobs will enable further the role unpaid working consumers play in the con(pro)sumption process.

Although the fast-food restaurant certainly did not create the yearning for efficiency (Taylor and scientific management played a big role in this; see Chapter 2), or the methods used to increase it, it has helped turn efficiency into an increasingly universal reality. Many sectors of society have had to change in order to operate in the efficient manner demanded by those accustomed to, among other things, life in the drive-through lane of the fast-food restaurant. This is even more the case online where the level of efficiency far exceeds that found in brick-and-mortar sites. While many manifestations of efficiency can be traced directly to the influence of the fast-food restaurant, many more of them predated and helped shape the fast-food restaurant. Others postdate the founding of McDonald's and are traceable to the coming of age of the Internet in the late 20th century. Nonetheless, they all contribute to the concern, even preoccupation, with efficiency—a central aspect of what is still best described by McDonaldization. The Internet has greatly enhanced that yearning for efficiency as people nearly effortlessly handle tasks, or more likely have them handled for them, without ever leaving their home. What could be more efficient than that?

Streamlining the Process

Efficiency will be discussed under three broad headings: streamlining the process, simplifying the product, and putting consumers (as prosumers) to work.

The Fast-Food Industry: Speeding the Way From Secretion to Excretion

As pointed out in Chapter 1, Ray Kroc was obsessed with streamlining McDonald's operations in order to increase efficiency not only for its workers, but also for those who consume its food. For its customers, McDonald's has done "everything to speed the way from secretion to excretion."[6] For example, the process of getting diners into and out of the fast-food restaurant has been streamlined in various ways. Parking lots adjacent to the restaurant offer readily available parking spots. It's a short walk to the counter, and although customers sometimes have to wait in line, they can usually quickly order, obtain, and pay for their food. The highly limited menu makes the diner's choice easy, in contrast to the many choices available in traditional restaurants. ("Satellite" and "express" fast-food restaurants in, for example, gasoline stations, are even more stream-lined.) With the food obtained, it is but a few steps to a table and the beginning of the "dining experience." With little inducement to linger, diners generally eat quickly and then gather the leftover paper, cardboard, and plastic, discarding them in a nearby trash receptacle, and return to their cars to drive to the next (often McDonaldized) activity.

Those in charge of fast-food restaurants discovered that the drive-through window made this whole process far more streamlined. Instead of requiring diners to undertake the "laborious" and "inefficient" process of parking their cars, walking to the counter, waiting in line, ordering, paying, carrying the food to the table, eating, and disposing of the remnants, the drive-through window offered diners the streamlined option of driving up to the window and driving off with the meal. If they wanted to be even more efficient, diners could begin to eat as they were driving away from the drive-through. Drive-through windows are also efficient for fast-food restaurants. As more and more people use drive-through windows, fewer parking spaces, tables, and employees are needed. Furthermore, consumers take their debris with them as they drive away. This reduces the need for employees to clean up after customers, for trash receptacles, and for workers to empty those receptacles periodically and dispose of all that trash.

Modern technology offers further advances in streamlining. Here is a description of some of the increased efficiency at a Taco Bell in California:

> Inside, diners in a hurry for tacos and burritos can punch up their own orders on a touch-screen computer. Outside, drive-through customers see a video monitor flash back a list of their orders to avoid mistakes. They then can pay using a pneumatic-tube like those many banks employ for drive-up transactions. Their food, and their change, is waiting for them when they pull forward to the pickup window. And if the line of cars grows too long, a Taco Bell worker will wade in with a wireless keyboard to take orders.[7]

Customers' and employees' use of touch screens (at Taco Bell and others, including McDonald's) streamlines the ordering and paying for food thereby reducing the need for counter people and cashiers.[8]

Further increasing efficiency is the growing use of credit and debit cards in fast-food restaurants. Fumbling for cash, and dealing with change, especially increasingly useless coins, is far less efficient for consumers (and workers) than swiping their cards or inserting those with a built-in chip in a terminal at the checkout counter. Coming are cards with radio-frequency identification which will read cards that are a short distance away and eliminate all that swiping and inserting.

Home Cooking (and Related Phenomena): "I Don't Have Time to Cook"

In the early 1950s, at the dawn of the fast-food restaurant era, the major alternative to fast food was the home-cooked meal, made mostly from ingredients purchased beforehand at various local stores and early supermarkets. This was clearly a more efficient way of preparing meals than earlier methods, such as hunting game and gathering fruits and vegetables. Cookbooks also made a major contribution to efficient home cooking. Instead of inventing a dish every time a meal was prepared, the cook could follow a recipe and thus more efficiently produce the dish.

Soon, the widespread availability of the home freezer led to the expanded production of frozen foods.[9] The most efficient frozen food was (and for some still is) the "TV dinner." Swanson created its first TV dinner, its meal-in-a-box, in 1953 and sold 25 million of them in the first year.[10] The large freezer also permitted other efficiencies, such as making fewer trips to the market for enormous purchases rather than making many trips for smaller ones.

However, with the advent of microwavable meals,[11] frozen dinners began to seem comparatively inefficient. Microwaves usually cook faster than stovetops and other ovens, and people can prepare a wider array of foods in them. Perhaps most important, microwave ovens spawned a number of food products (including microwavable soup, pizza, hamburgers, fried chicken, French fries, and popcorn) similar to the fare people had learned to love in fast-food restaurants. For example, one of the first microwavable foods was Hormel's array of biscuit-based breakfast sandwiches similar to the Egg McMuffin popularized by McDonald's.[12] As one executive put it, "Instead of having a breakfast sandwich at McDonald's, you can pick one up from the freezer of your grocery store."[13] In some ways, "homemade" fast foods seem more efficient than the versions offered by fast-food restaurants. Instead of getting into the car, driving to the restaurant, and returning home, consumers need only pop their favorite foods into the microwave. However, the microwaved meal does require a prior trip to the market.

Supermarkets have long been loaded with other kinds of products that streamline "cooking" at home and eliminate trekking to a fast-food restaurant. Instead of starting from scratch, the cook can use prepackaged mixes to make "homemade" cakes, pies, pancakes, waffles, and many other foods. In fact, entire meals are now available right out of the box. Dinty Moore's Classic Bakes promise to be "hot and hearty, quick and convenient, ready in minutes." Dinty Moore also offers "Big Bowls" of, for example, beef stew, which can be microwaved and served in the bowls in which they are sold. The bowls are then to be tossed in the garbage thereby eliminating the inefficiencies associated with washing and drying them.

An increasingly important alternative is the fully cooked meal consumers may now buy at the supermarket. People can simply stop on the way home and purchase main courses, sides and even entire meals, which they "prepare" by unpacking the food and perhaps reheating it—no actual cooking required.

The meal-kit delivery business involves a fascinating new example of McDonaldized meals, albeit ones that *do* require cooking. The industry leader is Blue Apron, but there are others such as Plated, Sun Basket, Hello Fresh, Marley Spoon, as well as Amazon, which entered the online meal-kit business in mid-2017 with the slogan, "We do the prep. You be the chef."[14] The enterprises differ slightly, but the main point from the perspective of McDonaldization is that they provide consumers with the recipes and all of the ingredients needed for several meals a week; no trips to the supermarket required. Blue Apron's customers often receive ingredients (e.g., fairy tale eggplant, pink lemon) not typically found in supermarkets. However, the production of those unique ingredients, as well as the rest of Blue Apron's processes, is highly McDonaldized. Once consumers receive their kits, they become prosumers doing the work involved in producing the meal—chopping, stirring, cooking the provided ingredients—as well as cleaning up afterwards.[15] Nevertheless, one of the company's owners claims: "The food almost cooks itself."[16] One of Blue Apron's competitors, Munchery, goes much further in this direction and provides meals that only require "cooking" in the microwave.

Blue Apron has basically helped to rationalize everything from farm production, to the delivery of the kit, to the cooking of the meal. It increases predictability by matching the supply of various ingredients to the expected customer demand. Long before ingredients are shipped to Blue Apron's customers, the company creates its "shopping lists" and farmers are organized to plant and produce the various ingredients, including such exotica as those fairy tale eggplants. This is made efficient by the fact that farmers produce only as much as Blue

Apron projects it will need; there is no excess in the crops. This requires a high degree of control, coordination, and organization because plans for what a farm will produce are laid a year, or more, before the products are needed for the kits to be delivered to the customers. However, adjustments are made along the way; there is flexibility in case, for example, a given crop fails. There is still much non-McDonaldized hand-cutting and packaging at Blue Apron's fulfillment centers, but the company is moving in the direction of increased automation. The supply chain is so highly organized that it is likely for ingredients to remain in one of the centers for only a few hours before they are combined, boxed, and sent out for next-day delivery.

In terms of the meals themselves, they are highly calculable in the sense that consumers receive the precise amounts of each ingredient needed for a given recipe. However, each ingredient is packaged separately thereby creating a great deal of waste. Online consumers order the meals they want (out of a limited set of options) and the ingredients for those meals arrive each week on their doorsteps. The beauty of the Blue Apron system is that consumers believe that they have been creative in cooking their meals, sometimes with unique ingredients, but everything involved has been highly McDonaldized. As one chef put it, "To me, meal kits sound like cheating, not cooking."[17] Everything is disenchanted, especially quantified. Lost is the "heart, and joy, of cooking."[18] Blue Apron customers can feel that they are rejecting McDonaldization while remaining safely within the constraints of a highly McDonaldized, farm-to-table, system.

The McDonaldization of food preparation and consumption closely relates to the booming diet industry. For example, eating too much fast food tends to lead to obesity. Losing weight is normally difficult and time-consuming, but diet books promise to make it quicker and easier. The preparation of low-calorie food has thus also been streamlined. Instead of cooking diet foods from scratch, dieters may purchase an array of prepared diet foods in frozen or microwavable form, for example, from Weight Watchers. Nutrisystem sells dieters, at substantial cost, streamlined and prepackaged freeze-dried food. Those who do not wish to go through the inefficient process of eating these diet meals can consume products such as diet shakes and bars (Slim-Fast, for example) in a matter of seconds. Dieters seeking even greater efficiency can turn to various pills that expedite weight loss—the now-banned "fen-phen" and the still available (by prescription) Xenical (Orlistat). The same drug can be obtained even more efficiently over-the-counter under the name Alli. Further streamlining radical weight loss is cosmetic surgery to quickly drop pounds of fat. Even more radical and invasive is gastric bypass surgery.

There are efficiencies in dieting outside the home as well. There are, for example, brick-and-mortar diet centers such as Jenny Craig[19] and Weight Watchers.[20]

In many cases, streamlined online consultations have replaced the more time-consuming ones that require trips to brick-and mortar diet centers. Beyond online consultations, there are now even a large number of apps available on smartphones dealing with weight loss and health. They can be accessed easily and they make obtaining information on how to lose weight even more efficient.

Shopping: Creating Ever More Efficient Selling Machines

Shopping for all kinds of goods and services, not just food, has also been streamlined. The now declining department store was obviously a more efficient place in which to shop than a series of specialty shops dispersed throughout neighborhoods, cities, and suburbs. In its day the shopping mall streamlined shopping by bringing a wide range of department stores and specialty shops to one location and under one roof.[21] It was cost-efficient for retailers because the "mall synergy" created by a number of shops and department stores in close proximity to one another brought in throngs of people. And it streamlined consumption for consumers because, in one stop, they could visit numerous shops and stores, have lunch at a "food court" (likely populated by many fast-food chains), see a movie, have a drink, and, perhaps, go to an exercise or diet center.

While malls may still seem streamlined and appear to offer various efficiencies, they pale in comparison to those available on online sites such as Amazon. This is a major reason for the decline of malls, as well as of the department stores and chains that are often found in them.

Consumers who do not feel that they have the time to visit the mall are able to shop from the comfort of their homes through catalogs such as IKEA's. Such catalogs are now increasingly available and accessed online.[22] Another alternative to visiting the mall is home television shopping. The efficiency of shopping via catalogs, on TV, and especially online is increased even further by express package delivery systems, overnight or even same day, from FedEx and UPS.

The drive for shopping efficiency did not end with the malls. 7-Eleven and its clones (for example, Circle K, ampm, and Wawa) have become drive-up, if not drive-through, minimarkets. Efficiency is further increased for consumers because these stores almost always also offer gasoline pumps out front and only a few steps away. For those customers who need only a few items, pulling up to a highly streamlined 7-Eleven (more than 56,000 locations worldwide)[23] is far more efficient (albeit more costly) than running into a supermarket. Shoppers have no need to park in a large lot, obtain a cart, wheel it through myriad aisles in search of needed items, wait in line at checkout, and then tote purchases back to a sometimes distant car. At 7-Eleven, they can park right in front and quickly find what they need. Like the fast-food restaurant, which offers a highly circumscribed menu, 7-Eleven has sought to fill its shops with a limited array of commonly sought goods: bread, milk, cigarettes, aspirin, even videos, and self-serve items such as hot coffee, hot dogs, hoagies, microwaved sandwiches, cold soda, and Slurpees. 7-Eleven's efficiency stems from the fact that it ordinarily sells only one brand of a highly limited number of items.

For greater selection, consumers must go to the relatively inefficient supermarket. Of course, supermarkets have sought to streamline shopping for consumers who might otherwise frequent convenience stores by institutionalizing automated self-checkout lanes (see below) and 10-to-15-item-limit, no-checks-accepted, lines.

Higher Education: Multitasking in McUniversity

In the contemporary rationalized university[24] (now often dubbed "McUniversity"),[25] students (the consumers in a university) are increasingly able to be more efficient *in* class by using their laptops and smartphones to multitask in various ways. This can be educationally beneficial when it involves doing relevant Google searches during a lecture, but it can have adverse effects when students are playing games online, writing on someone's Facebook wall, or texting on their smartphones. Also worth noting is RateMyProfessors.com, where students can efficiently evaluate their professors as well as find such ratings by other students.

Wikipedia has become an efficient source of information for both professors and students. There was a time when most professors were critical of the use of Wikipedia, but more and more have come to embrace it. They may use it themselves and allow, even encourage, their students to use it.

One other academic efficiency worth noting is the ability of students to purchase already completed term papers online. A variety of websites[26] now promise to deliver original, customized research papers on any topic for a "low, low fee" of, say, $12.99 per page. You could (although it is not advised) purchase a 10-page paper on McDonaldization on one website for less than $130.[27] Websites even have quick service and express delivery available ($14.99 per page if you need the paper in 48 hours) for those students who have put off academic dishonesty to the last moment. Beware, however, for there are also other websites (e.g., Turnitin .com) that help professors detect plagiarism, thereby combating student gains in efficiency through plagiarism with an efficient system to detect it.[28]

Health Care: Docs-in-a-Box

It might be assumed that modern medicine and its consumers—the patients—are immune to the drive for efficiency and invulnerable to rationalization more generally. However, medicine has been McDonaldized.

Perhaps the best example of the streamlining of visits to medical practices in the United States is the growth of walk-in/walk-out surgical or emergency centers such as DR (Duane Reade) Walk-In Medical Care clinics in New York City.[29] "McDoctors," or "docs-in-a-box," serve patients who want highly efficient medical care. Each center is streamlined to handle with great dispatch a limited number of minor problems. Although stitching a patient with a minor laceration cannot be done as efficiently as serving a customer a hamburger, many of the same principles apply. It is more streamlined for the patient to walk into a neighborhood McDoctors without an appointment than to make an appointment with a regular physician, perhaps travel great distances to her office, and to wait, sometimes quite a long time, until the appointed time arrives. For a minor emergency, such as a slight laceration, using a McDoctor's office is a far more streamlined process than the cumbersome process of working one's way through a large hospital's emergency room. Hospitals are set up to handle serious problems for which efficiency is not (yet) the norm, although many hospitals employ specialized emergency room physicians and teams of medical personnel in order to further streamline emergency care. Docs-in-a-box are also more efficient than private doctors' offices because they are not structured to permit the kind of personal (and therefore inefficient) attention patients expect from their private physicians; in other words, they streamline the doctor–patient relationship.

"Minute clinics" are increasingly found in pharmacies (e.g., CVS) and even in supermarkets, discounters, and big-box stores.[30] Nurse practitioners and physician assistants may staff these and offer streamlined help in the case of minor medical matters. It has become increasingly common to get shots (for flu, etc.) in a neighborhood pharmacy or supermarket (perhaps offered adjacent to the meat department and by a butcher—just kidding!).

Entertainment: Moving People (and Trash) Efficiently

Many people no longer deem it efficient to trek to their local theater to see a movie. For a time, DVDs, and the stores that rented them, boomed. Blockbuster, at one time the largest video rental firm in the United States, considered "itself the McDonald's of the video business."[31] However, Blockbuster went bankrupt in late 2010, mainly because it was inefficient in comparison to a number of newer, more streamlined, alternatives.

One example is the video rental machine. Redbox—once owned by McDonald's—is the major player in this area. However, this is far less popular (and efficient) than streaming movies, for a fee, from Netflix, Amazon, iTunes, Hulu, and others. Then there are the on-demand and pay-per-view movies offered by many cable companies. Offerings from these providers can be viewed at home as well as on a variety of mobile devices. DVRs and TiVos permit customers to record their favorite shows while they are watching something else or to rewind or pause live television. Viewers can even stream movies free of charge, often illegally.

Then there are the satellite networks that streamline the process of watching football games by allowing viewers to watch several football games at once. With "NFL RedZone," viewers can watch all games on a given day when the ball is within the opponent's 20-yard line. Thus, a football game is streamlined by eliminating all the "unnecessary" action between the 20-yard lines; in other words, it is unnecessary to watch 60% of the football field, of the game, and of the action that takes place there.

Another sort of efficiency in the entertainment world is the system for moving people at modern amusement parks, particularly Disneyland and Disney World.[32] A series of roads filters thousands of cars each day into the appropriate parking lots. Jitneys whisk visitors to the gates of the park. Once in the park, they find themselves in a vast line of people on what is, in effect, a huge conveyor belt that leads them from one ride or attraction to another. Once visitors actually reach an attraction, conveyances such as cars, boats, submarines, planes, rockets, or moving walkways move them rapidly through, into, and out of the attraction.

Disney World has been victimized by its own success: Even its highly efficient systems cannot handle the hordes that descend on the park at the height of the tourist season. Since 1999, Disney has sought to deal with this problem with its even more streamlined FASTPASS system that allows a visitor to arrange a specific time to be at a given attraction and to enter via a separate and much faster-moving FASTPASS line. Of course, there are limits on the number of FASTPASSes that can be issued. It would be self-defeating if every visitor used a FASTPASS for every trip to every attraction. There are still long lines at Disney resorts; even the FASTPASS lines may not be so fast. In 2014, in an effort to further increase efficiency and reduce wait times, Disney introduced the still more streamlined FASTPASS+ system, which allows visitors to reserve times in advance for up to three attractions.[33]

The movement of people is not the only thing Disney World has streamlined.[34] The throngs of visitors who frequent such amusement parks eat a great deal (mostly fast food, especially finger foods) and therefore generate an enormous amount of trash. If Disney World emptied trash receptacles only at the end of each day, the barrels would be overflowing most of the time. To prevent this eyesore (and it must be prevented since order and cleanliness—some would say sterility—are key components of the McDonaldized world in general and Disney World in particular), hordes of employees constantly sweep, collect, and empty trash. To take a specific example, a group of cleaners brings up the rear in the nightly Disney parade. They almost instantly dispose of whatever trash and animal droppings have been left behind. Within a few minutes, they have eliminated virtually all signs of a parade. Disney World also employs an elaborate system of underground tubes. Garbage receptacles are emptied into this system, which whisks the trash away at about 60 miles per hour to a central trash-disposal plant far from the view of visitors. Disney World is thus a "magic kingdom" in more ways than one. Here is the way one observer compares another of the modern, highly rational amusement parks—Busch Gardens—to ancestors such as county fairs and Coney Island: "Gone is the dusty midway. . . . In its place is a vast, self-contained environment . . . endowed with the kind of *efficiency* beyond the reach of most cities."[35]

Internet Consumption Sites and Streamlining

The Internet (as well as the augmented reality it creates with brick-and-mortar consumption sites) is clearly the most important factor in greatly increased efficiency in consumption. As we saw in Chapter 1, Amazon, via Amazon Go and its physical bookstores, is making brick-and-mortar shopping more efficient in a variety of ways, but those gains in efficiency pale in comparison to the efficiency of shopping on Amazon.com and other Internet sites. For example, unlike brick-and-mortar shops, Internet shopping sites are "open" 24/7, 365 days a year. Much of the guesswork is taken out of consumption online as a great deal of product information (including photos) is on the site or readily obtainable online. Reviews, often written by the prosumers who have bought the products in question, are on the site (or on dedicated sites) for all to see. Other peer reviews and recommendations can be found on social media sites. Making decisions about a purchase even easier are summary ratings and comparative rankings on various products. No need to even read reviews—all one needs to do is to quickly scan those ratings or rankings. Search engines allow online consumers to quickly and easily find the lowest price.

Instead of traveling to a perhaps distant brick-and-mortar shop, one can find virtually everything online via one's computer or cell phone. Specifically, in the case of books, instead of trekking to one of the few remaining book superstores or wandering from one small bookshop to another, one can, as is well known, access Amazon.com, which offers visitors millions of different book titles at their fingertips.[36] After selecting and charging the desired book titles—to say nothing of the innumerable other products available on Amazon.com—all consumers need to do is sit back and wait for the books to be delivered to their doors, usually within a day (via Amazon Prime) or two. In addition, there are no shipping charges on Amazon Prime; other online retailers have adopted similar enticing policies. For instance, at Zappos, there is no charge for returning shoes.

The advent of e-books and e-readers such as Amazon's Kindle and Barnes & Noble's Nook have made shopping for, and reading, books infinitely more efficient. The immaterial books can now be ordered and downloaded almost instantaneously and flipped through more quickly. For the first time in 2011, Amazon sold more Kindle books than it did both hardcover and paperback print books.[37] As of 2014, and the percentages today are certainly higher, almost 20% of books sold in the United States were Kindle titles and, more generally, e-books accounted for about 30% of all book sales; Amazon has about 65% of the e-book market.[38]

Similarly instantaneous and efficient is the streaming music on Apple Music, Google Play Music, Spotify, Pandora, YouTube, and similar sites. In spite of a big increase (up 11.4% in 2016) in revenue from these digital sources of music, overall sales revenue in the music industry is still down from its peak in 1999 when sales of CDs were at their height (they are now dropping dramatically). Not coincidentally, it was in 1999 that the first source of digital music—Napster— began operation.[39] The efficiency involved in using these digital sites is that one can listen to virtually anything one wants without venturing out to one of the few stores that still stock CDs (let alone vinyl records). As the number of stores that sell CDs and records continues to dwindle, the inefficiencies associated with them will increase further as it requires even more time and effort to travel to these stores in order to make a purchase.

A similar story is to be told about video games where digital access is far more efficient than trekking to, for example, one of the over 7,000 brick-and-mortar Game Stop shops in the world. As a result, Game Stop is in decline. Rather than going to a Game Stop store, more and more gamers are getting their games more efficiently through such online sites as Xbox Live and PlayStation Network.

There are innumerable other Internet sites (e.g., Overstock) where one can efficiently engage in e-tailing and shop for virtually anything. Among the other examples are online banking (the leader is Ally), pharmacies (e.g., Express Scripts, as well as a number in Canada where drug prices are lower than in the United States), grocery delivery (e.g., Amazon and FreshDirect), and flower delivery (e.g., ProFlowers). Consultations with "online doctors" are also available via, for example, TelaDoc and Doctor on Demand.[40] Then there is the leading online auction and shopping site eBay (another is eBid), which allows buyers and sellers, both consumers and businesses, to deal with one another, and to buy and sell, in a highly efficient manner. Imagine how difficult and inefficient it would be for such buyers and sellers to find, let alone deal with, one another without eBay. Stubhub, purchased by eBay in 2007, allows for online ticket trading for a wide range of events. Consider how inefficient such trading was before sites like Stub-Hub when, for example, buyers and sellers had to rely on chance meetings outside an event venue. PayPal, also owned by eBay, makes paying for online purchases easy and efficient. An often overlooked aspect of the efficiency of cybershopping is that it can be done while you are at work.[41] Although employers are likely to feel that shopping from work adversely affects worker efficiency, it is certainly very efficient from the perspective of the worker/consumer.

The drive to make Internet shopping ever more efficient continues. There are shopping robots, or "online comparison services," that automatically surf the Web for specific products, lowest prices, and shortest delivery dates.[42] For example, Google has "Google Shopping": "Browse by category—apparel, computers, flowers, whatever—or enter a query term, and it will present a list of matching products, each with a thumbnail sketch on the left and description, price and retailer on the right."[43] However, it is now even more efficient just to go online to Amazon.com, which has virtually everything one might want at competitive prices and without the need for online comparison price services.

All types of shopping, but particularly ordering online from perhaps distant merchants, have become far more efficient with the near-universal use of credit and debit cards (as well as such online payment systems as PayPal). Transactions by these means are obviously more efficient than cash transactions (no need to occasionally stop at the ATM or bank to load up with cash), or paper transactions by check or money order. In any case the enormous number of online transactions would be impossible on a cash, check, or money order basis.

For the consumer, virtually every digital site is more efficient, often *infinitely* more efficient, than comparable locales in the more material world. Almost all transactions are much more streamlined on websites than they are in the material world.

As a result, to take one example, bookstores and even book superstores seem to be dying. There has been a 50% decline of bookstores in recent years. Then there is the 2011 bankruptcy and closing of all Borders superstores and the economic difficulties Barnes & Noble has been experiencing. However, as we've seen, Amazon has run counter to this trend with its purchase of Whole Foods supermarkets and the opening of several brick-and-mortar bookstores, with plans to open more in various locations in the United States.[44] Of course, its brick-and-mortar presence is still minuscule in comparison to its online business.

Uberization: It's all About Efficiency. Uber is just one of a number of "ride-sharing," or transportation network, companies that are competing with one another and with the traditional taxicab industry—both within the United States and globally—to streamline and dominate the transportation business, especially in urban areas. Uber has been of such overwhelming importance in this industry that we can use a term like *uberisation* both to reflect its preeminence *and* to offer a parallel to the concept of McDonaldization. The great advantage of these ride-sharing companies over taxicabs is that while they, like taxicabs, offer a very material mode of transportation (and automobile), they are deeply embedded in the digital world. The cars are usually summoned through an app on the passenger's cell phone linked via the Internet to apps on the phones of available drivers. Those drivers closest to the potential passenger are most likely to respond and to get the job. Once a passenger and a driver are connected through their apps, the rider is informed how quickly the car will arrive. In a big city such as New York with many Uber drivers competing for work, a car is likely to arrive in minutes. Riders are also informed about the nature of the car that is to pick them up and where to meet it, usually very close by. Riders will also be informed of the cost of the ride to the chosen destination and that amount will automatically be charged to their credit card accounts (on file with the company). Tipping is rare and discouraged so there is no inefficient calculation of what the tip should be (although some taxi meters now tell passengers how much to tip, with several percentages of the total offered as alternatives). When the destination is reached, the passenger is able to leave the car immediately without any additional steps needed. In these ways, an Uber ride is far more streamlined than one taken in a taxicab.

It is clear that one of the defining characteristics of Uber is its efficiency. The controversial former chief executive of Uber, Travis Kalanick (who lost his job in mid-2017), is famous for his hard-driving pursuit of dominance, profits, *and* efficiency. In fact, prior to Uber, he had founded two other Internet-based start-ups, Scour (peer-to-peer file sharing, especially of music and media files) and Red Swoosh (sharing of large data files). Of these two companies, as well as of Uber, a former executive at Red Swoosh said, "Scour was about *efficiency.* Swoosh was about *efficiency.* It's just the way his [Travis Kalanick's] brain works. It's like the way Uber works right now: 'What's the fastest, cheapest, *most efficient* way to get from point A to point B.'"[45]

In contrast, traditional taxicabs are inefficient in a variety ways, but most important, given the focus of this section, in how a passenger obtains a ride. While it is possible that a taxi will be available at a taxi stand (not necessarily nearby) when it is desired, or a taxi might be passing by just as it is needed, the likelihood is that a potential passenger will need to wait as long as it takes for an available taxi to pass by. It is not always obvious that a taxi is available and taxis don't always stop for a fare or the drivers may refuse to go to a given location (too far, in too dangerous an area, etc.). Getting a taxi in a busy city is especially difficult at "rush hours," or in bad weather, and under various other circumstances. This is another advantage of ride-sharing companies. They offer higher "surge pricing" in such conditions. This makes picking up passengers more attractive to drivers because they earn more money (although it costs passengers more) under those circumstances; their percentage is of a higher total fare.

Online Dating: Show Your Interest With Just a "Wink". For young people, dating has become "dated," inefficient in an era in which they can simply "hang out" together, or "hook up." However, hanging out is inefficient, time-consuming for everyone, and becomes less possible and attractive as people grow a bit older. Dating is a highly inefficient process that has been streamlined as a result of the Internet and the ability to find and make dates with online services such as eHarmony.com and Match.com.[46] (For those who are more interested in sex than the less efficient process of dating, there are sites such as Tinder, www.findsex .com, and Craigslist Casual Encounters.)[47] With a single click, one can find men or women within a specified age group and a given distance from one's zip code (no long, unnecessary trips needed). Key words are provided on the site (e.g., *charming, energetic*), making it easier to find a particular kind of person. It is possible to scroll quickly through hundreds of profiles of potential dates who meet given criteria. Once a profile or photo of interest is located, a simple click indicates a "wink" at a potential date. Other clicks can organize potential dates into a "favorites" list so that, if one possibility does not pan out, another can be located quickly and contacted.

If a date is chosen, it is likely that sooner or later, the relationship will not work out. Once that happens, it is possible to block the spurned suitor's access to one's profile. Best of all, a person can be back on the dating scene in an instant with a plethora of alternatives on the website or on one's favorites list.

Online dating sites offer a variety of quantifiable (see below) advantages as far as consumers (users) are concerned. For example, one will meet far more people this way than would ever have been possible in, for example, a bar or a club. This is especially clear on the aptly-named site PlentyofFish. Indeed, one of the attractions of almost all of these sites is that they offer infinitely more potential dates than any of the other alternatives. One can find a date online much more quickly than, for example, hanging out at a bar. Tinder allows one to plow quickly through a large number of photos of potential "dates." If users swipe a Tinder photo to the left, they are indicating that they are not interested in pursuing a relationship with the person in the photo. A swipe to the right indicates interest in such a pursuit. One then has the possibility of chatting with that person and, if interested, in taking the relationship further. On most occasions meeting through one of these sites is likely to lead to a predictably short meeting ("meet up for coffee") or relationship. Many sites such as Tinder are mainly designed for brief and transient "hookups" rather than for long-term relationships.

Even more recent and efficient is the use of smartphones and mobile dating services, relevant apps, and geo-locating technology to find a date, even with one who is close by. This means that all of this can be done on the go; one does not need to be tied to a computer. As a result, the process of arranging dates is streamlined as they can be arranged even more quickly and efficiently via a smartphone.

Simplifying the Product

Complex foods based on sophisticated recipes are, needless to say, not the norm at fast-food restaurants. The staples of the industry are foods (e.g., hamburgers, slices of pizza) that require relatively few ingredients and are simple to prepare, to serve, and most importantly from the perspective of consumers, to eat. In fact, fast-food restaurants generally serve "finger food," which can be eaten without utensils.

Many innovations over the years have greatly increased the number and types of finger foods available to consumers. The Egg McMuffin is an entire breakfast— egg, Canadian bacon, English muffin—combined into a handy sandwich. For consumers, eating such a sandwich is far more efficient than sitting down with knife and fork and devouring a plate of eggs, bacon, and toast. The creation of the Chicken McNugget, perhaps the ultimate finger food, reflects the fact that chicken is pretty inefficient as far as McDonald's is concerned. The bones, gristle, and skin that are such a barrier to the efficient consumption of chicken have all been eliminated in the Chicken McNugget. Customers can pop the bite-sized morsels of fried chicken into their mouths even as they drive. Were they able to, the mass purveyors of chicken would breed a more efficiently consumed chicken free of bones, gristle, and skin.[48] Another example of efficiency is McDonald's apple pie, completely encased in dough, so it can be munched on like a sandwich.

However, what may be efficient from the point of view of the customer may not be efficient for the restaurant and its employees. Take, for example, McDonald's snack wrap.[49] This is a classic McDonaldized food. For one thing, it is another form of "finger food" that customers can eat quickly and efficiently. For another, it uses ingredients already in McDonald's restaurants and used in other menu items—breaded chicken strips, flour tortillas, shredded lettuce and cheese, and ranch sauce. However, McDonald's has largely discontinued the sale of wraps. They, firstly, proved to be not very popular with consumers who were more drawn to other innovations such as the all-day breakfast.[50] The bigger problem with the wraps was that while they could be eaten efficiently, the same was not true of their production by McDonald's employees. It took time to steam the tortilla, but even more time-consuming was all the chopping of the ingredients, the stuffing them into the tortilla, rolling it, and then fitting it into the narrow cardboard container.[51]

Given their obvious attraction from the point of view of consumers and efficiency in terms of consumption, many other fast-food restaurants (e.g., KFC, Wendy's) continue to serve, and even feature, wraps of various kinds. Taco Bell has its "Breakfast Crunchwrap," as well as its "Triple Double Crunchwrap." The burrito, perhaps the classic wrap, is popular in many fast-food restaurants, especially Chipotle.

The limited number of menu choices also contributes to customer efficiency in fast-food restaurants. McDonald's does not serve egg rolls, and Taco Bell does not offer fried chicken. Advertisements like "We do it your way" and "Your way, right away" imply that fast-food chains happily accommodate special requests. But pity the consumers who have such requests in a fast-food restaurant. Because much of these restaurants' efficiency stems from the fact that they virtually always do it one way—*their way*—the last thing fast-food restaurants want is to do it your way. Customers with the temerity to ask for a less well-done burger or well-browned fries are likely to cool their heels for a long time waiting for such "exotica." Few customers are willing to wait because, after all, that undermines the main advantages of going to a fast-food restaurant. Long ago, Henry Ford said: "Any customer can have a car painted any color that he wants so long as it is black."[52] In the fast-food restaurant, the parallel would be: "Any customer can have any hamburger she wants as long as it is well-done."

Many food products other than fast food have been simplified in the name of efficiency. Energy drinks such as 5-hour ENERGY and Red Bull are basically simplified beverages designed to quickly deliver large amounts of caffeine. Soylent (based on the dystopian 1973 sci-fi movie *Soylent Green* in which corpses are converted into edible wafers to deal with a shortage of food) is a powder designed to be transformed into a drink that provides all the nutrients needed by the human body. A journalist who consumed the drink for most of his meals for a week and a half found it to be "punishingly boring, joyless . . . everything about Soylent screams function, not fun. It may offer complete nourishment, but only at the expense of the aesthetic and emotional pleasures many of us crave in food."[53]

Bananas are an interesting example of product simplification. The banana itself has, of course, not been simplified, but the market for it, at least in the United States, has been simplified by the dominance of one variety of banana. In fact, this kind of simplification is true of other kinds of fruits and vegetables such as apples. At one time it was the "Gros Michel" banana that was dominant, but it was decimated by disease and was replaced in the United States and much of the rest of the world by the Cavendish banana. It was chosen for its resistance to disease and *not* for its quality or flavor. As a result, it has been called "the McDonald's of bananas."[54] In contrast, India has hundreds of breeds of bananas; the Cavendish is called there "the hotel banana."

Simplified products and services are increasingly on offer in many settings. AAMCO Transmissions works mainly on transmissions, and Midas Muffler largely restricts itself to the installation of mufflers. H&R Block does millions of simple tax returns in its roughly 12,000 offices, many of which are overseas. Because it uses many part-time and seasonal employees and does not offer the full array of tax and financial services available from a certified public accountant (CPA), it is undoubtedly not the best place to have complicated tax returns completed.[55] "McDentists" (e.g., AspenDental) may be relied on for simple dental procedures, but patients are ill advised to have root canal work done by one. Pearle Vision centers offer eye examinations, but clients should go to an eye doctor for any major vision problem. And, *USA TODAY* offers readers highly simplified "News McNuggets."

Putting Customers to Work

A final mechanism for increasing efficiency in a McDonaldized world is to put customers to work. It is more efficient for workers—and their employers (but not necessarily customers)—to have customers do the work. Consumers who also produce (work) are engaging in prosumption.[56] As mentioned earlier, *prosumption* involves the interrelated processes of production and consumption. McDonald's customers, and those in many other settings, are one type of "prosumer"; they are *working consumers*.[57] More specifically, they engage in unpaid "self-service work."[58] Also as pointed out earlier, all production involves some consumption of, for example, raw materials or ingredients. Similarly, all consumption involves some production, or work.

Many people like being prosumers because it gives them a sense of freedom, even empowerment, in areas such as shopping, education, and health care. On the other hand, prosumption can be alienating, leaving people with the feeling that they are largely on their own and unable to interact with others.

Fast-Food Restaurants: Doing It All for Them

Fast-food customers perform many more unpaid tasks than those who dine at full-service restaurants. "McDonald's came up with the slogan 'We do it all for you.' In reality, at McDonald's, we [the customers] do it all for them. We stand in line, pick up food, take it to the table, dispose of the waste, and stack our trays. As labor costs rise and technology develops, the consumer often does more and more of the work."[59] The customers who use drive-through windows can also be seen as doing the work involved in disposing of the garbage associated with their meal. While it is efficient for the fast-food restaurant to have consumers wait in line or dispose of their own waste, doing so is inefficient for consumers. Is it more efficient to order your own food rather than having a waiter do it for you? Or to bus your own paper, plastic, and Styrofoam rather than having a bus person do it? Or to figure out what to do with those things once a meal devoured in your car is finished?

The tendency to put customers to work was underscored by Steak 'n Shake's (over 500 restaurants in the United States, as well as in Europe and the Middle East)[60] TV advertisements describing fast-food restaurants as "workaurants."[61] In contrast to workaurants, Steak 'n Shake emphasizes its use of china plates and the fact that the food is actually served by a wait staff. Virtually all fast-food restaurants today can be thought of as workaurants.

The salad bar is a classic example of putting the consumer to work. The customer loads up on the array of vegetables and other foods available that day. Quickly seeing the merit in this system, many supermarkets installed their own, often more elaborate, salad bars. Salad lovers can thus work as salad chefs at lunch hour in the fast-food restaurant and then do it all over again in the evening at the supermarket. The fast-food restaurant and the supermarket achieve huge increases in efficiency because they need only a relatively small number of employees to keep the various compartments well stocked.

There is an all-you-can-eat restaurant chain, Souplantation (called Sweet Tomatoes in most areas), with 128 outlets in 15 states in the United States.[62] Although it filed for bankruptcy in late 2016, it expects to emerge from bankruptcy with roughly 100 restaurants. Its main attraction is a lengthy salad bar (really a kind of assembly-line) that customers encounter as they enter the restaurant. At lunch and dinner times, there are often long lines on both sides of the salad bar. In fact, at particularly busy times, the lines snake out the door and into the parking lot. As diners move slowly along the salad bar, they fill their plates with the desired foods. At the end of the salad bar are two cash registers where those in each line pay for their food. Various other foods and desserts are available at counters in the restaurant, and after they have finished their salads, customers trek to these additional counters, sometimes over and over again.[63] At Burger King and most other fast-food franchises, people must fill their own cups with ice and soft drinks, thereby spending a few moments as "soda jerks." Similarly, customers serve themselves in the popular "fresh food" buffets at Shoney's or the lunch buffets at Pizza Hut at a price in 2017 of $4.99 plus the cost of a soft drink. The buffet includes all the pizza, pasta, salad, "and more" that one can eat.

As pointed out earlier, McDonald's is using digital self-ordering kiosks in some of its restaurants and they will undoubtedly become increasingly common in the coming years. They allow customers to use touch screens to place their food orders (Chili's has such screens at its tables). They allow consumers— as prosumers—to do the work currently performed by counter people at McDonald's; they find and touch the picture on the screen that matches the food being ordered.[64] McDonald's has also rolled out an online app allowing the prosumer a greater role in the ordering process, as well as a role in speeding it up.[65] Also of note is the trend toward self-ordering food kiosks at gas station travel plazas, such as Sheetz and Wawa. One company that makes these kiosks for a wide variety of restaurants at airports, drive-throughs, and casinos is Nextep. It claims that these systems outperform humans by displaying attractive pictures of food and offering extras to entice the customer to purchase more food.[66]

A fairly recent example of putting the customer to work is the self-serve, touchscreen "freestyle Coke machines that offer more than 100 flavors."[67] They are found in and among an increasing number of locations, including various fast-food chains and AMC movie theaters. By making a series of choices the prosumer can create such customized drinks as a peach Sprite.

Other Brick-and-Mortar Sites: Working While Consuming

Food shopping also offers many examples of imposing work on the consumer. The old-time grocery store, where the clerk retrieved the needed items, has been replaced by the supermarket, where a shopper may put in several hours a week "working" as a grocery clerk, seeking out wanted (and unwanted) items during lengthy treks down seemingly endless aisles. Having obtained the groceries, the shopper then unloads the food at the checkout counter and, in some cases, even bags the groceries.

Of course, many supermarket checkout stands now require the customer to do the scanning, thereby eliminating the need for a checkout clerk.[68] Such self-checkout terminals are increasing rapidly in the United States and throughout the world; the number has multiplied greatly in recent years.[69] These systems allow customers to pay with credit cards and are, therefore, another method for eliminating the need for cashiers. The developer of one scanning system predicted, perhaps over-optimistically, that soon "self-service grocery technology could be as pervasive as the automatic cash machines used by bank customers."[70] One customer, apparently a strong believer in McDonaldization, said of such a system, "It's quick, easy and efficient. . . . You get in and out in a hurry."[71] But as an official with a union representing supermarket clerks put it, "To say it's more convenient for the customer is turning the world upside down. . . . In general, making customers do the work for themselves is not customer service."[72]

Virtually gone are gas station attendants who fill gas tanks, check the oil, clean windows, and take your cash or scan your credit card; drivers now put in a few minutes a week as unpaid attendants. Although one might think that eliminating gas station attendants leads to lower gasoline prices (and indeed it does in the short run), a comparison of gas prices at stations with and without attendants shows little difference in price. In the end, the gasoline companies and service station owners have simply found another way to force the consumer to do the work on an unpaid basis that employees once had to be paid to perform.

In some doctors' offices, patients must now weigh themselves and take their own temperatures. More important, patients have been put to work in the medical world through the use of an increasingly wide array of do-it-yourself medical tests. Two basic types are available: monitoring instruments and diagnostic devices.[73] Monitoring devices include blood pressure monitors and glucose and cholesterol meters, as well as at-home kits marketed to parents to allow them to test their children for the use of marijuana, heroin, and other drugs. Among the diagnostic tests are pregnancy detectors, ovulation predictors, HIV test kits, and fecal occult blood detectors. Thus, patients are now being asked to familiarize themselves with technologies that were formerly the exclusive province of physicians, nurses, or trained technicians. In addition, patients are being asked to provide samples of bodily fluids (blood) or waste products (urine, fecal matter) that were once handled (very carefully) by professional medical people. But in an era of high medical costs, it is cheaper and more efficient (no unnecessary trips to the doctor's office or to the lab) for patients to monitor and test themselves. Such home testing may identify problems that otherwise might not be discovered, but it can also lead to unnecessary worry, especially in the case of "false-positive" results. In either case, many of us are now "working," at least part-time, as unpaid medical technicians.

The automated teller machine (ATM) in the banking industry allows (forces) consumers to work, for at least a few moments, as unpaid bank tellers (and often pay fees for the privilege). To encourage the use of ATMs, some banks are charging customers a fee for having the temerity to use human tellers.[74]

When a satellite-TV receiver fails, DISH mails its customers a new one as a replacement. The customer is expected to return the defective one in the same box that contained the new one. More important, it is up to the consumer to install the new receiver. There is, of course, help available online and by phone if necessary—*and it is necessary*. DISH will send someone to install the new receiver, but the time delay involved and the relatively high cost discourage most customers from taking this option.

When calling many businesses these days, instead of dealing with a human operator, consumers must push a bewildering sequence of numbers and codes before they get, they hope, the desired extension.[75] Here is the way one humorist describes such a "conversation" and the work involved for the caller:

> The party you are trying to reach—Thomas Watson—is unavailable at this time. To leave a message, please wait for the beep. To review your message, press 7. To change your message after reviewing it, press 4. To add to your message, press 5. To reach another party, press the star sign and enter the four-digit extension. To listen to Muzak, press 23. To transfer out of phone mail in what I promise you will be a futile effort to reach a human, press 0—because we treat you like one.[76]

Instead of being interviewed by the government census taker, people usually receive a questionnaire (one that is supposedly self-explanatory) in the mail to fill out on their own. The self-response rate for occupied housing units was 74% in the 2010 census.[77] Census takers obtained the information only about a quarter of the time, and even then they were deployed only after people failed to respond to the mailed questionnaire.[78]

Internet Consumption Sites and the Working Consumer: Reaching Unprecedented Heights

While the role of the prosumer is undoubtedly becoming more and more significant in areas described above, it is on digital consumption sites that the tasks required of the working consumer have reached unparalleled heights. Because there are no human beings online when consumers click on these sites, consumers are responsible for all of the actions required to navigate them and, in the case of consumption, to complete their purchases. On many sites it is purposely made difficult to contact people associated with the site by e-mail or phone. Online sites discourage such contact because it is inefficient from their perspective in comparison to having the consumer do everything on the site. And, of course, such a "service" is much more costly to the company that owns the site. In fact, in some cases it is impossible to find a way of contacting a person associated with a given site. This leads to great efficiency for the site and enormous inefficiency for those seeking to consume something on the site.

For seasoned Internet users and visitors who frequent specific sites, actions required on digital sites may seem trivial. Taken alone they are trivial, but they do add up. To many, especially those who are older, these actions are difficult and sometimes impossible. They may even be shut out of the process or have to consult someone younger (say a grandchild) in order to navigate consumption (and other) sites. Of course, as these consumers age, they will pass from the scene making this a temporary problem. Let us look at one digital subscription music site—Spotify—and examine just some of the steps and options available to one seeking to navigate it and to play some music.

One first encounters an album that is at the top of the screen, perhaps, because its producer has paid for that prime spot. Below that are a series of categories—charts, genres, new releases, discover, and concerts. Clicking on genres, one soon encounters a much more detailed list of 40 genres and moods such as Christian, country, workout, sleep, K-pop, and funk. Choosing any of those leads to a number of choices within that category. For example, within funk, one can choose among popular playlists, choices in the category of funk machine, new releases, and a number of selections in rotation.

The ubiquity of such trivial online and offline activities means that the modern consumer spends an increasing amount of time and energy doing unpaid labor. Although organizations are realizing greater efficiencies, customers are often sacrificing convenience and efficiency. However, it is clear that increasing numbers of them are not cognizant of the difficulties and enjoy navigating Internet sites on their own. Over time, we can expect such a perspective to expand among those using digital sites and any lingering awareness that they are actually working on these sites to dissipate.

It is thus on Internet sites that the tasks facing the consumer as prosumer reach unprecedented heights. While paid employees do a great deal of work constructing, monitoring, and updating Internet sites, once those sites are up and running, prosumers are largely on their own to navigate them (such as Spotify), appraise the various offerings, choose one or more of them, and provide all of the information needed for the product(s) to be delivered. This is work that in the past, in brick-and-mortar sites, was done by paid employees, but is now done free of charge by prosumers. While it is more efficient, in many ways, for a prosumer to stay at home and order books (and innumerable other products) from Amazon than to trek to one of the relatively few remaining brick-and-mortar book stores, it is *certainly* more efficient for Amazon to have prosumers do the work than it is to have thousands of paid employees do the same work.

CALCULABILITY: BIG MACS, ALGORITHMS, AND BIG DATA

McDonaldization also involves calculability: calculating, counting, and quantifying many different things. With this, quantity tends to become a surrogate for quality.[79] Numerical standards are set for both processes (e.g., production) and end results (e.g., goods). In terms of processes, the emphasis is on speed (usually high), whereas for end results, the focus is on the number of products produced and served or on their size (usually large).

This calculability has a number of positive consequences, the most important being the ability to produce and consume large amounts of a wide variety of products and services very rapidly. Customers in fast-food restaurants get a lot of food quickly; managers and owners get a great deal of work from their employees and prosumers, and the work is done, and the services are provided, speedily. However, the emphasis on quantity tends to affect adversely the quality of both the process and the result. For customers, calculability often means eating on the run or in their cars (hardly a "quality" dining experience) and consuming food that is almost always prepared quickly, and at the lowest possible cost, so that it is almost always mediocre. For employees, calculability often means obtaining little or no personal meaning from their work; therefore, the work, products, and services are likely to suffer.

Calculability is intertwined with the other dimensions of McDonaldization. For instance, calculability makes it easier to determine *efficiency;* that is, those steps that take the least time and energy are usually considered the most efficient. Once quantified, products and processes become more *predictable* because the same amounts of materials or time are used from one place or time period to another. Quantification is also linked to *control,* particularly to the creation of nonhuman technologies that perform tasks in a given amount of time or make products of a given weight or size. Calculability is clearly linked to *irrationality* because, among other things, the emphasis on quantity tends, in many ways, to affect quality adversely.

While calculability has long been important to consumption sites, it has reached, as we will discuss later in this section, a whole new level on digital sites and their use of highly mathematical algorithms to analyze the "big data" produced on, and used by, them.

Emphasizing Quantity Rather Than Quality of Products

McDonald's has always emphasized bigness; it and the other fast-food chains have a "bigger-is-better mentality."[80] For a long time, the most visible symbols of this emphasis were the large signs, usually beneath the even larger golden arches, touting the millions and, later, billions of hamburgers sold. This was a rather heavy-handed way of letting everyone know about McDonald's great success. (With the broad recognition of its success in recent years, there is less need for McDonald's to be so obvious—thus the decline of such signs, as well as the decline in the size of the golden arches. Public protests against the size of the golden arches have also played a role in this reduction.[81]) The mounting number of hamburgers sold not only indicated to potential customers that the chain was successful but also fostered the notion that it was the high quality of the burgers that accounted for the immense sales. Hence, quantity appeared to equal quality.

The Fast-Food Industry: Of "Big Bites" and "Super Big Gulps"

The emphasis on quantity is abundantly clear in the names of McDonald's offerings. The best-known example is the "Big Mac." A large burger is considered desirable simply because consumers are receiving a large serving. Furthermore, consumers are led to believe that they are getting a great deal of food for a low price. Calculating consumers come away with the feeling that they are getting a good deal—and maybe even getting the best of McDonald's.

Many other fast-food restaurants mirror the emphasis by McDonald's on quantity. Burger King points to the large amount of meat in the "Big King," as well as the "Whopper," the "Double Whopper," and even the "Triple Whopper." Burger King's fish sandwich is "Big Fish." Not to be outdone, Jack in the Box has its "Jumbo Jack with Cheese," Hardee's offers a "Monster Thickburger" (two thirds of a pound of beef), KFC has "Value Boxes" and "Double Down" (no bun, but two pieces of fried chicken, two pieces of bacon, and two pieces of cheese), and Taco Bell offers the "Big Box."[82] Similarly, 7-Eleven has a large soft drink called the "Big Gulp" and the even larger "Double Gulp." It also offers a "Big Bite" hot dog.

However, it is the case that fast-food restaurants have come under pressure to eliminate their most obscene offerings. For example, Burger King no longer offers

BK Stackers. The idea was that people could supersize their hamburger sandwich by including up to *three* (!) hamburger patties, two cheese slices, and three half-slices of bacon. In one advertisement, the foreman at the "BK Stacker factory" is shown yelling "more meat" to workers struggling to produce a bigger burger. Of the product, Burger King said, "It's the flame-broiled meat lover's burger, and it's here to stay—no veggies allowed."[83] A meat lover who maximized the Stacker would have consumed about 650 calories (the Triple Whopper had 1,140 calories), 1,020 milligrams of sodium (the Triple Whopper had a bit more), and about half of a day's allowance of saturated fat. Not to be outdone, Carl's Jr. has a "Six Dollar Thickburger," although the "Double Six Dollar Burger," with about 75% of a day's suggested intake of calories (what does one do about eating for the rest of the day?), apparently went too far and was dropped.

Then there is Denny's, which is well-known for its various "Slam" breakfasts—"Grand Slam," "All-American Slam," Lumberjack Slam," and so forth. The emphasis is on not only the size of the meal, but also its seeming low price. This is clear in one commercial in which a man proclaims, "I'm going to eat too much, but I'm never going to pay too much."[84] Of course, he and other consumers of Grand Slam breakfasts are likely to "pay" in the long run (with poorer health) because those meals have many calories as well as large amounts of fat and sodium.

Fast-food restaurants now offer a range of products that provide a lot for a low price. For example, KFC offers an array of "$5 Fillups," which include a "main course" (e.g., two pieces of chicken), a "larger" (than what?) serving of mashed potatoes, a biscuit, a medium drink, and a chocolate chip cookie. In 2016 McDonald's once again offered its "McPick 2 for $5" special, which includes a choice of two of the following: Triple Cheeseburger, Quarter Pounder with Cheese, Filet-O-Fish, and 10-piece chicken McNuggets (note the emphasis on size in three of the four alternatives).

For years, McDonald's offered to "supersize" orders of its fries, 20% larger than a large order, and customers were urged to supersize their meals.[85] However, the uproar over Morgan Spurlock's critical documentary, *Super Size Me*, helped lead McDonald's to drop the term, although it continues to offer menu items that emphasize large size (e.g., "Daily Double"). Nevertheless, McDonald's lags behind Hardee's and Carl's Jr. and their larger burgers.[86] Interestingly, the controversy over large size led some fast-food restaurants to offer smaller portions of some menu items, although the emphasis is still on size rather than quality. Examples include Burger King's BK Burger Shots and Jack in the Box's Jr. Bacon Cheeseburger. In this context, it is hard to know what to make of Hardee's Little Thick Cheeseburger—it is *both* little and big!

All this emphasis on quantity suggests that fast-food restaurants have little interest in communicating anything directly about quality to their customers.[87] Were they interested, they might give their products such names as "McTasty," "McDelicious," or "McPrime." But the fact is that typical McDonald's customers know they are not getting the highest-quality food: "No one . . . knows exactly what's in those hamburger patties. . . . Let's face it. Nobody thinks about what's between the bun at McDonald's. You buy, you eat, you toss the trash, and you're out of there like the Lone Ranger."[88] Another observer has argued that customers go to McDonald's not for a delicious, pleasurable meal but, rather, to "refuel."[89] McDonald's is a place to fill our stomachs with lots of calories, sugar, and carbohydrates so that we have the energy to move on to the next rationally organized activity. Eating to refuel is far more efficient than having a culinary experience.

The propensity for fast-food restaurants to minimize quality is well reflected in the sad history of Colonel Harland Sanders, the founder of KFC. The quality of his cooking techniques and his secret seasoning (which his wife originally mixed, packed, and shipped herself) led to about 400 franchised outlets by 1960. Sanders had a great commitment to quality, especially to his gravy: "To Sanders himself the supreme stuff of his art was his gravy, the blend of herbs and spices that time and patience had taught him. It was his ambition to make a gravy so good that people would simply eat the gravy and throw away 'the durned chicken.'"[90] After Sanders sold his business in 1964, he became little more than the spokesman and symbol for KFC. The new owners soon made clear their commitment to speed over quality: "The Colonel's gravy was fantastic, they agreed . . . but it was too complex, too time-consuming, too expensive. It had to be changed. It wasn't fast food." Ray Kroc, who befriended Colonel Sanders, recalls him saying, "That friggin' outfit . . . they prostituted every goddamn thing I had. I had the greatest gravy in the world and those sons of bitches they dragged it out and extended it and watered it down that I'm so goddamn mad."[91] At best, what customers expect from a fast-food restaurant is mediocre but strong-tasting food—hence, the salty/sweet French fries, highly seasoned sauces, and saccharine shakes. Given such modest expectations of quality, customers do, however, have greater expectations of quantity. They expect to get a lot of food and to pay relatively little for it (they think they are getting a bargain).

Even the more upscale McDonaldized restaurant chains are noted for the size of their portions and the mediocrity of their food. Of the Olive Garden, one reviewer said, "But what brings customers in droves to this popular chain remains a mystery. The food defined mediocrity. Nothing was bad, but nothing was especially good, and it certainly isn't authentically Italian." Of course, the reason is quantity: "Portions . . . are large. . . . So you'll probably end up leaving stuffed, which is not to say satisfied."[92] The Cheesecake Factory, started in Beverly Hills in 1978 and now with 185 full-service restaurants, is another example of an upscale restaurant known for its huge portions (although many devotees consider its food to be higher in quality than, say, Olive Garden). Quantity is also in evidence in the menu, which contains over 250 highly varied items, including over 50 varieties of cheesecake and other desserts.[93] The cost of a meal at Cheesecake Factory is considered low for the amount of food one gets.

Higher Education: Grades and Scores

In education, most college courses run for a standard number of weeks and hours per week. Little attention is devoted to determining whether a particular subject is best taught in the given number of weeks or hours per week. The focus also seems to be on how many students (the consumers) can be herded through the system and what grades they earn rather than the quality of what they have learned and of the educational experience.

A student's entire high school or college experience can be summed up in a single number, the grade point average (GPA). Armed with their GPAs, students can take advanced examinations with quantifiable results, such as the MCAT, LSAT, SAT, and GRE. Colleges, graduate schools, and professional schools can thus focus on three or four numbers in deciding whether or not to admit a student.

For their part, students may choose a university because of its rating. In the United States we might ask whether it is one of the top 10 universities in the country. (Such ratings might have become universal if President Obama's controversial proposal for a rating system for all of the 7,000 colleges and universities in the United States had been implemented.[94] However, it is unlikely that President Trump will institute such a ranking system.) Is a university's physics department in the top 10? Are its sports teams usually top ranked? Most important, at least to many students, is it one of the top 10 party schools?

The ranking of universities is even more prevalent in the United Kingdom, where a number of "league tables" rank universities in various ways. These rankings are very important to UK universities. Rewards (especially funding) flow to those universities with high rankings while those with low rankings tend to get fewer rewards. Those whose rankings are very low might even be forced to cut back or even close. "Universities, therefore, have to spend an inordinate amount of time ensuring their position or trying to move up a few places on the growing number of league tables."[95]

The success of online universities (now threatened by revelations about their abuses) is traceable to various quantitative factors. For one thing, courses are far less expensive than those at four-year residential colleges, and credits can often be transferred to traditional colleges. For example, in one case, a student paid $750 for seven credits that would have cost $2,800 at a nearby college. In another, a master's degree in health care management from online Western Governors University cost only $9,000 rather than the approximately $40,000 it would have cost at a traditional university.[96] At the online company StraighterLine, which has had more than a thousand students, it costs $99 *per month* to register, plus $59 for various courses. A full "freshman year" would cost slightly more than $1,000.[97] As of early 2017, StraighterLine claims to have saved students (and taxpayers) almost $130 million.

Potential employers are likely to decide whether to hire graduates on the basis of their scores, their class ranking, and the ranking of the university from which they graduated. To increase their job prospects, students may seek to amass a number of different degrees and credentials with the hope that prospective employers will believe that the longer the list of degrees, the higher the quality of the job candidate. Personal letters of reference, however important, are often replaced by standardized forms with quantified ratings (for example, "top 5% of the class," "ranks 5th in a class of 25").

The number of credentials a person possesses plays a role in situations other than obtaining a job. For example, people in various occupations can use long lists of initials after their names to convince prospective clients of their competence. (My BA, MBA, and PhD are supposed to persuade the reader that I am competent to write this book, although a degree in "hamburgerology" from Hamburger University might be more relevant.) Said one insurance appraiser with ASA, FSVA, FAS, CRA, and CRE after his name, "The more [initials] you tend to put after your name, the more impressed they [potential clients] become."[98] The sheer number of credentials, however, tells little about the competence of the person sporting them. Furthermore, this emphasis on quantity of credentials has led people to make creative use of letters after their names. For example, one camp director put "ABD" after his name to impress parents of prospective campers. As all academics know, this informal (and largely negative) label stands for "all but dissertation" and is the label for people who have completed their graduate courses and exams but who have *not* written their dissertations. Also noteworthy here is the development of organizations whose sole reason for existence is to supply meaningless credentials, often through the mail.

Internet Consumption Sites: Of Big Data and the Algorithms Used to Analyze Them

Crucial to any discussion of McDonaldization in general, especially calculability, in contemporary society is the impact of the computer, smartphones, and, of course, the Internet.[99] The proliferation of personal computers and smartphones allows more of us to do more calculations with increasing speed and to access quantified data on a wide range of matters. Most important for our purposes, these devices allow us to access the Internet where our key strokes create intentionally, and increasingly unintentionally, mountains of easily quantifiable data for a wide range of websites. The real revolution today is *not* in the technology, but rather in the data produced and their massive accumulation, especially on many websites. Many aspects of today's quantity-oriented society could not exist, or would need to be greatly modified, were it not for all that data and the modern computer with its ability to accumulate, to store, and to have the power to process those enormous bodies of data. Those organizations that have large amounts of that data (Google, Facebook, Amazon, Twitter, to say nothing about governments, especially the U.S. government), and are continually accumulating more of it, have become enormously powerful entities. They can use it in myriad ways, especially given the concerns of this book, to shape what we buy. Although society was already moving toward ever-increasing calculability before computer technology advanced to its current level, computers have greatly expedited and extended that tendency.

For example, Google convinced many school districts to use its low-cost Chromebooks and its apps (while Google accounted for less than 1% of mobile devices shipped to primary and secondary schools in 2012, by 2016 it accounted for whopping 58% of those shipments). As a result, Google is gaining an enormous amount of data about these students (and the educational process) that they can use not only now, but long into the future to shape, among other things, their consumption choices and practices.[100] Of course, there are even graver concerns about these technologies and the data accumulated by them. These concerns include surveillance and intrusion in, and control over, people's lives.

Google's success with school districts is explained, in part, by its clever use of prosumers. In developing its "Classroom" app, it managed to get 100,000 teachers to test it out and to help Google refine it, in part by providing Google with invaluable data. Google needed the support of teachers in order to get school administrators to purchase the app (and the associated Chrome computers) and ultimately to get it into the hands of students. The point is that, as in the case of many prosumers today, those teachers were doing work for Google without being paid for it. Imagine the cost if Google had hired 100,000 teachers to do this work.

Google's success in this area is but a small part of what it, and many other entities, is doing in ushering us into the computational culture's[101] era of "datafication."[102] That is, in this era the goal is to turn as many things as possible, even the self through self-tracking devices such as Fitbit, into data; to replace subjectivity with objectivity.[103] Datafication is well illustrated in the 2011 movie (and book)[104] *Moneyball*, which, among things, depicts a debate about team personnel moves. On the one side are grizzled baseball scouts arguing on the basis of tradition and their subjective judgments of ball players. One the other side are those who are drawing conclusions about the players on the basis of "sabermetrics,"[105] that is, analysis of hard data on what actually transpires on a baseball field. The sabermetricians are shown to win the argument about the personnel directions the team involved ought to take.

Digital sites lend themselves easily to the collection of massive amounts of data—part of the new and increasingly important world of big data.[106] These data are provided, usually free of charge and often unknowingly, by users and providers. The users provide that data (e.g., preferences for various products) every time they click, for example, on products available on Amazon. The latter then turns around and extracts and uses that data in various ways, most obviously in targeting users with ads for products related to their preferences. Google uses extracted search data to "sell targeted ad space to advertisers through an increasingly automated auction system."[107] Such data were the basis of almost 90% of Google's and almost 96% of Facebook's revenue in the first quarter of 2016. Remember that virtually all of these data come from users (prosumers) who receive no monetary reward for their contributions.

Amazon's recent purchase of Whole Foods reflects the growing importance of big data. Supermarket chains have not been able to create, or to have access to, the abundance of big data that will be available to Whole Foods when it is under the Amazon umbrella. The fear is that such data, along with Amazon's other advantages, will allow Whole Foods to become a dominant player in the supermarket business, much bigger than it heretofore has been. Established supermarket chains will find it increasingly difficult to compete, and even survive, in this market. Furthermore, the addition of Whole Foods will enable Amazon to gather much more big data on food shopping. It can then use that not only to enhance Whole Foods' position in the supermarket world, but also to improve its role in the online sale of food.

Another major example of quantification on digital sites is the wide range of rating systems, with the ratings provided, once again, by users free of charge. Among the rating (actually ranking) systems on Amazon are its rankings of all books, as well as rankings in specific categories (for example, of books in sociology). Passengers rate Uber drivers from 1 to 5 stars on each ride. The driver's average rating is crucial; if that average falls below a certain number (4.6 leads the company to become concerned) they are let go by Uber. Drivers get an e-mail each week that includes their rating and a clear indication (in red) when it is below average; they also get some of the comments made about them by passengers. The most likely cause of a low rating is taking a bad route and not knowing the city well enough.[108] Another statistic collected by Uber is the number of requests, or "pings," accepted by drivers. The rate is expected to be above 80%, but the closer to 100%, the better. (Airbnb does not quantify users' ratings, but instead reports subjective comments.)

Uber collects other types of data for other purposes. For example, it uses its data to be sure that its drivers are not also working for other ride-sharing (or taxi) companies. Data on traffic patterns is used to determine the most efficient route for a trip. Data also allow Uber to predict where demand is likely to arise and to match passengers with the closest drivers. All of this "enables Uber to have a service that is quick and efficient from the passenger's point of view, thereby drawing users away from competitors."[109] Of course these data can be used for more nefarious purposes such as, in China, where Uber monitors whether drivers attend protests.

As will be discussed below, datafication is particularly important in relationship to Internet sites, especially, given our interests in this book, those that involve consumption of goods and services. The Internet has played a huge role in the emergence of the era of big data.[110] Machine technologies are crucial in this new era, especially their ability to learn over time, to be able to collect information, and to be able to communicate (especially exchange data) with other machines in the "Internet of things" (IoT).[111] Much of that data has been accumulating over a long period of time. Furthermore, the amount of data is now growing exponentially, especially on such sites as Facebook. Data not previously quantified are now being counted and being transformed into formats that enable tabulation and analysis. These data can be used in a multitude of ways. They also can be reused over and over. Data sets can be combined and data from different sets can be commingled in a multitude of ways. Every time anyone does anything on the Internet in general, and particularly on Facebook, they leave a digital trail that adds to the body of big data that can be analyzed in many ways. The Internet and its many sites have made it possible for those sites to capture an enormous amount of highly complex digitized data on many things, especially, in the case of sites like Amazon, on consumers and their consumption preferences.

As a result, these data become monetizable assets and are, in many ways, the most important corporate (intangible) asset to Facebook, Twitter, Google, Amazon, and many other Internet giants. These data can be used by the company collecting them to earn money and increase profits. Money can also be earned by leasing the data to others who can use them in unlimited, often novel, ways.

It is no longer necessary to limit analysis to samples of large data sets; we are now able to deal with huge bodies of data in their totality. This avoids many problems, especially sampling errors of various kinds. In some cases conscious consumer actions and choices are the basis of big data, but increasingly that data involves innumerable digital traces left, usually unwittingly, by visitors to a wide range of sites. In addition, such data are being gathered by sensors accumulating data unbeknownst to consumers. Automated systems now exist to rapidly search, aggregate, and cross-reference these incredibly vast bodies of data. Based on these data, among many other things, patterns of consumer preferences and trends, both individual and collective, can be described and, based on probabilities, predictions made about them. Amazon.com, for example, uses its data to make personalized recommendations on what other products a user might be interested in buying based on, among other things, previous clicks on the site. In accumulating these data, the goal is not, as it was in the past, to find out causes, why something is the case, but rather to simply uncover what the data show. To put this another way, the goal is not to deal with causality, but rather with the patterns of correlations that emerge. For example, are those who buy Stephen King books on Amazon.com also more likely to buy knives and hatchets offered on the site? These descriptions and predictions affect, among many other things, what Internet sites offer for sale to given individuals as well as to large collectivities. Internet sites also frequently use such information to deploy online ads tempting consumers into further purchases of goods and services, as their clicks indicate what they are interested in.

While in many ways big data speak for themselves, it is beyond the capabilities of humans to deal with these huge and complex data sets. This brings us to the importance of algorithms for analyzing big data, especially to those who control the websites devoted to consumption. Algorithms involve a set series of steps that lead rapidly to an automated computation of, for example, what a specific visitor to a site might be interested in purchasing (and to pop-up ads aimed at that visitor). More generally, algorithms can reveal large-scale patterns derived from composite data, and specifically, the algorithms indicate what thousands, or even millions, of consumers might be interested in purchasing. This leads to a far less targeted approach to ads, as well as to decisions by those associated with sites on what products to stock, to push, or to phase out. This, in turn, affects the actions of manufacturers who, in any case, have their own big data and algorithms informing them independently on what they do, and do not, need to produce based on expected demand.

Many companies both off- and online have proprietary algorithms that allow them to make calculations based on their own information and needs. (They can also earn money by leasing those algorithms to noncompeting companies that can gain from them without threatening the business of the algorithm's owner and creator.) The "bigger" the big data, the more likely they are to lead to algorithms that produce useful results.[112] Outside of the realm of consumption in, for example, criminal justice, proprietary algorithms can, among other things, "set bail, determine sentences, and even contribute to determinations of guilt or innocence."[113] Google has very sophisticated algorithms that allow it to make predictions on a wide variety of things, especially, in terms of consumption, what goods and services are of interest to consumers and which ones they are likely to buy. This leads to, for example, the appearance of paid ads when consumers are searching for something of interest on the Internet. These ads are a huge source of revenue and profits to Google and many other Internet sites.

There are more and more of these paid ads everywhere on the Internet. They are a variant on "product placement" seen, among other places, in movies where a particular brand of, for example, automobile or breakfast cereal is highly visible in various scenes. Such ads are likely to appear on Google at the top of a list of relevant sites. This placement makes it more likely that they will be accessed than the unpaid listings that appear farther down on the list. Furthermore, many users are unaware of this practice and therefore are likely to click naively on sites that they do not realize are listings rather than ads for less- or noncommercialized information.

Users are also likely to be unaware of the many other ways in which Internet companies get access to and use their data. A scandal occurred in mid-2017 when it was revealed that Uber was using data collected by Slice Intelligence to spy on Lyfft, one of its main competitors. Slice runs a free service called Unroll.me that allowed users to clean up their mailboxes by unsubscribing from e-mail lists. It appears that Uber either bought or stole information gleaned by Slice from users' mailboxes that included, among other things, receipts for services by Lyfft. Slice, like almost all other such data service businesses (the major ones are Acxiom, CoreLogic, Datalogix, and ID Analytics), adheres to a privacy policy and does not sell personally identifiable data. However, the collective body of big data is highly useful to buyers of the data such as Uber, as well as Lyfft. Slice users, like users of many other sites, did not know that, or how, their data were being used, especially in this way.

While Unroll.me has a written policy on this, few users bother to read it. The policy is: "We may collect, use, transfer, and disclose *nonpersonal information* for *any purpose*." The data can then be used by Unroll.me "to build anonymous market research products and services." Uber could use such information to undermine Lyfft's business by figuring out why, where, and how people were using Lyfft and then adjusting its operations to make itself more attractive to consumers of Lyfft's service. This was not an isolated event, but rather is "part of an expansive and largely unregulated world of selling personal data collected by online consumer services."[114]

This is also related to the replacement of human by nonhuman technologies. While humans can, at least theoretically, do the computations needed to analyze big data, the fact is that the data sets are far too large and complex to be analyzed in that way, especially in a timely manner. Thus, it is increasingly machines, employing artificial intelligence (AI), that are doing the computations much more quickly and accurately than humans could ever do them.

Along with the previous examples, big data and their analysis using algorithms can be used in many other ways and for many different purposes. Take, for example, Didi Chuxing, the competitor in China to Uber in the ride-sharing business. It is using big-data algorithms that aim to help ease congestion on roadways. "By analyzing commuter patterns, Didi may help traffic jams go the way of the flip phone."[115] While Didi is interested in reducing traffic jams, it is most interested in increasing its profitability through the use of these algorithms to produce better knowledge of traffic jams and how to circumvent them. Didi hopes that this knowledge will give it a big leg up on its competition in the ride-sharing business in China and perhaps ultimately elsewhere in the world.

Jeff Bezos, the head of Amazon, has said that in at least some cases he is more interested in collecting data on consumers than in selling products, some of which is, in any case, offered at a price that brings little profit or may even be sold at a loss.[116] These data are of great importance to Amazon and its ability to predict trends and target sales in the future. They also become part of big data sets that can be sold to others. For example, information on what books groups of visitors to Amazon.com click on, and in some cases buy, is of great interest to publishers who might purchase such information from Amazon, or other sites.

Quantification on Augmented Sites

Amazon has succeeded in creating a highly sophisticated augmented reality in its developing relationship between its online site, especially as it relates to books, and its burgeoning brick-and-mortar bookstores. This augmentation was made clear by the president of Amazon Books on the 2017 opening of its book shop in Manhattan: "We call this a physical extension of Amazon.com. . . . We incorporate [online] data about what people read, how they read it and why they read it."[117] Thus, on entering the New York bookstore (and presumably others), customers first encounter a display table packed with "Highly Rated" books, or those that have gotten an average rating of 4.8 (out of 5) online. Then there is another table, "Page-Turners," which includes books that Kindle readers have completed in less than three days. Still another table includes books that have been reviewed online by at least 10,000 customers. It is expected that using these data will serve to pique the interest of customers in Amazon's stores and lead them to buy at least some of the books on those tables.

Mimicking the look of the Amazon.com website, books are displayed face out on those and other tables. There is a card under each book with quantitative data derived from the website such as its average rating and the number of online reviews; there is also one qualitative review from an Amazon.com reader. One number that is *not* immediately visible is the price of the book. Customers must either use an Amazon app on their smartphones, or a digital kiosk in the store, to find the price. This allows Amazon to alter the price depending on supply and demand. Akin to Uber's "surge pricing," Amazon's dynamic pricing allows it to raise the price of books when demand is high and to reduce it when demand flags.

What makes Amazon's book stores unique is their access to, and use of, the big data constantly accumulating on its website (and soon to be augmented, if only minimally, by data from the stores). Instead of the largely hit-or-miss approach of traditional book shops, Amazon bases its stocking decisions on its proprietary logarithms analyzing its own unparalleled body of big data. Thus, it is producing its own "unfiltered and unedited" (or so it says) best-seller list, Amazon Charts, to compete with the filtered and edited industry leaders such as the *New York Times* best-seller lists. While the latter presumably merely reflect book sales, Amazon's charts attempt to shape future sales by including Amazon's own self-published (it now has nine imprints), Kindle, and Audible books. As one executive of a book consulting firm said, "They are hijacking the best-seller list to conform to what they are doing."[118]

User-Consumable Data

In addition to being a source of data, consumers themselves can find a great deal of useful data on Amazon.com. For example, in looking at the site for a previous edition of this book, a potential buyer learns all of the following:

- Number of pages in the book
- Most recent edition

- Publication date of that edition

- ISBN numbers

- Product dimensions—inches thick, width, and height

- Shipping weight and rate

- Average customer review

- Whether it is in the top 100 in all books

- Its overall rank in a list of all books

- Where it ranks in terms of social science books

- Sale price

- Rental price

- Kindle price

Amazon also sells used textbooks, although most of them are offered by resellers through the Amazon site. For such books, the potential buyer can view a long list of used books available, and their highly variable prices, and cost of shipping. Furthermore, each of these sellers is rated. The buyer can find such information as how many people have rated each seller in the last year and the sellers' average rating (percentage positive). This allows the buyer to choose among sellers on the basis of those ratings, as well as price.

Ratings and rankings of books are regularly updated (sometimes on an hourly basis) and this is especially the case at the beginning of each academic semester when such books are most likely to be in high demand and to sell.

Similar data are available on many other products available on Amazon.com. Take, for example, Samsung's 4K, Ultra HD Smart LED TV:

- Price

- Product dimensions

- Shipping weight

- ASIN—Amazon Standard Identification Number

- Item model number

- Number of customer reviews

- Average rating—1 to 5

- Ranking among all electronics
- Ranking among television and video

There are also subjective reviews (814 of them linked to this site when I checked). There is much to be gleaned from them, but many may find the overall average numerical rating sufficient for their purposes.

On eBay, quantified information on a similar television includes list price, discounted price, number of ratings, average rating (perhaps top-rated plus), number remaining in stock, shipping cost (if any), and how many people happen to be looking at that product.

Thus, consumers on these sites have a massive amount of quantitative (and some qualitative) data to help them make a decision on the purchase of, for example, textbooks or television sets. This is another of the great advantages of digital over brick-and-mortar sites where such information is comparatively meagre, difficult to come by, and harder to compare to data on similar products.

Of course, the most important data, at least as far as Amazon is concerned, is the massive amount it collects for its own use as well as to sell to a wide range of interested businesses.

PREDICTABILITY AND CONTROL

Consumers 2

The focus in this chapter is, once again, on consumers, but this time on their relationship to the two other dimensions of McDonaldization: predictability and control. (See Chapter 3 for a discussion of efficiency, calculability, and consumers.) Once again, the concern is with the relationship between dimensions of McDonaldization and those who consume the offerings of McDonaldized systems.

PREDICTABILITY: IT NEVER RAINS ON THOSE LITTLE HOUSES ON THE HILLSIDE

In a rationalized society, consumers prefer to know what to expect in most settings, most of the time. They neither desire nor expect surprises. They want to know that when they order their Big Macs today, those burgers will be identical to the ones they ate yesterday and that they will eat tomorrow. Consumers would be upset if the special sauce was used one day but not the next or if it tasted differently from one day to another. They want to know that the McDonald's franchise they visit in Des Moines, Los Angeles, Paris, or Beijing will appear and operate much the same as their local McDonald's. To achieve predictability, a rationalized society and its systems emphasize discipline, order, systematization, formalization, routine, consistency, and methodical operation.

From the consumer's point of view, predictability makes for much peace of mind in day-to-day dealings. It is also the case that predictability makes tasks easier for workers (see Chapter 6). In fact, some workers prefer effortless, mindless, repetitive work because, if nothing else, it allows them to think of other things, even daydream, while they are performing their tasks.[1] For managers and owners, too, predictability makes life easier: It helps them manage both workers and customers and aids in anticipating needs for supplies and materials, personnel requirements, income, and profits.

Predictability, however, has a downside. It has a tendency to turn consumption (as well as work and even management) into a mind-numbing routine.

Predictability is discussed in this chapter under the headings of predictable consumption settings and predictable products and processes. It is also dealt with under the heading of efforts to minimize danger and even unpleasantness.

Predictable Consumption Settings

Long before McDonald's arrived on the scene, motel chains were engaged in the rationalization process. The most notable are Best Western, founded in 1946 (more than 4,100 hotels in 100 countries),[2] and Holiday Inn (and Holiday Inn Express), which started in 1952. Holiday Inn is now part of the InterContinental Hotels Group, which claims to be the world's largest hotel chain with about 4,600 hotels in nearly 100 countries; over 2,600 of them carry the Holiday Inn logo.[3] By the late 1950s, about 500 Howard Johnson's restaurants (only two remain) were scattered around the United States, many with standardized motels attached to them. Unlike other motel chains, Howard Johnson's has stagnated, but it still has almost 400 international locations; it is now part of Wyndham Worldwide.[4] These motel chains, and others, opened in anticipation of the massive expansion of highways and highway travel. Their ability to bring consistency to the motel and hotel industry was the basis of their success and has been widely emulated.

Motel Chains: "Magic Fingers" but No Norman Bates

Before the development of such chains, motels were very diverse and highly unpredictable. Run by local owners, motels may not have been very good, but they were unique, albeit mostly in their negative characteristics. Because the nature and quality of the owners and employees varied from one locale to another, guests could not always feel fully safe and or sleep soundly. One motel might be quite comfortable, even luxurious, but another might well be a hovel. People could never be sure which amenities would be present—soap, shampoo, telephones, radio (and later television), air-conditioning, and please don't forget the much-loved "Magic Fingers" massage system. Checking into a motel was an adventure; travelers never knew what to expect, or what they would find, when they entered their rooms.

In his classic thriller *Psycho* (1960), Alfred Hitchcock exploited beautifully consumers' anxieties about old-fashioned, unpredictable motels. The motel in the movie was creepy but not as creepy as its owner, Norman Bates. Although it offered few amenities, the Bates Motel room (more recently there was a TV show titled *Bates Motel* on A&E that dealt with the horrors of Norman's early years) did come equipped with a peephole (something most travelers could do without) so that Norman could spy on his victims. Of course, the Bates Motel offered the ultimate in unpredictability: a homicidal maniac and a horrible death to unsuspecting guests.

Although very few independently owned motels actually housed crazed killers, all sorts of unpredictabilities confronted travelers at that time. In contrast, the post-WWII motel chains took pains to make their guests' experience predictable. They developed tight hiring practices to keep "unpredictable" people from managing, or working in, them. Travelers could anticipate that a motel equipped with the then-familiar orange and green Holiday Inn sign (now gone the way of McDonald's oversized golden arches) would have most, if not all, of the amenities they could reasonably expect in a moderately priced motel. Faced with the choice between a local, no-name motel and a Holiday Inn, many travelers preferred the predictable—even if it had liabilities (the absence of a personal touch, for example). The success of the early motel chains has led to many imitators, such as Ramada Inn and Rodeway Inn (now part of Choice Hotels International).

The more price-conscious chains—Super 8, Days Inn, and Motel 6—are, if anything, even more predictable.[5] The budget motel chains are predictably barren; guests find only the minimal requirements. But they expect the minimum, and that's what they get. They also expect, and receive, bargain-basement prices for the rooms.

While all of this predictability remains, and if anything has increased, there are exceptions where unpredictability has increased. One is associated with the rise of home stays booked through Airbnb, HomeAway, Homestay.com, and others. The number of home stays is projected to increase from about 8 million in 2014 to almost 20 million by 2020.[6] Home stays allow tourists to "live like a local,"[7] rather than in a generic hotel or motel from nowhere. Because we are being offered idiosyncratic houses and apartments, there is no way that they can be as predictable as centrally conceived and controlled motel rooms at, say, Holiday Inn. In fact, hotel and motel chains are being forced to offer, at least to some degree, less uniform, more local, experiences in order to compete with home stays. In contrast to hotel and motel chains, there is no powerful central home stay organization to guarantee uniformity. While much information is available online about these short-term rentals, the fact is that in many cases they are nowhere as complete, or often as out front on what they offer in these homes and apartments, as hotel and motel chains. While many like the unpredictability of home stays, the major concern of those who have never booked a home stay is that they "don't know what to expect."[8]

I learned about the problems associated with home stays the hard way when I rented a large, very expensive house for a week in Costa Rica for me and my extended family. It was obvious that the owner had brought in nice furniture for the online photos on which we based our decision to rent the house, but then brought back the old, threadbare furniture once the photos were completed. There were many other problems with the house—a lack of railings (my grandson fell about 3 feet, but fortunately was not hurt), one of the bedrooms was *under the pool* and proved unusable, and so on. When I complained to the owner by e-mail (he lived in California), he was completely unresponsive. While it is not impossible, it is very unlikely that a chain motel would have presented these kinds of problems or that it would have been unresponsive to my complaints. All of this is why, of course, many people prefer McDonaldized motels and hotels to other vacation possibilities.

That my experience was not unique is clear in the case of a man who rented a lake house in New Jersey. The online photos looked good and previous visitors rated it at 4.5 out of 5. However, the house was a huge disappointment to the renter and was very different from the photos: "The sofa had huge tears in its cushions, as if someone had stabbed it with a knife. There were burn marks all over the carpet, like someone had put out cigars on the floor . . . There was no toilet paper, and one of the air mattresses the host provided deflated in the middle of the night because it had a hole in it."[9] Generalizing this perspective, a regular Airbnb user said: "The big downside of using Airbnb instead of the hotel is the risk, because of the potential lack of consistency. . . . When Airbnb is bad, it's really bad."[10]

Because of issues such as these, Airbnb has recently sought to have its hosts operate their sites more predictably, that is, more like hotels. The view has emerged that "to expand further, Airbnb must attract travelers who prefer the *predictability* of hotels to the quirky array of spare rooms."[11] Guests also increasingly expect "that hosts will act like hotel staff members."[12]

Home stays can never be as predictable as stays at hotel and motel chains, in part because Airbnb (and others) cannot force its hosts to follow its guidelines and rules. However, in most cases that unpredictability remains an attraction rather than a liability. Home stays are by their nature less McDonaldized than those in hotel and motel chains. They are, for example, likely to be quite unique, one-of-kind domiciles and to offer similarly unique vacations.

The Fast-Food Industry: Thank God for Those Golden Arches

The fast-food industry quickly adopted and perfected practices pioneered by, among other precursors, the motel chains. In fact, Robin Leidner argues that "the heart of McDonald's success is its uniformity and predictability, . . . [its] relentless standardization." She argues that "there is a McDonald's way to handle virtually every detail of the business, and that doing things differently means doing things wrong."[13] Although McDonald's allows its franchisees and managers to innovate, "The object is to look for new innovative ways to create an experience that is exactly the same no matter what McDonald's you walk into, no matter where it is in the world."[14] As discussed, like the motel chains, McDonald's (and many other franchises) devised a large and garish sign that soon became familiar to customers. McDonald's "golden arches" evoke in consumers a sense of predictability: "Replicated color and symbol, mile after mile, city after city, act as a tacit promise of *predictability* and stability between McDonald's and its millions of customers, year after year, meal after meal."[15] Even though the signs are now smaller and less obtrusive, they still conjure a feeling of familiarity and predictability for consumers. Furthermore, each McDonald's presents the consumer with a series of predictable elements—counter, menu marquee above it, "kitchen" visible in the background, tables and uncomfortable seats, prominent trash bins, drive-through windows, and so on.

This predictable setting appears not only throughout the United States but also in many other parts of the world. Thus, homesick American tourists can take comfort in the knowledge that nearly anywhere they go, they will likely run into those familiar golden arches and the restaurant to which they have become so accustomed. Interestingly, even many non-Americans now take comfort in the appearance of a familiar McDonald's restaurant when they journey to other countries, including the United States itself.

This kind of predictability is much the same in all fast-food chains. Starbucks has its familiar green and white sign, mermaid (streamlined a few years ago), counter for placing and paying for orders, display case filled mainly with pastries, and separate counter where specialty drinks are made and retrieved. Then there is KFC with its cartoonish image of Colonel Sanders; Wendy's little girl with red pigtails; Taco Bell with its logo featuring a bell; Papa John's red, white, and green logo designed to remind us of Italy by replicating the colors of the Italian flag; and In-N-Out Burger's sweeping yellow arrow.

Although they strive hard to be as predictable as possible, some of the more recent chains are finding achieving a high degree of predictability elusive. For example, haircutting franchises such as Hair Cuttery and its offshoots (about 1,000 salons in 14 states)[16] cannot offer customers a uniform haircut because every head is slightly different and every barber or hairdresser operates in a slightly idiosyncratic fashion. To reassure the anxious customer longing for predictability, Supercuts, Great Clips, Hair Cuttery, and other haircutting franchises offer a common logo and signs, a similar shop setup, and perhaps a few familiar products.

Other Brick-and-Mortar Settings: E.T. Can't Find His Home

Megachurches are defined as churches with more than 2,000 members (the largest one is Lakewood Church in Houston, Texas, with an average attendance of 52,000 people).[17] The roughly 1,300 megachurches in the United States[18] play a central role in the McDonaldization of religion. A number of megachurches now have satellite locations. While there might be some variation, some customization, from one satellite to another (live music, local pastors), all of the participants hear a portion of the same sermon at the same time via television. This serves to bring a polished, predictable, and "branded" performance to every location the megachurch serves.[19]

Modern suburban housing also demonstrates the predictability of settings in a McDonaldized society. In fact, a famous folk song characterizes the suburbs as

Little boxes on the hillside,

Little boxes made of ticky-tacky,

Little boxes, little boxes,

Little boxes all the same.[20]

In many suburban communities, interiors and exteriors are little different from one house to another. Although some diversity exists in the more expensive developments, many suburbanites could easily wander into someone else's house and not realize immediately that they are not in their own home.

Furthermore, the communities themselves look very much alike. In new developments rows of saplings (many of which will die or not develop fully) held up by posts and wire are planted to replace mature trees ripped out of the ground to allow for the more efficient building of houses. Similarly, hills are often bulldozed to flatten the terrain. Streets are laid out in familiar patterns with, for example, many cul-de-sacs. With such predictability, suburbanites may well enter the wrong suburban community or get lost in their own community.

Several of Steven Spielberg's early movies take place in these rationalized suburbs. Spielberg's strategy is to lure viewers into this predictable world and then confront them with an unpredictable event. For example, in *E.T.* (1982), an extraterrestrial wanders into a suburban development of tract houses and is discovered by a child there who, until that point, has lived a highly predictable suburban existence. The unpredictable E.T. eventually disrupts not only the lives of the child and his family but also the entire community. Similarly, *Poltergeist* (1982) takes place in a suburban household, with evil spirits disrupting its predictable tranquility. The great success of several of Spielberg's movies may be traceable to people's longing for some unpredictability, even if it is frightening and menacing, in their increasingly predictable suburban lives.

The Truman Show (1998) takes place in a community completely controlled by the director of a television show. The movie can be seen as a spoof of, and attack on, the Disneyesque "planned communities" that have sprung up throughout the United States (and elsewhere in the world). These are often more upscale than the typical suburban community. The leading example of a planned community is, not surprisingly, Disney's town of Celebration, Florida. Potential homeowners must choose among approved options and are strictly limited in what they can do with their homes and property.[21] These communities go farther than traditional suburban developments in seeking to remove as much unpredictability as possible from people's lives.

Another 1998 movie, *Pleasantville,* depicts a tightly controlled 1950ish community that is characterized by a high degree of conformity and uniformity. This is reflected in the fact that everything is depicted in black and white. As the story unfolds, however, things grow less and less predictable, and color is gradually introduced. In the end, a far more unpredictable Pleasantville is shown in full color. The remakes of *Fun With Dick and Jane* (2005) and *Revolutionary Road* (2008) deal with couples who have, and then gradually lose, the seemingly ideal suburban home and lifestyle.

Predictable Online Consumption Settings:
They Look and Operate Much the Same

Perhaps the most predictable thing about online consumption sites, taken collectively, is that consumers know, assuming they try hard enough, that they will be able to find almost literally anything they might want. This not something that brick-and-mortar sites—even the largest Wal-Mart or shopping mall—can promise. It is almost impossible to fail in consuming online. Perhaps the same could be said about brick-and-mortar consumption sites, but one would need to be willing to travel great distances and spend much time in pursuit of one's objective. Even if one is so inclined, the outcome of the trip would still be in doubt.

Online consumption settings tend to adopt a format that is well known to those who click on them. Those who create and run these sites do not want visitors to be surprised or to be put off by differences in their sites in comparison to others with which consumers are familiar.

A visitor to any of these sites is likely to be greeted with a website that looks much like every other one of that genre. A very unusual looking website is likely to put consumers off; they are likely to retreat to more familiar ones. Most consumption-oriented websites include such categories as "special sales"; "gifts for upcoming holidays"; a menu of departments offering different kinds of products; items suggested by algorithms analyzing previous visits by the consumer; items that have been clicked on in the past, especially those that have been purchased previously; a history of previous orders; items in one's "cart" but not yet purchased; a search box for other items, and so forth. Consumers have learned to expect these, as well as how to work their way through them and the sites more generally in order to get what they want; their actions on the sites tend to be quite predictable. Furthermore, the sites are structured on the basis of what visitors have done in the past. Thus, predictable past actions lead to predictable sites that, in turn, lead to further predictable choices. While they can certainly act in surprising ways, consumers generally do what their past behavior, and that of perhaps millions of others, indicates they will do and what the site's algorithms anticipate they will do. In any case, the site's preexisting structure makes it nearly impossible for consumers to act in very unpredictable ways.

Even though it offers a wider range of new, used, and unusual things for sale, eBay's site looks like most of the other consumption sites online. Similar sites such as uBid.com look much the same. So, even those sites that offer the most surprising goods and services are set up so that consumers encounter few, if any, surprises.

Predictable Products and Processes

The drive for increased predictability extends, unsurprisingly, to the goods and services being sold in McDonaldized settings, as well as to the methods used to produce and deliver them. Consider the uniformity that characterizes the chain stores (Apple, Banana Republic, Foot Locker, Old Navy, United Colors of Benetton, Victoria's Secret, etc.) dominating virtually all remaining malls. Few of the products are unique—indeed, many are globally available brand names— and procedures for displaying merchandise, greeting customers, ringing up purchases, and so on are amazingly similar.

The Fast-Food Industry: Even the Pickles Are Standardized

Needless to say, the food purveyed in fast-food restaurants is highly predictable. A short menu of simple foods helps ensure predictability. Hamburgers, fried chicken, pizza, tacos, French fries, soft drinks, shakes, and the like are all relatively easy to prepare and to serve in a uniform fashion. Predictability in such products is made possible by the use of uniform raw ingredients, identical technologies for food preparation and cooking, similarity in the way the food is served, and identical packaging. As a trainer at Hamburger University put it, "McDonald's has standards for everything down to the width of the pickle slices."[22] Packaging is another important component of predictability in the fast-food restaurant.

Despite the fast-food restaurants' best efforts, unpredictabilities can creep in because of the nature of the materials—the food might not be hot enough, the chicken might be gristly or tough, or there may be too few pieces of pepperoni on a slice of pizza. Whatever the (slight) unpredictabilities in the food, the packaging—containers for the burgers, bags for the small fries, cardboard boxes for the pizzas—will always be the same and imply to the customers that the food will be, too.

Predictable food also requires predictable ingredients. McDonald's has stringent guidelines on the nature (quality, size, shape, and so on) of the meat, chicken, fish, potatoes, and other ingredients purchased by each franchisee. The buns, for example, must be made of ordinary white bread from which all the chewy and nutritious elements of wheat, such as bran and germ, have been milled out. (One wit said of mass-produced white bread, "I thought they just blew up library paste with gas and sent it to the oven."[23]) Because buns otherwise might grow stale or moldy, preservatives are added to retard spoilage. Precut, uniform, frozen French fries rather than fresh potatoes are used.

The increasing use of frozen (or freeze-dried) foods addresses unpredictabilities related to the supply of raw materials. One of the reasons Ray Kroc eventually substituted frozen for fresh potatoes was that for several months a year, it was difficult to obtain the desired variety of potato. Freezing potatoes made them readily available year-round. In addition, the potato peelings at each McDonald's outlet often created a stench that was anathema to Kroc and the sanitized (sterile?) world he sought to create. Frozen, peeled, and precut French fries solved this problem as well.

The predictability of foods in a McDonaldized society has led to a disturbing fact: "Regional and ethnic distinctions are disappearing from American cooking. Food in one neighborhood, city, or state looks and tastes pretty much like food anywhere else. . . . Sophisticated processing and storage techniques, fast transport, and a creative variety of formulated convenience-food products have made it possible to ignore regional and seasonal differences in food production."[24]

Entertainment: Welcome to McMovieworld

The earlier discussion of *Psycho* (and the *Bates Motel* TV show) brings to mind the fact that the movie industry, too, values predictability. *Psycho* was followed by several sequels (as well as a later [1998] shot-by-shot remake of the original). In 2017 an unusually large number of sequels, including *John Wick: Chapter 2; Wolverine 3: Weapon X; Fast 8; Pirates of the Caribbean: Dead Men Tell No Tales; War for the Planet of the Apes; Alien: Covenant; Blade Runner 2;* and *Star Wars Episode VIII*. The all-time leaders among sequels are the 12 *Friday the 13th* movies and the 23 *James Bond* movies. These predictable products generally attract a large audience, and they often succeed at the expense of movies based on new concepts, ideas, and characters.

The studios like sequels ("Welcome to McMovieworld")[25] because the same characters, actors, and basic plotlines can be used again and again. Furthermore, sequels are more likely to succeed at the box office than completely original movies; profits are therefore more predictable. Viewers (consumers) presumably like sequels because they enjoy the comfort of encountering favorite characters played by familiar actors who find themselves in accustomed settings. Like a McDonald's meal, many sequels are not very good, but at least consumers know what they are getting.

Movies themselves seem to include increasingly predictable sequences and highly predictable endings. Dustin Hoffman contends that today's movie audiences would not accept the many flashbacks, fantasies, and dream sequences of his classic 1969 movie, *Midnight Cowboy.* He believes that this may be "emblematic of the whole culture . . . now people want to know what they're getting when they go to the movies."[26]

On television, the parallel to sequels is "copycatting" or producing sitcoms and comedies "that are so similar as to be indistinct."[27] For example, "They all gather in apartments and offices that tend to have heightened, overly colorful, casual-by-design look, and they exchange jokes that frequently depend on body parts or functions for their punch."[28] Among syndicated or current TV fare, *Seinfeld, Friends,* and *The Big Bang Theory* come to mind. A variety of successful shows such as *CSI* and *NCIS* (as well as spinoffs *NCIS: Los Angeles* and *NCIS: New Orleans*) all follow a given formula. Successful TV shows such as *Survivor* and *American Idol* have spawned a number of shows (e.g., *America's Got Talent, The Voice*) that emulate the model they created. *The Real Housewives of Orange County* spawned, among others, *The Real Housewives of New York City, Atlanta, Miami,* and *Beverly Hills.* "Like McDonald's, prime time wants you to know exactly what you'll get no matter where you are, emphasizing the comforts of predictability over nutrition."[29] Then there the revivals of once successful TV shows such as *24, Lethal Weapon, Prison Break,* and *Roseanne* (coming in 2018). In fact, *American Idol,* which went off the air in 2016, will become its *own sequel* when it returns in 2017–2018.

Another form of entertainment aiming to provide consumers with no surprises is the cruise, which is as oriented to predictability as it is to efficiency. A cruise originating from the United States will likely be made up of like-minded Americans. Cruise ship operators have turned travel into a highly predictable product by creating trips that allow consumers minimal contact with the people, culture, and institutions of visited countries. This result creates a paradox: Consumers go to considerable expense and effort to go to foreign countries, where they have as little contact as possible with native culture.[30] American package tour agencies use American air carriers wherever possible or local transports that offer the amenities expected by American tourists (perhaps even air-conditioning, private bathrooms, or flat-screen TVs). Tour guides are usually Americans or people who have spent time in America—at the very least, natives fluent in English who know all about the needs and interests of Americans. Restaurants visited on the tour either are American (perhaps associated with an American fast-food chain) or cater to the American palate. Hotels are also likely to be either American chains, such as Sheraton and Hilton, or European hotels that have structured themselves to suit American tastes.[31] Each day offers a firm, often tight schedule, with little time for spontaneous activities. Tourists can take comfort from knowing exactly what they are going to do on a daily, even hourly, basis.

John Urry argues that the package tour has declined in popularity in recent years.[32] How do we reconcile this contention with the idea that McDonaldization is increasing? The answer lies, in part, in the growing popularity of highly McDonaldized cruises to and around, among many other places, the Caribbean, the Mediterranean, South America, Southeast Asia, and Alaska. Relatively recent are river cruises on, for example, the Danube and Rhine rivers in Europe. Events on the cruise ships and river cruise boats follow a familiar pattern and there are many guided side trips that resemble, especially if the traveler goes on a number of them, the old packaged tours.

The other part of the answer is to be found in the fact that most societies have grown increasingly McDonaldized, with the result that there may be less need for McDonaldized tours. After all, because tourists traveling practically anywhere are likely to find McDonald's, Holiday Inn, Hard Rock Cafe, *USA TODAY,* and CNN, they may feel less need to be protected from unpredictabilities; many of them have already been eliminated.

Minimizing Danger and Unpleasantness

Brick-and-Mortar Settings: Antiseptic, Climate-Controlled, Plastic Worlds

The attraction of the shopping mall can be credited, at least in part, to its ability to make shopping more predictable. For example, "One kid who works here [at a mall] told me why he likes the mall. . . . It's because no matter what the weather is outside, it's always the same in here. He likes that. He doesn't want to know it's raining—it would depress him."[33] Consumers who wander through malls are also relatively free from the crime that might beset them in city streets. The lack of bad weather and the relative absence of crime point to another predictable aspect of shopping malls—they are always upbeat.

Avoiding crime is a key factor in the rise of so-called family fun or pay-to-play centers. (Often, children pay an entrance fee, although, in a cute gimmick, parents may be "free.") These centers offer ropes, padded "mountains," tubes, tunnels, giant blocks, trapezes, and so on. They have proven popular in urban areas because they provide a safe haven in crime-ridden cities.[34] Children are also seen as less likely to injure themselves in fun centers than in community playgrounds because of the nature of the equipment and the presence of staff supervisors. And there are safety checks to be sure that children do not leave with anyone but their parents. However, although fun centers are undoubtedly safer and less unpredictable, they have also been described as "antiseptic, climate-controlled, plastic world[s]."[35]

Modern amusement parks are in many ways much safer and more pleasant than their honky-tonk ancestors. The Disney organization quite clearly knew that to succeed, it had to overcome the unpredictability of old amusement parks. Disneyland and Walt Disney World take great pains to be sure that the consumer is not subject to any disorder. We have already seen (in Chapter 3) how the garbage is whisked away so that people do not have to be disturbed by the sight of trash. Vendors do not sell peanuts, gum, or cotton candy because those items would make a mess underfoot. Consumers will not likely have their day disrupted by the sight of public drunkenness. Crime in the parks is virtually nonexistent. Disney offers consumers a world of predictable, almost surreal, orderliness.

While there have been some highly publicized accidents in recent years, few unanticipated things happen on any of the rides or in any of the attractions in contemporary theme parks. Of the Jungle Cruise ride at Disney World, a company publication says, "The Jungle Cruise is a favorite of armchair explorers, because it compresses weeks of safari travel into ten minutes [efficiency!] of fun, *without mosquitoes, monsoons, or misadventures.*"[36]

At one time, people went camping to escape the predictable routines of their daily lives. City dwellers fled their homes in search of nature, with little more than a tent and a sleeping bag. Little or nothing lay between the camper and the natural environment, leading to some unpredictable events. But that was the whole point. Campers might see a deer wander close to their campsite, perhaps even venture into it. Of course, they might also encounter the unexpected thunderstorm, tick bite, or snake, but these were accepted as an integral part of escaping one's routine activities.

Some people still camp this way; however, many others have sought to eliminate unpredictability from camping. Said the owner of one campground, "All they wanted [in the past] was a space in the woods and an outhouse. . . . But nowadays people aren't exactly roughing it."[37] Instead of simple tents, modern campers might venture forth in a recreational vehicle (RV) such as a Winnebago or take a trailer with an elaborate pop-up tent to protect them from the unexpected. Of course, "camping" in an RV also tends to reduce the likelihood of catching sight of wandering wildlife. Furthermore, the motorized camper carries within it all the familiar elements one has at home—refrigerator, stove, television, portable DVD player, iPad, smartphone, and iPod base.

Camping technology has not only made for great predictability but has also changed modern campgrounds. Relatively few people now pitch their tents in the unpredictable wilderness; most find their way into rationalized campgrounds, even "country-club campgrounds," spearheaded by franchises such as Kampgrounds of America (KOA), the latter with almost 500 sites.[38] Even being labeled the "McDonald's of camping" does not cause KOA's vice president for marketing to blanch: "We never took that as sort of a knock on the vacation experience or it being a cheap vacation, because it's more talking about consistency, and McDonald's is a franchise that really delivers consistency."[39] Said one camper relaxing in his air-conditioned, 32-foot trailer, "We've got everything right here. . . . It doesn't matter how hard it rains or how the wind blows."[40] Modern campgrounds are likely to be divided into sections—one for tents, another for RVs, each section broken into neat rows of usually tiny campsites. Hookups allow those with RVs to operate the various technologies encased within them. Campsite owners might also provide campers who are "roughing it" with amenities such as a well-stocked delicatessen, bathrooms and showers, heated swimming pools, a game room loaded with video games, a Laundromat, a TV room, a movie theater, and even entertainment such as bands or comedians.

KOA has moved away from homogeneous budget campgrounds to differentiate among "Journey" (basic campgrounds mainly for one-night stays), "Holiday" (more destinations with picturesque settings and more upscale amenities), and "Resort" (more upscale amenities for large groups such as family reunions) campgrounds. While this creates more differentiation among campgrounds, KOA will undoubtedly seek to create some level of predictability within each of these categories.

One of the things chains of campgrounds offer is freedom from danger. There is certainly nothing wrong with wanting to be safe from harm. However, society as a whole has surrendered responsibility for providing safe environments to commercial interests. Because our city streets can be unsafe, consumers shop in malls. Because our playgrounds are sometimes unsafe (and greatly limited), children play in commercial "fun" centers. The problem is that people are therefore spending large amounts of leisure time in commercial environments eager to lead them into a life of consumption. If the larger society provided safe and attractive recreation centers for both adults and children, we would not be forced to spend so much of our lives, and do so many things, in commercial venues.

The irony is that, despite their claim to safety, McDonaldized locations, especially fast-food restaurants, seem particularly prone to crime and violence. Said the owner of a fast-food outlet, "Fast food for some reason is a target."[41]

Perhaps the iron cage sometimes forces consumers to lash out in the setting that is its leading example.

Online Settings: The Danger Is Rarely Physical

Most, but not all, of the physical dangers that confront consumers offline are absent on online sites, but there are a range of other kinds of potentially more dangerous situations encountered online. While there have been scary stories of online stalking,[42] the danger is rarely physical. Economic dangers, on the other hand, to both individuals and large groups of people, can be extraordinary. Valuable information on many millions of consumers (e.g., social security and credit card numbers) have been stolen from a variety of sites, including those associated with consumption. For example, thefts of millions of credit card numbers have occurred in recent years from, among other places, Home Depot, Target, and Neiman Marcus. In addition, consumers have been defrauded in various ways on such sites. In late 2017, the credit-reporting company Equifax was hacked, exposing the personal information of nearly 150 million people, as well as the credit card numbers of over 200,000 of them.

Hacking of accounts reached something of a peak in May 2017 when hackers were able to attack computer systems in about 150 countries, including those of FedEx, the Russian Interior Ministry, and Britain's National Service. Using "ransomware" called Wannacry 2.0, the hackers locked the computers and demanded payment of $300, or more, to prevent data loss and to unlock the devices.[43] In this case, it was organizations that were compromised, but many consumers these organizations serve were affected indirectly. For example, in China some ATMs and e-payment systems at gasoline stations ceased working, at least for a time.[44] In Britain, the National Health Service postponed scheduled surgeries for non-life-threatening maladies, in some cases even as patients were about to be wheeled into the operating room. Patient care suffered as, among other things, their records could not be accessed and their test results were unobtainable.[45]

CONTROL: HUMAN AND NONHUMAN ROBOTS

The fourth dimension of McDonaldization is increased control of humans through the use of nonhuman technology. Technology includes not only machines and tools but also materials, skills, knowledge, rules, regulations, procedures, and techniques. Technologies thus encompass not only the obvious, such as robots and computers, but also the less obvious, such as the assembly-line, bureaucratic rules, and manuals prescribing accepted procedures and techniques. A *human technology* (a screwdriver, for example) is controlled by people; a *nonhuman technology* (e.g., the order window at the drive-through, a logarithm) controls people.

The great source of uncertainty, unpredictability, and inefficiency in any rationalizing system is people—either those who work within it or those served by it. Hence, efforts to increase control are usually aimed at employees (see Chapter 6) as well as customers, although processes and products may also be the targets. A wide array of consumers are discussed in this section. Beyond the usual consumers of fast food, we also deal with consumers of the processes of both birth and death. That the latter have become processes to consume (and to McDonaldize) is a powerful indication of the extent to which we have come to live in a society increasingly characterized and dominated by consumption.

Controlling Consumers

Employees are relatively easy to control because they rely on employers for their livelihood. Customers have much more freedom to bend the rules and go elsewhere if they don't like the situations in which they find themselves. Still, McDonaldized systems have developed and honed a number of methods for controlling customers.

The Fast-Food Industry: Get the Hell Out of There

Whether customers go into a fast-food restaurant or use its drive-through window, they enter a kind of conveyor system that moves them through the restaurant in the manner the management desires. It is clearest in the case of the drive-through window (the energy for this conveyor comes from the consumer's own automobile), but it is also true for those who enter the restaurant. Consumers know that they are supposed to line up, move to the counter, order their food, pay, carry the food to an available table, eat, gather their debris, deposit it in the trash receptacle, and return to their cars.

Three mechanisms help control customers:[46]

1. Customers receive cues (e.g., the presence of lots of trash receptacles, especially at the exits) that indicate what is expected of them.

2. A variety of structural constraints lead customers to behave in certain ways. For example, the drive-through window, as well as the written

instructions on the menu marquee above the counter (and elsewhere), give customers few, if any, alternatives.

3. Customers have internalized taken-for-granted norms and follow them when they enter a fast-food restaurant.

When my children were young, they admonished me after we finished our meal at McDonald's (before I "saw the light," I occasionally ate in fast-food restaurants) for not cleaning up the debris and carting it to the trash can. My children were, in effect, serving as agents for McDonald's, teaching me the norms of behavior in such settings. I (and most other consumers) have long since internalized these norms, and I still dutifully follow them these days on the rare occasions that a lack of any other alternative (or the need for a reasonably clean restroom) forces me into a fast-food restaurant.

One goal of control in fast-food restaurants is to influence customers to spend their money and leave quickly. (Starbucks is an exception, at least to some degree, in encouraging a few customers to linger over their coffee and laptops in order to support its image as a modern version of an old-fashioned coffee shop that welcomes customers. Actually, the vast majority of customers are not welcome, could not be welcome, there and they recognize this by getting their coffee to go or using the drive-through window.) The restaurants need tables to be vacated rapidly so other diners will have a place to eat their food. A famous old, but now defunct, chain of cafeterias, the Automat,[47] was undermined in part, by people who occupied its tables for hours on end. The Automat became a kind of social center, leaving less and less room for diners to eat the meals they had purchased. The deathblow was struck when street people began to monopolize the Automat's tables. Interestingly, McDonald's is now experiencing a similar problem in China with homeless people ("McRefugees") who beg in the restaurants, eat leftover scraps of food, and sleep there.[48] In at least one McDonald's in downtown New York City, the problem is not so much the homeless as it is drug addicts who congregate there (informally called "junkie" or "zombie" McDonald's), come down from their drugs, hustle more drugs, and sleep them off.[49]

Some fast-food restaurants employ security personnel (however, the "zombie" McDonald's is usually overwhelmed by the addicts and, in this case, the security guard is known to leave by 2pm) to keep street people on the move or, in the suburbs, to prevent potentially rowdy teenagers from monopolizing tables or parking lots. There have even been instances where the police have been called to remove customers, even senior citizens, who linger.[50] In some cases, fast-food restaurants have put up signs limiting a customer's stay in the restaurant (and even its parking lot) to, say, 20 minutes. More generally, fast-food restaurants have structured themselves so that consumers do not need or want to linger over meals. Easily consumed finger foods make the meal itself a quick one. Some fast-food restaurants have even created special chairs designed to make customers uncomfortable after about 20 minutes.[51] Much the same effect is produced by the colors used in the décor. For example, at McDonald's, "From the scarlet and yellow of the logo to the maroon of the uniform, everything clashes. It's designed to stop people from feeling so comfortable they might want to stay."[52]

Other Brick-and-Mortar Settings: It's Like Boot Camp

Grade schools have developed many ways to control students. For example, kindergarten has been described as an educational "boot camp."[53] Students are taught not only to obey authority but also to embrace the rationalized procedures of rote learning and objective testing. More important, spontaneity and creativity tend not to be rewarded and may even be discouraged, leading to what one expert calls "education for docility."[54] Those who conform to the rules are thought to be good students; those who don't are labeled bad students. As a general rule, the students who end up in college are the ones who have successfully submitted to the control mechanisms. Creative, independent students are often, from the educational system's point of view, "messy, expensive, and time-consuming."[55]

The clock and the lesson plan also exert control over students, especially in grade school and high school. Because of the "tyranny of the clock," a class must end at the sound of the bell, even if students are just about to comprehend something important. Because of the "tyranny of the lesson plan," a class must focus on what the plan requires for the day, no matter what the class (and perhaps the teacher) may find interesting. Imagine "a cluster of excited children examining a turtle with enormous fascination and intensity. Now children, put away the turtle, the teacher insists. We're going to have our science lesson. The lesson is on crabs."[56]

In the health care industry, the patient (along with the physician) is increasingly under the control of large, impersonal systems. For example, in many medical insurance programs, patients can no longer decide on their own to see a specialist. The patient must rather first see a primary care physician, who must decide whether a specialist is necessary. Because of the system's great pressure on the primary care physician to keep costs down, fewer patients visit specialists, and primary care physicians perform more functions formerly handled by specialists. Interaction with physicians is often limited, sometimes to 10 minutes, including time to enter notes in the patient's digital record.

The supermarket scanners that control checkers also control customers. When prices were marked on all the products, customers could calculate roughly how much they were spending as they shopped. They could also check the price on each item to be sure that they were not being overcharged at the cash register. But with Universal Product Codes (UPCs) and scanners, it is almost impossible for consumers to keep tabs on prices and on the cashiers. More recently, supermarkets have placed scanners in the markets to allow customers to check on the prices of items they are interested in buying. However, these are sometimes difficult to find and my impression is that they are not widely used. In any case, a quick scan or two is not likely to be as useful as having prices marked on every item. Not having prices marked on food items makes it easier for the markets to change prices quickly and in a way that consumers might not notice.

Supermarkets also control shoppers with food placement. For example, supermarkets take pains to put the foods that children find attractive in places where youngsters can readily grab them (i.e., on low shelves). Also, what a market chooses to feature via special sale prices and strategic placement in the store profoundly affects what is purchased. Manufacturers and wholesalers battle one another for coveted display positions, such as at the front of the market or at the "endcaps" of aisles. Foods placed in these positions will likely sell far more than they would if they were relegated to their usual positions.

Malls also exert control over customers, especially children and young adults, who are programmed by the mass media to be avid consumers. Going to a mall, as well as trekking through it, can become deeply ingrained habits. Some people are reduced to "zombies," walking the malls hour after hour, weekend after weekend.[57] More specifically, the placement of food courts, escalators, and stairs forces customers to traverse corridors and pass attractive shop windows. Benches are situated so that consumers might be attracted to certain sites, even though they are seeking a brief respite from the labors of consumption. The strategic placement of shops, as well as goods within shops, leads people toward products in which they might not otherwise have been interested.

Control in Online Settings: Amazon's Increasing Power and the Drive to Limit Net Neutrality

While users have lots of options once they log on to online consumption sites, once there, they are controlled to a large degree. Of course, consumers can freely choose among available options on those sites, but their choices are generally restricted to those items. They cannot order items that are unavailable on those sites. For example, logging into Amazon.com in search of books, one of the first things that consumers see are lists of books related to their previous searches. Next might be a list of various other kinds of books (e.g., those relating to an upcoming holiday). At the bottom of the screen is a list of recently clicked-on books. If, and when, the consumers click on one of the books, a variety of (mostly) quantified information appears. In addition, a list of books bought by people who also looked at the same book is offered in the hope that consumers might also be interested in one or more of them. In these and other ways the users are led in the direction that sites want them to go and, in at least some cases, to purchase items that they might not have anticipated wanting. While they can opt to go in other directions and make other choices—and they often do—the fact is that they have to resist the sites and choices that a given site has prioritized. They have to search harder for other options. Of course, Amazon is happy for them to search out other options because that means additional sales (and data; see Chapter 3). If consumers are determined to buy a particular item, they will search it out. Amazon is interested in laying before them options that they might not have thought of initially.

A much broader form of control is exercised by the corporations and organizations that collect and sort big data. As a result, they know a great deal about us as large collectivities, smaller groups, and even as individuals. Among other things, they can surveille us and affect our ability to get products and services. Most important, they know what goods and services we—as collectivities, groups, and individuals—have purchased or even thought about purchasing. As a result, they can target ads based on that knowledge and make it difficult for us to learn about alternatives in the marketplace.

I have some personal experience in terms of the latter. Amazon's online power allows it to get concessions from publishers (and other manufacturers) that none of it competitors can get. Amazon demanded concessions from the relatively small press—Sage—that publishes a number of my books, including this one. For a time, Sage refused to meet their demands with the result that Amazon refused to order new copies of my books. As a result, the new copies were unavailable on the site, especially during the period at the beginning of a semester when students were buying books for their courses. Students could buy used books sold by or through Amazon and, of course, there are other ways they could have gotten the books, but the lack of a listing on Amazon adversely affected the sales of this book. Sage eventually reached an understanding with Amazon (I don't know how many of Amazon's demands they acceded to), but new books of mine again became available on Amazon's website.

A more general example of the effort to gain control over access to the Internet is the drive to limit or eliminate net neutrality. That is, instead of giving users equal access to various sites, Internet Service Providers (ISPs) have been seeking to limit access to, or at least limit the speed of access to, certain sites. This serves to advantage the most powerful and profitable Internet sites. The federal government has sought, so far unsuccessfully, to pass laws that would restrict access to the Internet; that would violate the idea of net neutrality. Such laws would serve to give ISPs such as Comcast and Verizon and the most powerful Internet sites (e.g., Google) much greater control over the information available to users.

Birth and Death: The Ultimate Examples of Control

In this concluding section, we turn to two very different kinds of consumption—birth and death—that are not usually thought of in those terms. But, as we will see, we do consume both of them in several ways. Beyond that, we will discuss some of the controls that are exercised over the consumption of birth and death. The fact is that the processes of birth and death, as well as those who "consume" those processes (give birth, die), have come under increasing control.

Controlling Conception: Even Granny Can Conceive. Conception is rapidly becoming McDonaldized. For example, the problem of male impotence[58] has been attacked by burgeoning impotence clinics (some of them chains,[59] e.g., National Male Medical Clinics) and low-T (Testosterone) centers. Male impotence has also been dealt with by an increasingly wide array of technologies, including medicine (especially Viagra,[60] Cialis, and others), surgical implants, and mechanical devices. Many males are now more predictably able to engage in intercourse and to play a role in pregnancies that otherwise might not have occurred.

Similarly, female infertility has been ameliorated by advances in the technologies associated with artificial (more precisely, "donor") insemination,[61] in vitro fertilization,[62] intracytoplasmic sperm injection,[63] various surgical and nonsurgical procedures associated with the Wurn Technique,[64] at-home fertility kits,[65] and so on. Some fertility clinics have grown so confident that they offer a money-back guarantee if there is no live baby after three attempts.[66] For those women who still cannot become pregnant or carry to term, surrogate mothers can do the job.[67] Even postmenopausal women now have the chance of becoming pregnant ("granny pregnancies");[68] the oldest, thus far, is a 70-year-old Indian woman who gave birth to twins in 2008.[69] These developments and many others, such as ovulation-predictor home tests,[70] have made having a child far more predictable. Efficient, easy-to-use home pregnancy tests are widely available to take the ambiguity out of determining whether a woman has become pregnant.

One of the great unpredictabilities tormenting some prospective parents is whether their baby will turn out to be a girl or a boy. Sex selection[71] clinics can be found in the United States, Canada, Australia, England, India, and Hong Kong, as part of what may eventually become a full-scale chain of "gender choice centers." The technology, developed in the early 1970s, is actually rather simple: Semen is filtered through albumin to separate sperm with male chromosomes from sperm with female chromosomes. The woman (the consumer in this case) is then artificially inseminated with the desired sperm. A recent technique uses staining of sperm cells to determine which cells carry X (male) and Y (female) chromosomes. Artificial insemination or in vitro fertilization then mates the selected sperm with an egg. MicroSort technology offers a couple a 93% chance of creating a girl; the probability of creating a boy is 82%.[72] The goal is to achieve 100% accuracy in using "male" or "female" sperm to tailor the sex of the offspring to the needs and demands of the parents.

Consumers' increasing control over the process of conception delights some but horrifies others: "Being able to specify your child's sex in advance leads to nightmare visions of ordering babies with detailed specifications, like cars with automatic transmission or leather upholstery."[73] Furthermore, said a medical ethicist, "Choosing a child like we choose a car is part of a *consumerist mentality*, the child becomes a 'product' rather than a full human being."[74] By turning a baby into just another "product" to be McDonaldized—engineered, manufactured, and commodified—people are in danger of dehumanizing the birth process.

Of course, we are just on the frontier of the McDonaldization of conception (and just about everything else). For example, the first cloned sheep, Dolly (since deceased), was created in Scotland in 1996, and other animals have since been cloned, opening the door to the possibility of cloning humans. Cloning involves creating identical copies of molecules, cells, or even entire organisms.[75] This conjures up an image of the engineering and mass production of a "cookie-cutter" race of people, all good-looking, athletic, intelligent, free of genetic defects, and so on—the ultimate in the control of conception. And a world in which everyone was the same would be a world in which people might be ready to accept a similar sameness in everything around them. Of course, this is a science fiction scenario, but the technology needed to take us down this road is already here.

Controlling Pregnancy: Choosing the Ideal Baby. Some parents wait until pregnancy is confirmed before worrying about the sex of their child, but then, amniocentesis can be used to determine whether a fetus is male or female. First used in 1968 for prenatal diagnosis, amniocentesis is a process whereby fluid is drawn from the amniotic sac, usually between the 14th and 18th weeks of pregnancy.[76] With amniocentesis, parents might choose to exert greater control over the process by aborting a pregnancy if the fetus is of the "wrong" sex. This technique is clearly far less efficient than pre-pregnancy sex selection because it occurs after conception. In fact, very few Americans (only about 5% in one study) say that they might use abortion as a method of sex selection.[77] Amniocentesis does, in any case, exemplify the notion of control by allowing parents to know well in advance what the sex of their child will be and, if they wish, to do something about it.

Concern about a baby's sex pales in comparison to concerns about the possibility of genetic defects. In addition to amniocentesis, a variety of tests can be used (consumed) to determine whether a fetus carries genetic defects such as cystic fibrosis, Down syndrome, Huntington's disease, hemophilia, Tay-Sachs disease, and sickle cell disease.[78] These tests include the following:

- Chorionic villus sampling (CVS): Generally done earlier than amniocentesis, between the 10th and 12th weeks of pregnancy, CVS involves taking a sample from the fingerlike structures projecting from the sac that later becomes the placenta. These structures have the same genetic makeup as the fetus.[79]

- Maternal serum alpha-fetoprotein (MSAFP) testing: This procedure is a simple blood test done in the 16th, 17th, or 18th week of pregnancy. A high level of alpha-fetoprotein might indicate spina bifida; a low level might indicate Down syndrome.

- Ultrasound: This technology, derived from sonar, provides an image of the fetus by bouncing high-frequency energy off it. Ultrasound can reveal various genetic defects, as well as many other things (sex, gestational age, and so on).

The use of all these nonhuman technologies has increased dramatically in recent years, with some (ultrasound, MSAFP) routine practices.[80] Many other technologies for testing fetuses are also available, and others will undoubtedly be created.

If one or more of these tests indicate the existence of a genetic defect, then abortion becomes an option. Parents who choose abortion are unwilling to inflict the pain and suffering of genetic abnormality or illness on the child, themselves, and other family members. Eugenicists feel that it is not rational for a society to allow genetically disabled children to be born and to create whatever irrationalities will accompany their birth. From a cost-benefit point of view (calculability), abortion is less costly than supporting a child with serious physical or mental abnormalities or problems, sometimes for a number of years. Given such logic, it makes sense for society to use the nonhuman technologies now available to discover which fetuses should be permitted to survive and which should not. The ultimate step would be a societal ban on certain marriages and births, something China has considered, with the goal of reducing the number of sick or intellectually disabled children that burden the state.[81] Efforts to predict and repair genetic anomalies are proceeding at a rapid rate. The Human Genome Project has constructed a map of the human genome's gene-containing regions.[82] When the project began, only about 100 human disease genes were known; today we know many more such genes.[83] This knowledge will allow scientists to develop new diagnostic tests and therapeutic methods. Identification of where each gene is and what it does will also extend the ability to test fetuses, children, and prospective mates for genetic diseases. Prospective parents who carry problematic genes may choose not to marry or not to procreate. Another possibility (and fear) is that, as the technology gets cheaper and becomes more widely available, people may be able to test themselves (home pregnancy tests are already widely used) and then make a decision to try a risky home abortion.[84] Overall, human mating and procreation will come to be increasingly affected and controlled by these new nonhuman technologies.

Controlling Childbirth: Birth as Pathology. McDonaldization and increasing control is also manifest in the process of giving birth. One measure is the decline of midwifery, a very human and personal practice. In 1900, midwives attended about half of American births, but by 1986, they attended only 4%.[85] Midwifery enjoyed a slight renaissance, however, because of the dehumanization and rationalization of modern childbirth practices,[86] and 6.5% of babies in the United States were being delivered by midwives in the late 20th century.[87] By 2014, midwives were involved in 12% of all U.S. births.[88] (The United States is atypical. Worldwide, two thirds of all births involve midwives.[89]) When asked why they sought out midwives, women mention things such as the "callous and neglectful treatment by the hospital staff," "labor unnecessarily induced for the convenience of the doctor," and "unnecessary cesareans for the same reason."[90] The use of midwives has also declined due to an increase in the control of the birth process by professional medicine,[91] especially obstetricians who are most likely to rationalize and dehumanize the birth process. Dr. Michelle Harrison, who served as a resident in obstetrics and gynecology, is but one physician willing to admit that hospital birth can be a "dehumanized process."[92] The increasing control over childbirth is also demonstrated by the degree to which it has been bureaucratized. "Social childbirth," the traditional approach, once took place largely in the home, with female relatives and friends in attendance. Now, childbirth takes place almost totally in hospitals, "alone among strangers."[93] In 1900, less than 5% of U.S. births took place in hospitals; by 1940, hospital births totaled 55%, and by 1960, the process was all but complete, with nearly 100% of births occurring in hospitals.[94] In more recent years, hospital chains and birthing centers have emerged, and they are modeled after the paradigm for the rationalization process—the fast-food restaurant.

Over the years, hospitals and the medical profession have developed many standard, routinized (McDonaldized) procedures for handling and controlling childbirth. One of the best known, created by Dr. Joseph DeLee, was widely followed throughout the first half of the 20th century. DeLee viewed childbirth as a disease (a "pathologic process"), and his procedures were to be followed even for low-risk births.[95]

1. The patient was placed in the lithotomy position, "lying supine with legs in air, bent and wide apart, supported by stirrups."[96]

2. The mother-to-be was sedated from the first stage of labor on.

3. An episiotomy[97] was performed to enlarge the area through which the baby must pass.

4. Forceps[98] were used, but now less commonly (see below), to make the delivery more efficient.

Describing this procedure, one woman wrote, "Women are herded like sheep through an *obstetrical assembly-line,* are drugged and strapped on tables where their babies are forceps delivered."[99]

DeLee's standard practice includes not only control through nonhuman tech-nology (the procedure itself, forceps, drugs, and an assembly-line approach) but most of the other elements of McDonaldization—efficiency, predictability, and the irrationality of turning the human delivery room into an inhuman baby fac-tory. The calculability that it lacked was added later in the form of Emanuel Friedman's "Friedman Curve." While it is now largely obsolete, this is an interest-ing example of the McDonaldization of the labor process. The curve prescribed three rigid stages of labor. For example, the first stage was allocated exactly 8.6 hours, during which cervical dilation was to proceed from 2 to 4 centimeters.[100] The moment babies come into the world, they are greeted by a calculable scor-ing system, the Apgar test. Babies receive scores of 0 to 2 on each of five fac-tors (e.g., heart rate, color), with 10 being the healthiest total score. Most babies have scores between 7 and 9 a minute after birth and scores of 8 to 10 after five minutes. Babies with scores of 0 to 3 are considered to be in very serious trouble. Dr. Harrison has wondered why medical personnel don't ask about more subjective variables, such as the infant's color, curiosity, and mood.[101]

The use of various nonhuman technologies for delivering babies has ebbed and flowed. The use of forceps, invented in 1588, reached a peak in the United States in the 1950s, when as many as 50% of all births involved their use. For-ceps fell out of vogue, however, and by the 1980s, only about 15% of all births employed forceps, and their use continues to decline.[102] Many methods of drug-ging mothers-to-be have also been widely used. The electronic fetal monitor became popular in the 1970s, and as discussed previously, ultrasound is now a popular and commonly used technology.

Another worrisome technology associated with childbirth is the scalpel. Many doctors routinely perform episiotomies during delivery so that the opening of the vagina does not tear or stretch unduly. Often done to enhance the pleasure of future sex partners and to ease the passage of the infant, episiotomies are quite debilitating and painful for the woman. Dr. Harrison expresses consider-able doubt about episiotomies: "I want those obstetricians to stop cutting open women's vaginas. Childbirth is not a surgical procedure."[103]

The scalpel is also a key tool in cesarean sections. Birth, a perfectly human process, has come to be controlled by this technology (and those who wield it) in many cases.[104] The first modern "C-section" took place in 1882, but as late as 1970, only 5% of all births involved cesarean. Its use skyrocketed in the 1970s and 1980s, reaching 25% of all births in 1987 in what was described as a "national epidemic."[105] By the mid-1990s, the practice had declined slightly, to 21%.[106] The rate in the United States rose to about 32% by 2015.[107] First-time C-sections were at an all-time high of almost 17% in 2005, and the rate of vaginal births after a previous cesarean was down to 16.5%.[108] This latter occurred even though the American Congress of Obstetricians and Gynecologists has formally abandoned the time-honored idea, "once a cesarean, always a cesarean." That is, it no longer supports the view that, once a mother has a cesarean section, all succeeding births must be cesarean.

In addition, many people believe that cesareans are often performed unnecessarily. The first evidence for this belief is historical data: Why did we see a sudden need for so many more cesareans? Weren't cesareans just as necessary a few decades ago? The second clue regarding unnecessary cesareans is data indicating that private patients who can pay are more likely to get cesareans than those on Medicaid (which reimburses far less) and are twice as likely as indigent patients to get cesareans.[109] Are those with higher incomes really more likely to need cesareans than those with lower incomes?[110] One explanation for the dramatic increase in cesareans is that they fit in well with the idea of substituting nonhuman for human technology, but they also mesh with the other elements of the McDonaldization of society:

- Cesareans are more predictable than the normal birth process, which can occur a few weeks (or even months) early or late. It is frequently noted that cesareans generally seem to be performed before 5:30 p.m. so that physicians can be home for dinner. Similarly, well-heeled female consumers may choose a cesarean so that the unpredictabilities of natural childbirth do not interfere with careers or social demands.

- As a comparatively simple operation, the cesarean is more efficient than natural childbirth, which may involve many more unforeseen circumstances.

- Cesarean births are more calculable, normally involving no less than 20 minutes and no more than 45 minutes. The time required for a normal birth, especially a first birth, is far more variable.

- Irrationalities exist (see Chapter 7 for more on the irrationality of rationality), including the risks associated with any surgery—anesthesia, hemorrhage, and blood replacement. Compared with those who undergo a normal childbirth, women who have cesareans experience more physical problems and a longer period of recuperation, and the mortality rate can be as much as twice as high. There are also higher costs associated with cesareans. One study indicated that physicians' costs were 68% higher and hospital costs 92% higher for cesareans compared with natural childbirth.[111] Cesareans are dehumanizing because a natural human process is transformed, often unnecessarily, into a nonhuman or even inhuman process in which women endure a surgical procedure. At the minimum, many of those who have cesareans are denied unnecessarily the very human experience of vaginal birth. The wonders of childbirth are reduced to the routines of a minor surgical procedure.

Above all, it is increasingly clear that cesareans have become just another service to be consumed.

Controlling the Process of Dying: Designer Deaths. We have now become consumers of death and dying, and ways have been found to rationalize the dying process, giving us at least the illusion of control. Consider the increasing array of nonhuman technologies designed to keep people alive long after they would have expired had they lived at an earlier time in history. In fact, some beneficiaries of these technologies would not want to stay alive under those conditions (a clear irrationality). Unless the physicians are following an advance directive (a living will) that explicitly states "do not resuscitate" or "no heroic measures," people lose control over their own dying process. Family members, too, in the absence of such directives, must bow to the medical mandate to keep people alive as long as possible.

Computer systems may be used to assess a patient's chances of survival at any given point in the dying process—90%, 50%, 10%, and so on. The actions of medical personnel are likely to be influenced by such assessments.

Death has followed much the same path as birth; that is, the dying process has been moved out of the home and beyond the control of the dying and their families and into the hands of medical personnel and hospitals.[112] Physicians have gained a large measure of control over death, just as they won control over birth. Death, like birth, is increasingly likely to take place in the hospital. In 1900, only 20% of deaths took place in hospitals; about a third of U.S. deaths in 2010 occurred in hospitals, while in 2008, 20% occurred in nursing homes, and in 2011 44.6% occurred in hospices.[113] The growth of hospital chains and chains of hospices, using principles derived from the fast-food restaurant, signals death's bureaucratization, rationalization, and even McDonaldization.

The McDonaldization of the dying process, as well as of birth, has spawned a series of counterreactions—efforts by consumers to cope with the excesses of rationalization. Advance directives and living wills tell hospitals and medical personnel what they may or may not do during the dying process. Suicide societies and books such as Derek Humphry's *Final Exit*[114] give people instructions on how to kill themselves. There is the growing interest in and acceptance of euthanasia,[115] most notably the work of "Dr. Death," Jack Kevorkian, whose goal was to return to people control over their own deaths. Finally, many people are choosing to die at home, and some are even opting to be buried there as well.[116] However, these counterreactions themselves have elements of McDonaldization. For example, Dr. Kevorkian (who died in 2011) used a nonhuman technology, a "machine," to help people kill themselves. More generally, and strikingly, he was an advocate of a "rational policy" for the planning of death.[117] The rationalization of death is thus found even in the efforts to counter it.[118]

Overall, the future will bring with it an increasing number of nonhuman technologies with ever-greater ability to control consumers and the consumption process. However, more and more people will lose the opportunity, and perhaps the ability, to think and to choose for themselves.

5

EFFICIENCY AND CALCULABILITY

McJobs and Other McDonaldized Occupations 1

While Chapters 3 and 4 dealt mainly with the consumers in McDonaldized settings, the focus shifts in this chapter and the next to those who work (or produce) in those settings. Workers will be dealt with using the same principles of McDonaldization—efficiency, calculability, predictability, and control—that were used to deal with consumers. It is important to remember that for the sake of convenience and clarity work (and production) and consumption are being clearly distinguished in this discussion. However, in many cases the McDonaldization of one is closely linked to the McDonaldization of the other. McDonaldized work settings tend to produce McDonaldized consumers, while those settings as well as the behavior and demands of McDonaldized consumers tend to create, or enhance, the McDonaldization of work and work settings.

McJOBS AND THE DIMENSIONS OF McDONALDIZATION

Virtually all occupations have, at least to some degree, been McDonaldized. The term "McJobs" has been reserved for those occupations most affected by the process of McDonaldization.[1] However, because of McDonaldization, especially when it is associated with technological changes such as automation and robotization, many McJobs have disappeared, or soon will be gone. The other major factor in the demise of McJobs is the increase in prosumption. As we've seen on several occasions, prosumers are now doing all kinds of work, at no cost, traditionally performed by those in McJobs. Companies would obviously prefer to have the work done at no expense to them than to pay those associated with McJobs. This is the case even though those employed in McJobs earn "McWages." For example, those who handled the position of gas station attendant are all but gone with prosumers doing the work of pumping their own gas. These prosumers often also use credit cards to pay at the pump thereby reducing the need for workers to swipe their cards. Similarly, cashier jobs in banks have been lost because prosumers are using ATMs, and self-service lanes at supermarkets are having a similar impact. The irony is that as a result of this change, many of us are doing elements of McJobs, at least part of the time. Most of us seem unaware of this or are unconcerned about it. Further, many, who would eschew McJobs, seem to enjoy doing this low-skilled work, at least for a few minutes a day. The concern here, however, is not with the consumers, but rather with the McJobs themselves.

While the existence of many McJobs is threatened in a variety of ways, some of them are likely to change and also to expand as technological change reduces the skill needed in various jobs thereby pushing them in the direction of becoming McJobs. This overlaps with the decline of the middle class as well as a decline of the higher skilled, higher paying jobs these middle-class workers once held. As the middle class and its traditional jobs shrink, many are thrust into the working class or, worse yet, pushed out of the labor force entirely. There is no shortage of stories about once well-paid, middle-class workers finding that the only work they could get afterwards were in McJobs, such as counter people at McDonald's or as baggers at supermarkets.

The term "McJobs" clearly applies, among others, to the occupations associated with the fast-food industry, but it can extend to many jobs at the low end of the occupational hierarchy that are poorly paid, require little skill and training, and offer little in the way of upward mobility. The term was first employed by the sociologist Amitai Etzioni in a *Washington Post* op-ed essay titled "McJobs Are Bad for Kids."[2] McJobs have since been dealt with by a number of popular[3] and academic authors[4] in a number of locations in United States and out of it (e.g., India and China).[5] The general tendency in this work is to be critical of McJobs as being bad not only for young people, but for virtually anyone who holds such jobs. We will deal with some of the problems associated with McJobs in Chapter 7, while addressing the irrationality of rationality.

While these problems abound, it is important to note that McJobs can also be defended for a variety of reasons.[6] For example, McJobs provide employment for millions of people who would otherwise be unemployed and who would therefore greatly inflate the unemployment rate; they are an especially important source of employment for teenagers, minorities, and even retirees (many of whom are baggers in supermarkets); these jobs often train people in the basic skills (e.g., reporting for work on time, following routines and orders) needed for other kinds of jobs; they can be a good first step to many different kinds of future careers; and so on. While these and other arguments, both pro and con, have merit, the focus here is on gaining a better understanding of the process—McDonaldization—by examining the impact it has on work and workers. We can do so by returning once again to the basic dimensions of McDonaldization and examining the impact of each of them on not only McJobs, but many other occupations.

We will discuss a wide range of McDonaldized occupations in this chapter and also Chapter 6, including not only those who work in fast-food restaurants, but also those who deliver pizzas, supermarket employees, manual workers, farmers, professors, scholars, schoolteachers, physicians, athletes, horse trainers, politicians, insurance salespeople, Disney "cast members," customer service representatives, Amazon warehouse workers, and pilots.

While all of these occupations are discussed in this chapter as workers, or producers, it is the case that they, like consumers, can also be seen as prosumers. We discussed prosumers as working consumers in Chapter 3, but we can also think of prosumers as "consuming workers." All workers consume all sorts of things as they work such as the raw materials they use and their own labor, time, and capacities.

EFFICIENCY: IT'S A FETISH

The Fast-Food Industry: "Burger Dressers" and "Factory Stores"

Today, all fast-food restaurants prepare their menu items on a kind of assembly-line involving a number of workers performing specialized operations (e.g., the burger "dresser"). The ultimate application of the assembly-line to the fast-food process is, as pointed out in Chapter 2, Burger King's conveyor belt: "Above and below the conveyor were two flames. Burgers were placed in this mesh, and they moved along the belt at a pre-set speed, were cooked on both sides simultaneously by the two flames, and then spilled out the other end into holding trays."[7] This system transforms those who work on them into assembly-line workers who are not dissimilar to those who work on automobile assembly-lines.

Similar techniques are employed throughout the fast-food industry. Take the example of Domino's and some of its employees:

> Lonnie Lane starts slapping and saucing: kneading and tossing the dough and then spooning the proper measure of sauce on it. He slides the tray down . . . and Victor Luna starts reaching for the toppings. A dozen bins are arrayed in front of him: cheese, pepperoni, green pepper. . . . Luna sprinkles stuff over the tray by the handful. . . . He eases the tray onto a conveyor belt that takes it through a 12-foot oven in six minutes. . . . The store manager is dispatching waiting drivers and waiting drivers are folding pizza boxes. . . . The crew chief and quality controller . . . slices it with a pizza wheel and slides it into a box that already bears a computer label with the customer's address.[8]

As another example, many Krispy Kreme shops are "factory stores" where the doughnuts are produced using a highly efficient conveyor belt system. The doughnuts produced in this way are sold in the factory stores and shipped to Krispy Kreme outlets without such factories, as well as to supermarkets and other locales where the doughnuts are sold.

Academia: Machine-Grading and Other Efficiencies

As discussed in Chapter 3, McUniversity is not only efficient for students, but also for the "producers" in universities, especially professors. Creating and assessing simple computerized exams and assignments that follow a rubric is easy, requiring little thought and effort on the part of teachers. More generally, in the university, the work lives of many instructors and professors (the "workers" in universities while students are the "customers") have been made more like McJobs. They have been made more efficient by, for example, the machine-graded, multiple-choice examination. In a much earlier era, students were examined individually in conference with their professors. Later, the essay examination became popular. Grading a set of essays was more efficient than giving individual oral examinations, but it was still relatively time-consuming. Enter the multiple-choice examination, the grading of which was a snap. In fact, graduate assistants could grade it, making evaluation of students even more efficient for the professor. Computer-graded examinations maximize efficiency for both professors and graduate assistants.

The computerized Blackboard system (and other learning management systems like it) has added still greater efficiencies. For example, it eliminates the need for professors to reproduce and distribute materials to class. Blackboard grades exams, adds them to the grade book, and even calculates a final grade. It also makes it possible for students to take exams online rather than in class. Other innovations in academia have further streamlined the educational process. Instead of professors composing multiple-choice questions, publishers provide digital, online sets of questions. Another advance is computer-based programs to grade essay examinations (and even term papers).[9] Professors can now choose to have very little to do with the entire examination process, from composing questions to grading, freeing up time for activities that many professors, but few students, value more highly, such as writing and research.

Publishers have provided other services to streamline teaching for those professors who adopt best-selling textbooks, including lecture outlines, powerpoints, text-related websites, computer simulations, discussion questions, DVDs, movies, and ideas for guest lecturers and student projects. Professors who choose to use all these devices need to do little or nothing on their own for their classes.

Students increasingly see themselves as customers and "going to college as a business transaction." Said one professor, "They view professors in a way similar to the person behind the counter getting their coffee." This professor is clearly implying that a college professorship is increasingly being seen as a McJob. As a result, students are more and more likely to treat their professors as just another kind of worker, as a "bunch of overeducated customer service representatives."[10] This means, among other things, that students are increasingly casual in their interaction and communication with their professors. They often don't address them as "professor." They may even call their professors by their first names. In another manifestation of this increasing disrespect, students are prone to send their professors casual, poorly written e-mails that the students have not had the courtesy too proofread.

Medicine: On the Medical Assembly-Line

In medicine, one example of increasing efficiency for physicians (and patients) is the recently deceased Dr. Denton Cooley, whose fetish was efficiency. Cooley's way of operating has had an effect on many other surgeons. He gained worldwide fame for streamlining delicate open-heart surgery in a "heart surgery factory" that operated "with the precision of an assembly-line."[11]

Even more striking is the following description of Russia's S.N. Fyodorov Eye Microsurgery Complex, which promises "efficient therapy of most serious ophthalmic diseases":[12]

> In many ways the scene resembles any modern factory. A conveyor glides silently past five work stations, periodically stopping, then starting again. Each station is staffed by an attendant in a sterile mask and smock. The workers have just three minutes to complete their tasks before the conveyor moves on; they turn out 20 finished pieces in an hour.

> Nearly everything else about the assembly-line, however, is highly unusual: the workers are eye surgeons, and the conveyor carries human beings on stretchers. This is where the production methods of Henry Ford are applied to the practice of medicine . . . a "medical factory for the production of people with good eyesight."[13]

Such assembly-lines are not yet the norm in medicine, but one can imagine that they will grow increasingly common in the coming years.

While not quite done on an assembly-line, I had laser eye surgery performed on the basis of a system that is very close to one. Ten patients requiring the same operation were instructed to report at a given hour, ushered into a room, and told to sit in a specific place in a line of chairs. On several occasions, assistants went down the line putting various drops into the eye that was to be operated on. When the surgeon arrived, each patient was hustled—in order of his or her position in the line of chairs—into another room, was told by another assistant to place his or her chin on a chin rest on the laser machine, and soon heard a series of zapping sounds. When the sound stopped and the surgery was completed, the patients were dismissed and ushered back to their original seats. When all 10 patients had their surgery, each in turn was brought back to the room where the surgery was performed, although by this time the surgeon was long gone. Other assistants checked the eye to be sure the surgery was successful, and if it was, the patient was told he or she could leave.

Also increasing is the use of robots to perform advanced forms of surgery. Perhaps the best known is the da Vinci robotic system that is revolutionizing various forms of surgery (e.g., for prostate cancer). In the old days, a prostatectomy was a major operation involving a large incision and substantial blood loss. In contrast, a robotic prostatectomy is minimally invasive. That not only makes the operation more efficient for the medical team, but also makes the process more efficient from a patient's point of view. Because only small incisions are made, blood loss is minimized, hospital stays are reduced to perhaps a day or two, and postoperative recovery time is relatively brief.[14] As for the surgeons, they can do the operation from the comfort of a computer console placed some distance from the patient and the rest of the operating team.

Work Efficiency on Digital Sites: It's Like Working in an Oven

As pointed out earlier, most of the work done on digital sites is performed by con(pro)sumers. In a way, this leads to the extreme of efficiency of work because no actual paid human labor is performed when consumers log onto a site. Of course, much work is performed behind the scenes in, for example, maintaining those sites and much of that work could qualify as McWork. However, a great deal more involves the actual creation of those sites by highly skilled and well-paid computer programmers. They are likely to be more valued for their skill than for their efficiency.

In January 2017, Amazon announced that it would be adding 100,000 jobs over the ensuing year and a half. These jobs were to include skilled software developers and engineers, but it is likely that most of them will be low-paid, hourly, warehouse workers. This expansion reflects the huge increase in digital consumption at Amazon and elsewhere on the Internet and the corresponding decline of brick-and-mortar sites such as department stores and shopping malls. The loss of McJobs in the latter settings is not likely to be made up by increases at sites such as Amazon's. According to one estimate, there are 1.2 million fewer jobs in retailing mainly because of the growth of online shopping. Further worsening the outlook for work at Amazon is the likelihood that automation and robots will even begin to replace workers in its warehouses. Other jobs are also being lost. For example, the truck drivers who pick up and deliver Amazon's goods are likely to suffer as self-driving trucks begin to take the road.

Then there is the issue of the nature of work in warehouses such as Amazon's. New employees are likely to be temporary workers with little chance of ever getting permanent jobs. While their hourly wage is about $5 more an hour than fast-food workers, it is unlikely that most warehouse workers can actually live on such a wage. Working conditions are far from ideal. Only one worker in an Amazon warehouse in Pennsylvania was willing to describe it as a good place to work. Among the complaints are the following: a work pace that employees could not sustain, oppressive heat in the warehouse causing some workers to require medical attention or hospitalization (one worker said that it resembled "working in a convection oven while blow-drying your hair"),[15] frequent reprimands for not working fast enough, being fired for not keeping up with company expectations, and being humiliated by being paraded out of the warehouse after being fired. New employees are hired by a temp agency and they are legally employed by the agency. As a result, they do not get the benefits accorded Amazon's full-time workers such as workers' compensation and unemployment insurance. Because of all of this, turnover is high at the warehouse with new employees lasting only a few months.[16]

CALCULABILITY: ZEAL FOR SPEED

Reducing Production and Service to Numbers

As it concerns the McDonaldization of work, calculability primarily involves reducing production and service to numbers.

The Fast-Food Industry: Hustle, and a
Precooked Hamburger Measures Exactly 3.875 Inches

There is great emphasis on the speed with which workers can serve a meal in the fast-food restaurant. In fact, Ray Kroc's first outlet was named McDonald's Speedee Service Drive-In. At one time, McDonald's sought to serve a hamburger, shake, and French fries in 50 seconds. The restaurant made a great breakthrough in 1959 when it served a record 36 hamburgers in 110 seconds.

Many other fast-food restaurants have adopted McDonald's zeal for speed. Burger King, for example, seeks to have its employees serve a customer within 3 minutes of entering the restaurant.[17] The drive-through window drastically reduces the time required to process a customer through a fast-food restaurant. Speed is obviously a quantifiable factor of monumental importance in a fast-food restaurant.

Speed is even more important to the pizza-delivery business. At Domino's, the mantra is "Hustle! Do It! Hustle! Do It! Hustle! Do It!" and the "Domino's goal is eight minutes out the door."[18] Employees are now expected to make the pizza itself in "less than a minute." A decades-old technological advance is the "spoodle . . . a ladle with a flat bottom that allows workers to spread the sauce evenly and quickly."[19] Not only does the number of pizzas sold depend on how quickly they can be made and delivered by the drivers, but it also depends on how quickly they need to be delivered in order to arrive hot. Special insulated containers now help keep the pizzas hot longer. This emphasis on rapid delivery has caused several scandals, however; pressure to make fast deliveries has led young delivery people to become involved in serious and sometimes fatal automobile accidents.

Pizza making and pizza delivery have speeded up greatly in recent years as Domino's has become more of a high-tech company relying on a digital ordering system—no more time wasted on phone orders and the possibility of errors in getting orders right. Now most orders come in by computer and are filled much more quickly than they are by phone.

Still another aspect of the emphasis on quantity lies in the precision with which employees measure every element in the production of fast food. At frozen yogurt franchises, containers are often weighed by workers to be sure they include the correct quantity of frozen yogurt, whereas in old-fashioned ice cream parlors, the attendants simply filled a container to the brim. McDonald's itself takes great care in being sure that each raw McDonald's hamburger weighs exactly 1.6 ounces—10 hamburgers to a pound of meat. The precooked hamburger measures precisely 3.875 inches in diameter and the bun exactly 3.5 inches. McDonald's invented the "fatilyzer" to ensure that its regular hamburger meat had no more than 19% fat.[20] Greater fat content would lead to greater shrinkage during cooking and prevent the hamburger from appearing too large for the bun. Grilling eight hamburger patties at a time takes 38 seconds.[21] Using the French fry scoop helps workers make sure that each package has about the same number of fries. The automatic drink dispensers ensure that each cup gets the correct amount of soft drink, with nothing lost to spillage. The average cash register transaction takes 12 seconds.[22]

Arby's has reduced the cooking and serving of roast beef to a series of exact measurements to be watched over and taken by its employees.[23] All roasts weigh 10 pounds at the start. They are roasted at 200°F for 3.5 hours until the internal temperature is 135°F. They are then allowed to cook in their own heat for 20 minutes more until the internal temperature is 140°F. By following these steps and making these measurements, Arby's doesn't need skilled chefs; virtually any employee who can read and count can cook an Arby's roast beef. When the roasts are done, each weighs between 9 pounds, 4 ounces, and 9 pounds, 7 ounces. Every roast beef sandwich contains 3 ounces of meat, allowing Arby's to get 47 sandwiches (give or take one) from each roast.

Burger King has also quantified quality control. Employees must serve hamburgers within 10 minutes of being cooked. French fries may stand under the heat lamp for no more than 7 minutes. A manager is allowed to throw away 0.3% of all food.[24] The performance of fast-food restaurants is also assessed quantitatively, not qualitatively. At McDonald's, for example, central management judges the performance of each restaurant "by 'the numbers': by sales per crew person, profits, turnover, and QSC [Quality, Service, Cleanliness] ratings."[25] While the fast-food restaurant has greatly increased the emphasis on calculability, it had many precursors, including the original *Boston Cooking-School Cook Book,* published in 1896, in which Fannie Farmer emphasized precise measurement and, in the process, helped rationalize home cooking (a kind of work): "She . . . changed American kitchen terminology from 'a pinch' and 'a dash' and 'a heaping spoonful' . . . to her own precise, standardized, scientific terms, presenting a model of cooking that was easy, reliable, and could be followed even by inexperienced cooks."[26]

The Workplace: A Penny the Size of a Cart-Wheel

It was F. W. Taylor's intention that scientific management transform everything work related into quantifiable dimensions (see Chapter 2). Instead of relying on the worker's "rule of thumb," scientific management sought to develop precise measurements of how much work was to be accomplished by each and every motion of the worker. Everything that could be reduced to numbers was then analyzed using mathematical formulas.

Calculability was clearly an aim when Taylor sought to increase the amount of pig iron a worker could load in a day: "We found that this gang were loading on the average about 12½ long tons per man per day. We were surprised to find, after studying the matter, that a first-class pig iron handler ought to handle between 47 and 48 long tons per day, instead of 12½ tons."[27] To try to nearly quadruple the workload, Taylor studied the way the most productive workers, the "first-class men," operated. He divided their work into its basic elements and timed each step with a stopwatch, down to hundredths of a minute.

On the basis of this careful study, Taylor and his associates developed the one best way to carry pig iron. They then found a worker they could motivate to work this way—Schmidt, who was able and ambitious and to whom, as one coworker said, a penny looked to be "about the size of a cart-wheel." Schmidt, furthermore, indicated that he wanted to be a "high-priced man." Taylor used a precise economic incentive: $1.85 per day, rather than the usual $1.15, if Schmidt agreed to work exactly the way Taylor told him to. After careful training and supervision, Schmidt successfully worked at the faster pace (and earned the higher pay); Taylor then selected and trained other employees to work the same way.

Schmidt and his successors, of course, were being asked to do about 3.6 times the normal amount of work for an approximately 60-percent increase in pay. For Taylor, "the pig iron handler with his 60-percent increase in wages is not an object for pity but rather a subject for congratulations."[28]

Academia: Ratings and Ranking

The emphasis on quantifiable factors is common even among college professors. For example, at more and more colleges and universities, students evaluate each course by answering questions with ratings ranging from, for example, one to five. At the end of the semester, the professor receives what is in effect a report card with an overall teaching rating. Students have little or no room to offer qualitative evaluations of their teachers on such questionnaires. Although student ratings are desirable in a number of ways, they also have some unfortunate consequences. For example, they tend to favor professors who are performers, who have a sense of humor, or who do not demand too much from students. Serious professors who place great demands on students are not likely to do well in such rating systems, even though they may offer higher-quality teaching (e.g., more profound ideas) than does the performer. Thus, the emphasis on quantifiable evaluations of professors can distort, even demean, the educational process.

Quantitative factors are important not only in teaching but also in research and publication. The "publish or perish" pressure on academicians in many colleges and universities leads to greater attention to the quantity of their publications than to the quality. In hiring and promotion decisions, a résumé with a long list of articles and books is generally preferred to one with a shorter list. Thus, an award-winning teacher was turned down for tenure at Rutgers University because, in the words of his department's tenure committee, his stack of publications was "not as thick as the usual packet for tenure."[29] The unfortunate consequence of this bias is publication of less than high-quality works, the rush to publication before a work is fully developed, or publication of the same idea with only minor variations in several different journals.

Another quantitative factor in academia is the ranking of the outlet in which a work is published. In the hard sciences, articles in professional journals receive high marks; books are less valued. In the humanities, books are of much higher value and sometimes more prestigious than journal articles. Being published by some publishers (for example, university presses) yields more prestige than being published by others (for example, commercial presses).

In sociology, a formal ratings system assigns points for publication in professional journals. A publication in the prestigious *American Sociological Review* receives 10 points, the maximum in this system, but the far less prestigious (and, in order not to hurt anyone's feelings, fictional) *Antarctic Journal of Sociology*, with a readership primarily composed of penguins, receives only 1 point. By this system, the professor whose journal publications yield 340 points is supposed to be twice as "good" as one who earns only 170 points.

However, as is usually the case, such an emphasis on quantity tends not to relate to quality:

- It is highly unlikely that the quality of a professor's life's work can be reduced to a single number. In fact, it seems impossible to quantify the quality of an idea, theory, or research finding.

- This rating system deals only indirectly with quality. That is, the rating is based on the quality of the journal in which an article was published, not the quality of the article itself. No effort is made to evaluate the quality of the article or its contribution to the field. Poor articles can appear in the highest-ranking journals, excellent ones in low-ranking journals.

- The academician who writes only a few high-quality papers might not do well in this rating system. In contrast, someone who produces a lot of mediocre work could well receive a far higher score. This kind of system leads ambitious sociologists (and those in most other academic fields) to conclude that they cannot afford to spend years honing a single work because it will not pay off in their point score.

Any system that places so much emphasis on quantity of publications will lead to the production of a great deal of mediocre work.

The sciences have come up with another quantifiable measure in an effort to evaluate the quality of work: the number of times a person's work is cited in the work of other scholars. In many fields, Google Scholar is used, and it relies heavily on such citation counts.[30] In fact, Google now has a "citations gadget" to allow one to get an instantaneous citation count for virtually any scholar.[31] The assumption is that high-quality, important, and influential work is likely to be used and cited by other scholars. However, once again, the problem of evaluating quality arises. Can the influence of a person's academic work be reduced to a single number? It is possible that a few central uses of one scholar's ideas will influence the field more than many trivial citations of another scholar's work. Furthermore, the mere fact that a work is cited tells us nothing about what other scholars thought about the work. A worthless piece of work attacked by many people and thereby cited in their work would lead to many citations for its creator. Conversely, scholars may ignore a truly important piece of work that is ahead of its time, leading to a minuscule number of citations for the author. Google has tried to deal with this problem by, not surprisingly, coming up with another number—its h-index, which measures both number of publications and citations per publication.[32]

When Donald Kennedy was president of Stanford University, he announced a change in that university's policies for hiring, promoting, or granting tenure to faculty members. Disturbed by a report indicating "that nearly half of faculty members believe that their scholarly writings are merely counted—and not evaluated—when personnel decisions are made," Kennedy said, "I hope we can agree that the quantitative use of research output as a criterion for appointment or promotion is a bankrupt idea. . . . The overproduction of routine scholarship is one of the most egregious aspects of contemporary academic life: It tends to conceal really important work by sheer volume."[33] To deal with this problem, Kennedy proposed to limit the extent to which the number of publications would be used in making personnel decisions. He hoped that the proposed limits would "reverse the appalling belief that counting and weighing are the important means of evaluating faculty research."[34] Despite protestations like this one, there is little evidence that there has been much progress in reducing the emphasis on quantity rather than quality in the academic world.

In fact, in recent years, there has been a massive increase in the emphasis on quantitative factors in the British academic world. "League tables of universities are now produced grading research and teaching. . . . These make the system subject to quantitative, rather than the previous qualitative evaluations and therefore clearly calculable."[35]

Health Care: Patients as Dollar Signs

In profit-making medical organizations (the largest is Hospital Corporation of America [HCA]; the Department of Veterans Affairs [VA] is larger, but it is nonprofit), physicians, along with all other employees, feel pressured to contribute to the corporation's profitability. Limiting the time with each patient and maximizing the number of patients seen in a day allow the corporation to reduce costs and increase profits. This emphasis on quantity can easily endanger the quality of medical care. Profits can also be increased by pushing doctors to turn down patients who probably can't pay the bills and to see only patients who have the kinds of diseases whose treatment is likely to yield large profits.

Following the lead of profit-making medical organizations, all medical bureaucracies are now pushing physicians in the direction of greater calculability. Even nonprofit medical organizations—for example, nonprofit hospitals and local clinics—increasingly employ professional managers and have sophisticated accounting systems.

The federal government, through Medicare, has created the prospective payment and diagnostic-related group (DRG)[36] programs, in which a set amount is reimbursed to hospitals for a given medical diagnosis, no matter how long the patient is hospitalized. Prior to 1983, the government paid whatever "reasonable" amount it was billed. Outside agencies have also grown increasingly concerned about spiraling medical costs and have sought to deal with the problem by limiting what they will pay for and how much they will pay for it. A third-party payer (an insurer) might thus refuse to pay for certain procedures or for hospitalization or perhaps pay only a given amount.

Doctors, who have traditionally placed quality of patient care above all else (at least ideally), often complain about the new emphasis on calculability. At least one physicians' union engaged in a strike centered on such issues as required number of visits, number of patients seen, and an incentive system tying physician salaries to productivity. As one physician union leader put it, however romantically, doctors are "the only ones who think of patients as individuals . . . not as dollar signs."[37]

Sports: Nadia Comaneci Scored Exactly 79.275 Points

The quality of various sports has been altered by, perhaps even sacrificed to, calculability. For instance, the nature of sporting events has been changed by the needs of television.[38] Because teams in many sports earn a large part of their revenue from television contracts, they will sacrifice the interests of paid spectators, even compromise the games themselves, to increase their television income.

A good example is the so-called TV timeout. In the old days, commercials occurred during natural breaks in a game—for example, during a timeout called by one of the teams, at halftime, or between innings. But these breaks were too intermittent and infrequent to bring in the increasingly large fees advertisers were willing to pay. Now regular TV timeouts are scheduled in sports such as football and basketball. In this way, the owners of sports franchises may be maximizing their incomes from advertising, but the momentum of the team may be lost because of an inopportune TV timeout. Players may cool off or lose their momentum. These timeouts not only alter the nature of some sports but may even affect the outcome of games. Also, these timeouts interrupt the flow of the game for the fans who watch in person (and pay high ticket prices for the privilege). The fans at home can at least watch the commercials (as well as run to the kitchen to grab a snack, or take a bathroom break); the spectators at the games have little to watch, except perhaps others in the crowd (as well as the jumbotron) until the commercial ends and the game resumes. But the owners consider such negative effects on the quality of the game insignificant compared with the economic gain from increased advertising.

Clearly, though, sports continue to place a premium on the quality of both individual *and* team performance. For instance, in the NBA, the offensive skills of the superstars of the 2017 Golden State Warriors—Stephen Curry and Kevin Durant—are complemented by the selfless teamwork of the team as a whole. The team has "turned sharing-is-caring into a high art."[39] At the same time, quantitative factors as they relate to individual performance continue to be enormously important in sports. In many cases, quality is directly related to quantity: the better the performance, the higher the score, and the greater the number of victories. Over the years, however, the emphasis on the quantifiable attributes of sports has increased:

> Modern sports are characterized by the almost inevitable tendency to transform every athletic feat into one that can be quantified and measured. The accumulation of statistics on every conceivable aspect of the game is a hallmark of football, baseball, hockey, and of track and field too, where the accuracy of quantification has, thanks to an increasingly precise technology, reached a degree that makes the stopwatch seem positively primitive.[40]

Even a highly aesthetic sport such as gymnastics has been quantified: "How can one rationalize and quantify a competition in gymnastics, in aesthetics? . . . Set up an interval scale and a panel of judges and then take the arithmetic mean of the subjective evaluations. . . . Nadia Comaneci [an Olympic champion in gymnastics] scored exactly 79.275 points . . . neither more nor less."[41]

The growing emphasis on quantity can sometimes adversely affect the quality of play in a sport. For example, the professional basketball star (a highly paid worker), motivated by a need to stand out individually and score as many points as possible, may negatively affect the play of individual teammates and the team's overall performance. The quality of play is even more compromised by owners' attempts to maximize points scored. Basketball, for example, was once a rather leisurely game in which a team could take as long as necessary to bring the ball down the court and get a player into position to take a good shot. Basketball fans enjoyed the strategies and maneuvers employed by the players. Toward the end of the game, a team holding a slim lead could attempt to "freeze" the ball—that is, not risk missing a shot and thereby giving their opponents a chance to take possession of the ball.

Several decades ago, however, the leadership of collegiate and professional basketball decided that fans raised in the McDonald's era wanted to see faster games and many more points scored. In other words, fans wanted from basketball what they got from their fast-food restaurant: great speed and large quantities. Hence, in college games, offensive teams were limited to 35 seconds in which to attempt a shot; in professional games, 24-second time clocks were established. Although the "run-and-shoot" style of play generated by the time clocks has created faster-paced, higher-scoring games, it may have adversely affected the quality of play. No longer is there much time for the maneuvers and strategies that made the game so interesting to "purists." But a run-and-shoot style of basketball fits in well with the McDonaldized "eat-and-move" world of dinners purchased at drive-through windows and consumed on the run. In 2016 the average score for NBA teams exceeded 100 points a game; the first time that had happened since the mid-1990s.[42] Some teams have flirted with an offense oriented to shooting the ball in 7 seconds or less.

Similarly, baseball owners decided long ago that fans prefer to see high-scoring games with lots of hits, home runs, and runs scored rather than the kind of game favored by "purists": pitchers' duels in which the final score might be 1–0. They took a number of steps to increase the number of runs scored. Livelier baseballs travel farther than old-fashioned "dead balls." In some baseball parks, outfield fences have been brought closer to home plate to increase the number of home runs (the new Yankee Stadium, opened in 2009, is notable in this regard). In 2017 a new single-season major league baseball record was set for the total number of home runs hit.[43]

The designated hitter, found in the American League but not in the more traditional National League, is the most important effort to increase hits and runs. Instead of the often weak-hitting pitcher taking his turn at bat, a player whose main (and sometimes only) skill is batting replaces him. Designated hitters get more hits, hit more home runs, and help produce more runs than pitchers who are allowed to bat.

Although use of the designated hitter in American League baseball has undoubtedly increased the number of runs scored, it has also affected, perhaps adversely, the quality of the game (which is why the National League has steadfastly refused to adopt the designated hitter). For example, when pitchers bat in certain situations, they often employ a sacrifice bunt, a very artful practice intended to advance a runner already on base. But a designated hitter rarely sacrifices an at-bat by bunting. In addition, pinch hitters play less of a role when designated hitters replace weak-hitting pitchers.[44] Finally, if there is less need to pinch hit for them, starting pitchers can remain in games longer, which reduces the need for relief pitchers.[45] In these and other ways, baseball is a different game when a designated hitter is employed. In other words, the quality of the game has changed, some would say for the worse, because of the emphasis on quantity.

A recent innovation is the installation in major league baseball parks of high-tech hardware, including Trackman radar, to measure precisely aspects of the game that, in the past, were dealt with in approximations or aphorisms such as home runs that "went a country mile," or were "tape-measure blasts."[46] As a result we know that current New York Yankee phenom, Aaron Judge, has hit a ball that traveled 470 feet (and would have gone farther had not a fan touched it), left his bat at 118.6 miles per hour, had a launch angle of 28.4 degrees, and arrived at the fan's hands at 84.7 miles per hour. More generally, we are in an era when "every swing, every step, every long ball is quantified, recorded and ranked." While this is all very rational, it is "devoid of all romance, exaggeration and mythology."[47] In other words, baseball has been further rationalized and, as a result, grows even more disenchanted.

The term *extreme* has been associated with all sorts of things (food [e.g., 7-Eleven's "X-Treme Gulp," Extreme Pita's Extreme Team pitas], candy, breath mints), although most typically with an array of sports activities. These include *extreme* snowboarding, skateboarding, BMX riding, and even bowling.[48] The use of this term implies that these sports offer something "more" than their traditional versions. Usually, the "more" translates into that which is faster, riskier, more innovative, more creative, and more outrageous. Most generally, extreme sports are associated with that which is more nonconformist, more daredevilish, and, in a word, "cooler" than traditional sports.

Politics: There Were No Sound Bites in the Lincoln-Douglas Debate

The political sector offers a number of revealing examples of the emphasis on calculability—for example, the increasing importance of polls in political campaigns.[49] Candidates and incumbents are obsessed by their ratings in political polls. This has been particularly true of Donald Trump both as a candidate and as president. Politicians often adjust their positions on issues or the actions they take on the basis of what pollsters say will increase (or at least not lower) their rankings. How a specific political position affects ratings can become more important than whether the politician genuinely believes in that position.

Television has affected politics in various ways. It has led to shorter conventions, for one thing, as well as shorter political speeches. In the famous Lincoln-Douglas debates of 1858, the candidates "spoke for ninety minutes each on a single topic: the future of slavery in the territories."[50] Prior to television, political speeches on radio at first often lasted an hour; by the 1940s, the norm had dropped to 30 minutes. In the early years of television, speeches also lasted about half an hour, but because political campaign speeches became more tailored to television coverage and less to the immediate audience, speeches have grown shorter, less than 20 minutes on the average. By the 1970s, speeches had been largely replaced by the 60-second (or less) advertisement. In today's televised presidential debates, candidates have a minute or two to offer their position on a given issue.

News reports of political speeches have contracted to fit the visual demands of television as well. By the 1984 presidential campaign, only about 15 seconds of a speech would likely find its way onto a national news program. Four years later, speaking time on such reports shrank to only 9 seconds.[51] As a result, political speechwriters concentrate on creating 5- or 10-second "sound bites" that are likely to be picked up by the national networks. This emphasis on length has clearly reduced the quality of public political speeches and, therefore, the quality of public discourse on important political issues. However, YouTube countered this trend when Barack Obama won the presidency in 2008 and 2012 partly because of Obama's savvy use of such Web 2.0 technologies. YouTube allowed him to stream more content in much more depth on the Web, with millions of people viewing online his famous speech on race.[52]

Obama's presidency now looks like an aberration in light of Donald Trump's extensive use, both as a candidate and as president, of Twitter and tweets limited to 140 words in order to get his messages across. (As of mid-2017 Trump had over 1.5 million followers on Twitter.) Not only are President Trump's tweets limited in terms of words, they are necessarily short on substance. This is a clear manifestation of the emphasis in a McDonaldized world on quantity (in this case short) rather than quality. The brevity of tweets makes it impossible for Trump to develop a cogent argument. Of course, this is not only true of Trump's tweets; it is true of *all* tweets.

The Digital: The Extreme of Calculability

It is in the digital world where calculability reaches an extreme and that extreme will be exceeded with new technological advances. The largely automatic collection of big data and their analysis by algorithms transforms virtually everything into data—numbers, ratings, rankings, and the like. Almost all of this is done electronically. It would be virtually impossible for humans to do the calculations on such large data sets. Thus, there are relatively few jobs associated with big data analysis and those that exist are likely to be mainly high-tech, professional jobs (e.g., computer systems analysts); they are not going to be McJobs. In the long term those who lose jobs as a result of these changes are either going to be more or less permanently unemployed or they are likely to drift into low-paying McJobs in the service industry. This will represent a huge and growing problem in the coming years as more and more people find themselves unemployed or underemployed.

PREDICTABILITY AND CONTROL

McJobs and Other McDonaldized Occupations 2

T his chapter picks up where the last one left off with a discussion of the ways in which the two other dimensions of McDonaldization—predictability and control—relate to workers.

PREDICTABILITY: SCRIPTING AND CONTROLLING EMPLOYEES

The Fast-Food Industry: "Howdy, Pardner" and "Happy Trails"

Because interaction between customer and counter person in the fast-food restaurant is limited in length and scope, it can be largely routinized. McDonald's thus has a series of regulations that employees must follow in their dealings with customers. There are, for example, seven steps to window service: greet the customer, take the order, assemble the order, present the order, receive payment, thank the customer, and ask for repeat business.[1] Fast-food restaurants also seek to make other work as predictable as possible. For example, all employees are expected to cook hamburgers in the same, one-best way. In other words, "Frederick Taylor's principles [see Chapter 2] can be applied to assembling hamburgers as easily as to other kinds of tasks."[2] Employees follow well-defined steps in preparing various foods. The following are those involved in preparing French fries in much of the fast-food industry: open the bag of (frozen) fries; fill the basket half full; put the basket in the deep-frying machine; push the timer; remove the basket from the fryer and dump the fries into holding trays; shake salt on the fries; push another timer; discard the fries that are unsold after several minutes; look at the computer screen to see what size fries the next customer requires; fill another fry container and put it in a holding bin in preparation for preparing the next batch of fries.

Fast-food restaurants try in many ways to make workers look, act, and think more predictably.[3] All employees must wear uniforms and follow dress codes for things such as makeup, hair length, and jewelry. Training programs are designed to indoctrinate the worker into a "corporate culture,"[4] such as the McDonald's attitude and way of doing things. Highly detailed manuals spell out, among other things, "how often the bathroom must be cleaned to the temperature of grease used to fry potatoes . . . and what color nail polish to wear."[5] Finally, incentives (e.g., awards) are used to reward employees who behave properly, as are disincentives, ultimately firing, to deal with those who do not.

Predictability is also created in fast-food restaurants by having employees follow scripts in their interaction with customers. Perhaps the best-known scripts at McDonald's are "Do you want fries with that?" and "Would you like to add an apple pie to that order?"[6] Such scripts help create highly predictable interactions between workers and customers. While customers do not follow scripts, they tend to develop their own simple recipe-like responses to the employees of McDonaldized systems.

The Roy Rogers chain used to have its employees, dressed in cowboy and cowgirl uniforms, say "Howdy, pardner" to every customer about to order food. After paying for the food, people were sent on their way with "Happy trails." Employees' repetition of these familiar salutations, visit after visit, was a source of great satisfaction to regulars at Roy Rogers. Many customers (including me) felt a deep personal loss when Roy Rogers ceased this practice. However, in a McDonaldized society, other types of pseudo interactions are increasingly the norm. Consumers have come to expect and maybe even like them, and they might even look back on them longingly when interactions with their favorite robot are all they can expect on their visits to fast-food restaurants.

Like all other aspects of McDonaldization, scripts can have positive functions. For example, scripts can be a source of power to employees, enabling them to control interaction with customers. Employees can fend off unwanted or extraordinary demands merely by refusing to deviate from the script. Employees can also use their routines and scripts to protect themselves from the insults and indignities frequently heaped on them by the public. Employees can adopt the view that the public's hostility is aimed not at them personally but at the scripts and those who created them. Overall, rather than being hostile toward scripts and routines, McDonald's workers often find them useful and even satisfying.[7] However, employees (and customers) sometimes go off, or even resist, scripts (and other routines). As a result, what those who give (and receive) services actually say "is never entirely predictable."[8] People do not yet live in an iron cage of McDonaldization. In fact, they are unlikely ever to live in a totally predictable, completely McDonaldized, world.

Nonetheless, what McDonald's workers could do to exert some independence in their work is hardly overwhelming. For example, they could say all sorts of things that are not in the script, go a "bit" beyond the routine by providing extra services or exchanging pleasantries, withhold smiles, act a bit impatient or irritated, or refuse to encourage the customer to return. These all seem like very small deviations from an otherwise highly routinized workday.

As in the case of workers, customers also gain from scripts and routines: "Routinization can provide service-recipients with more reliable, less expensive, or speedier service, can protect them from incompetence, can minimize the interactive demands on them, and can clarify what their rights are." Such routines help guarantee equal treatment of all customers. Finally, routinization can help "establish a floor of civility and competence for which many customers have reason to be grateful."[9] Some customers appreciate the polite, ritualized greetings they encounter at McDonaldized businesses.

However, there are exceptions. Some customers may react negatively to employees mindlessly following scripts, who seem "unresponsive" or "robot-like."[10] Arguments can ensue, and angry customers may even leave without being served. In a classic scene from *Five Easy Pieces* (1970), Jack Nicholson's character stops at a diner and encounters a traditional "greasy-spoon" waitress, who is following a script. He cannot get an order of toast, although he could order a sandwich made with toast. Nicholson's character reacts even more strongly and negatively to the unresponsive script than he does to the surly waitress.

The fake friendliness of scripted interaction reflects the insincere camaraderie ("have a nice day") that characterizes not only fast-food restaurants but also all other elements of McDonaldized society, a camaraderie used to lure customers and keep them coming back. For example, TV screens used to be saturated with scenes of Wendy's owner and founder, Dave Thomas, extending a "personal invitation" to join him for a burger at his restaurant.[11] To help ensure predictable thinking and behavior among restaurant managers, McDonald's has them attend its Hamburger University.[12] Even the full-time "professors" at Hamburger University behave predictably because "they work from scripts prepared by the curriculum development department."[13] Trained by such teachers, managers internalize McDonald's ethos and its way of doing things. As a result, in demeanor and behavior, McDonald's managers are difficult to distinguish from one another. More important, because the managers train and oversee workers to help make them behave more predictably, managers use elaborate corporate guidelines that detail how virtually everything is to be done in all restaurants. McDonald's central headquarters periodically sends forth "undercover" inspectors to be sure that these guidelines are being enforced. These inspectors also check to see that the food meets quality control guidelines.

Other Brick-and-Mortar Settings: Scripted Jokes and That Disney Look

The fast-food industry is far from the only place where we are likely to encounter employees engaging in scripted interaction. Telemarketing is another setting that usually provides scripts that workers must follow, often unerringly. The scripts are designed to handle most foreseeable contingencies. Supervisors often listen in on solicitations to make sure employees follow the correct procedures. Employees who fail to follow the scripts, or who do not meet the quotas for the number of calls made and sales completed in a given time, may be fired summarily.

Robin Leidner details how Combined Insurance tried to make life insurance sales predictable: "The most striking thing about Combined Insurance's training for its life insurance agents was the amazing degree of standardization for which the company was striving. The agents were told, in almost hilarious detail, what to say and do." In fact, a large portion of the agents' sales pitch was "supposed to be memorized and recited as precisely as possible." One of the trainers told of a foreign salesman whose English was poor: "He learned the script phonetically and didn't even know what the words meant. . . . He sold twenty applications on his first day and is now a top executive."[14] The insurance agents were even taught the company's standard joke, as well as "the Combined shuffle"—standardized movements, body carriage, and intonation.

McDonald's relies on external constraints on its workers, but Combined Insurance attempts to transform its workers. Combined workers are supposed to embrace a new self (a "McIdentity");[15] in contrast, McDonald's employees are expected to suppress their selves. This dissimilarity is traceable to differences in the nature of the work in the two settings. Because McDonald's workers perform their tasks within the work setting, they can be controlled by external constraints. In contrast, Combined Insurance salespeople work door-to-door, with most of their work done inside customers' homes. Because external constraints do not work, Combined tries to change the agents into the kind of people the company wants. Despite the efforts to control their personalities, however, the insurance agents retain some discretion as well as a sense of autonomy. Although control of Combined workers goes deeper, McDonald's workers are still more controlled because virtually all decision making is removed from their jobs. Leidner concludes, "No detail is too trivial, no relationship too personal, no experience too individual, no manipulation too cynical for some organization or person, in a spirit of helpfulness or efficiency, to try to provide a standard, replicable routine for it."[16]

Disney has developed detailed guidelines about what its employees should look like (the "Disney look") and how they should act. Disney has assembled a long list of "dos" and "don'ts" for employees. Female "cast members" (a Disney euphemism for its park employees) may not use beads as part of a braided hairstyle, shave their heads or eyebrows, or use extreme hair coloring. Only neutral nail polish is allowed, and fingernails must not be more than a quarter of an inch in length. Neat mustaches are permitted for male hosts, but beards and goatees are not. Male cast members are allowed to shave their heads but not their eyebrows. The list goes on and on.[17]

Disney is not alone among amusement parks in the effort to make employee behavior predictable. At Busch Gardens in Williamsburg, Virginia, "a certain amount of energy is devoted to making sure that smiles are kept in place. There are rules about short hair (for the males) and no eating, drinking, smoking, or straw chewing on duty (for everyone)."[18] Not only do the employees at Busch Gardens all look alike, but they are also supposed to act alike: "Controlled environments hinge on the maintenance of the right kind of attitude among the lower echelons. 'It is kind of a rah-rah thing. We emphasize cleanliness, being helpful, being polite.' . . . Consequently, there is a lot of talk at Busch Gardens about . . . keeping people up and motivated . . . there are contests to determine who has the most enthusiasm and best attitude."[19] Such techniques ensure that visitors to Busch Gardens and parks like it can expect to see and deal with highly predictable employees throughout their visit.

The Assembly-Line: Cars More Uniform Than Those Produced by Craftspeople

The assembly-line enhanced the likelihood of predictable work and products. The problem with the alternative is that the steps a craftsperson takes are somewhat unpredictable, varying from person to person and over time. Small but significant differences in the finished products crop up, and they lead to unpredictabilities in the functioning and quality of the goods. For instance, one car produced by a craftsperson would run far better or be much less prone to breakdowns than a car produced by another; cars produced on an assembly-line are far more uniform. Realizing the benefits to be gained from predictable worker performance, many nonmanufacturing industries now have highly developed systems for making employee behavior more routine.

Sports: There's Even a McStables

In tennis, the tiebreaker has made the length of tennis matches more predictable. Prior to tiebreakers, in order to win a set, a player needed to win six games with a two-game margin over his or her opponent. If the opponent was never more than one game behind, the set could go on and on. Some memorable, interminable tennis matches produced scores on the order of 12 to 10. With limitations imposed by television and other mass media, the tennis establishment decided to institute the tiebreaker in many tournaments. If a set is deadlocked at six games each, a 12-point tiebreaker is played. The first player to get 7 points with a 2-point margin wins. A tiebreaker might go beyond 12 points (if the players are tied at 6 points each), but it rarely goes on nearly as long as close matches occasionally did.

Prior to 1940, National Football League (NFL) games had no overtime period in order to decide the winner. However, even with the advent of an overtime period, the score could still end up being tied when the score was tied at the end of regulation play. Wanting to make at least playoff games predictable in terms of having a winner and a loser, the NFL instituted a sudden-death system in 1974. Additional 15-minute quarters were played until one team scored and thereby won the game. In 2010, the overtime rules for playoff games were changed once again. With that change, if one team scored a field goal or a touchdown in the overtime period, then the other team was given a chance to tie or win the game. If they tied the score, the game would proceed in similar fashion into additional overtime periods until there was a winner. In 2012 the rule was amended to say that if one team scored a touchdown, then the game is over. If a field goal was scored, then the opposing team was given a chance to win the game with a touchdown. Sudden death was extended to regular season games in 2012. There is *always* a winner in a professional football game.

In college football, there are now also overtime periods to create a winner rather than having the game end in a tie. In order to increase the chance of quick scores, in each overtime period there is no kickoff; the offensive team starts on the defensive team's 25-yard line. This makes a quick score, and ending, highly likely. If the offensive team scores, the defensive team, also starting from the other team's 25-yard line, is given an opportunity to tie or win. If the overtime ends in a tie, then other periods are played until there is winner. As in pro football, in the college game there is now the predictable outcome that one team will win and the other will lose.

An interesting example of predictability in a previously highly unpredictable area is in the rationalization of racehorse training. There is even a Circle McStables in Texas and a Three Bar McStables in Oklahoma. While these are one-of-a-kind operations, as mentioned in Chapter 1, trainer D. Wayne Lukas has set up a string of stables around the United States that some have labeled "McStables." In the past, training stables were independent operations specific to a given track. Training procedures varied greatly from one racetrack to another and from one stable to another. Lukas, however, has been successful by establishing and supervising far-flung divisions of his stable. He said, "The barns are the same. The feeding program is the same. . . . There's never an adjustment necessary. . . . *It's the McDonald's principle.*"[20]

Predictability Online: Not Taking No for an Answer

As we all know, there are no people on Internet sites, or at least readily available there. Thus, the greatest predictability is that workers will be difficult to reach or even be nonexistent. However, if customers look carefully enough and dig deeply enough, they will likely eventually find someone to e-mail or, astoundingly in this day and age, even talk to. When customers get in touch with such workers, the workers are likely to react in highly predictable ways. As in many brick-and mortar settings, they are likely to follow, and closely adhere to, scripts.

For example, recently on a trial basis, I tried Audible, a system—part of Amazon—for listening to books. However, I quickly decided that I didn't like it. So, I tried to cancel it early within the trial period. While I was told by phone that the account had been cancelled, the monthly charge continued to appear on my credit card bill. After several tries, I was finally able to talk to a representative by phone. He said the account would be cancelled, but as part of his scripted response, he wanted to give me a free gift card. I kept saying that I didn't want it, but just as we were about to finish our conversation, we lost phone contact. When I called back, I had to start the process all over with a different representative going through the same steps. What is most striking was that this representative—like the one before—kept trying to give me that gift card. Finally, after raising my voice several times, the representative finally gave up, abandoned the script, and canceled (I think) my account without that free card.

CONTROL: EVEN PILOTS AREN'T IN CONTROL

Organizations have historically gained control over employees (and others, including customers) gradually, through increasingly effective technologies.[21] With these technologies, organizations began reducing workers' behavior to a series of machine-like actions. And once employees were behaving like machines, they could be replaced with actual machines. The replacement of humans by machines is the ultimate stage in control over people; people can cause no more uncertainty and unpredictability because they are no longer involved, at least directly, in the process. As Erik Brynjolfsson and Andrew McAfee[22] point out in *Race Against the Machine: How the Digital Revolution Is Accelerating Innovation, Driving Productivity, and Irreversibly Transforming Employment and the Economy,* large numbers of people in the age of accelerating digital technology are losing the race against technology. Computerized technology, including the growing number of robots, including web-based e-bots, are now doing an increasing amount of the work (producing goods, finding products, comparing prices) that at one time was the domain of human employees.

The following discussion is mainly concerned with the ways in which nonhuman technologies have increased control over employees in a McDonaldizing society, as well as over the processes these employees engage in and the resulting products. However, control over workers is not the only goal associated with nonhuman technologies. These technologies are created and implemented for many reasons, such as increased productivity, improved quality, and lower cost.

Controlling Employees

The Workplace: Do as I Say, Not as I Do

Most workplaces are part of bureaucracies that can be seen as large-scale nonhuman technologies. Their innumerable rules, regulations, guidelines, positions, lines of command, and hierarchies dictate what people do within the system and how they do it. The consummate bureaucrat thinks little about what is to be done; he or she simply follows the rules, deals with incoming work, and passes it on to its next stop in the system. Employees need to do little more than fill out the required forms, these days most likely right on the computer screen.

At the lowest levels in the bureaucratic hierarchy (the now declining manual, "blue-collar work"), scientific management clearly strove to limit or replace human technology. For instance, the "one best way" required workers to follow a series of predefined steps in a mindless fashion. More generally, Frederick Taylor believed that the most important part of the work world was not the employees but, rather, the organization that would plan, oversee, and control their work.

Although Taylor wanted all employees to be controlled by the organization, he accorded managers much more leeway than manual workers. The task of management was to study the knowledge and skills of workers and to record, tabulate, and ultimately reduce them to laws, rules, and even mathematical formulas. In other words, managers were to take a body of human skills, abilities, and knowledge and transform them into a set of nonhuman rules, regulations, and formulas. Once human skills were codified, the organization no longer needed skilled workers. Management would hire, train, and employ unskilled workers in accordance with a set of strict guidelines.

In effect, then, Taylor separated "head" work from "hand" work; prior to Taylor's day, the skilled worker had performed both. Taylor and his followers studied what was in the heads of those skilled workers, then translated that knowledge into simple, mindless routines that virtually anyone could learn and follow. Workers were thus left with little more than repetitive "hand" work. This principle remains at the base of the movement to replace human with nonhuman technology throughout our McDonaldizing society.

Behind Taylor's scientific management, and all other efforts at replacing human with nonhuman technology, lies the goal of being able to employ human beings with minimal intelligence and ability. In fact, Taylor sought to hire people who resembled animals, who had the mental makeup of oxen.[23] Not coincidentally, Henry Ford had a similar view of the kinds of people who were to work on his assembly-lines: "The average worker, I am sorry to say, wants a job in which he does not have to think."[24] The kind of person Taylor sought out was the same kind of person Ford thought would work well on the assembly-line. In their view, such people would more likely submit to external technological control over their work and perhaps even crave such control.

Not surprisingly, a perspective similar to that held by Taylor and Ford can be seen in the ideas of other entrepreneurs: "The obvious irony is that the organizations built by W. Clement Stone [the founder of Combined Insurance] and

Ray Kroc, both highly creative and innovative entrepreneurs, depend on the willingness of employees to follow detailed routines precisely."[25] Many workplaces have come under the control of nonhuman technologies. In the supermarket, for example, the checker once had to read the prices marked on food products and enter them into the cash register. As with all human activities, however, the process was slow, with a chance of human error. To counter these problems, many supermarkets installed optical scanners, which "read" a code preprinted on each item. Each code number calls up a price already entered into the computer that controls the cash register. This nonhuman technology has thus reduced the number and sophistication of the tasks performed by the checker. Only the less-skilled tasks remain, such as physically scanning the food and bagging it. And even those tasks are being eliminated with the development of self-scanning and having consumers bag their own groceries. In other words, the work performed by the supermarket checker, when it hasn't been totally eliminated, has been "de-skilled"; that is, a decline has occurred in the amount of skill required for the job.

The Fast-Food Industry: From Human to Mechanical Robots

Before the age of sophisticated nonhuman technologies, employees were largely controlled by their superiors. In the workplace, owners and supervisors controlled subordinates directly, face-to-face. But such direct, personal control is difficult, costly, and likely to engender personal hostility. Subordinates might strike out at an immediate supervisor or an owner who exercises excessively tight control over their activities. Control through a technology is easier, less costly in the long run, and less likely to engender hostility toward supervisors and owners. Over time, control by people has thus shifted toward control by technologies.[26] McDonald's controls employees by threatening to use, and ultimately using, technology to replace human workers. No matter how well they are programmed and controlled, workers can foul up the system's operation. A slow worker can make the preparation and delivery of a Big Mac inefficient. A worker who refuses to follow the rules might leave the pickles or special sauce off a hamburger, thereby making for unpredictability. And a distracted worker can put too few fries in the box, making an order of large fries seem skimpy. For these and other reasons, McDonald's and other fast-food restaurants feel compelled to control and ultimately replace human beings with machines. Technology that increases control over workers helps McDonaldized systems assure customers that their products and services will be consistent.

Fast-food restaurants have coped with problems of uncertainty by creating and instituting many nonhuman technologies. Among other things, they have done away with a cook, at least in the conventional sense. Of the cook, Jerry Newman says, "What a crock! Neither McDonald's nor Burger King had a 'cook.' Technology has all but eliminated this job."[27] Grilling a hamburger is so simple that anyone can do it with a bit of training. Even when more skill is required (as in the case of cooking an Arby's roast beef), the fast-food restaurant develops a routine involving a few simple procedures that almost anyone can follow. Cooking fast food is like a game of connect-the-dots or painting-by-numbers. Following prescribed steps eliminates most of the uncertainties of cooking.

Much of the food prepared at McDonaldized restaurants arrives preformed, precut, presliced, and "pre-prepared." All employees need to do, when necessary, is cook or often merely heat the food and pass it on to the customer. Instead of having employees cut lettuce at the local McDonald's restaurants in Great Britain, the following high-tech operation does it for them at a central location:

> The iceberg lettuce in the factory that supplies McDonald's is shredded at a rate of 1,000 kg an hour by a 22-blade machine you wouldn't under any circumstances want to fall into. After that, its ordeal is far from over. It drops onto a conveyor belt which propels it at four metres per second into a flurolaser optical-sorting machine that cost the company a cool 350,000 pounds. The machine uses the latest in laser and digital-camera technology to analyse the colour and density of the lettuce shreds. It takes tens of thousands of scans a second to identify rogue chunks, grit and discolouration. When an anomaly is spotted, the air guns 50 cm further along the belt are primed. One-eighth of a second later, the jets blast the offending matter out of the flow. . . . Of course, lettuce is just the tip of the iceberg. Each constituent part of a Big Mac, from the burger to the sesame-seed bun, has a process of massive industrial scale behind it.[28]

At Taco Bell, workers used to spend hours cooking meat and shredding vegetables. The workers now simply drop bags of frozen, ready-cooked beef into boiling water. They have used preshredded lettuce for some time, and more recently preshredded cheese and prediced tomatoes have appeared.[29] The more that is done by nonhuman technologies before the food arrives at the restaurant, the less workers need to do and the less room they have to exercise their own judgment and skill.

McDonald's has gone further than most other chains in developing technologies to control employees. For example, its soft drink dispenser has a sensor that automatically shuts off the flow when the cup is full. Ray Kroc's dissatisfaction with the vagaries of human judgment led to the elimination of French fry machines controlled by humans and to the development of machines that ring or buzz when the fries are done and that automatically lift the French fry baskets out of the hot oil. When an employee controls the French fry machine, misjudgment may lead to undercooked, overcooked, or even burned fries. Kroc fretted over this problem: "It was amazing that we got them as uniform as we did, because each kid working the fry vats would have his own interpretation of the proper color and so forth."[30] At the cash register, workers once had to look at a price list and punch the prices in by hand; hence, the wrong (even lower) amount could be rung up. Computer screens and computerized cash registers—point-of-sale registers— forestall that possibility.[31] All that the employees need do is press the image on the register that matches the item purchased; the machine then produces the correct price. Even that is being eliminated as consumers use iPads to do the ordering, leaving employees less to do and offering them even less decision making and therefore reducing their margin for error.

If the objective in a fast-food restaurant is to reduce employees to human robots, we should not be surprised if we see the spread of robots that prepare food. For example, a robot has cooked hamburgers at one college campus restaurant.[32] Robots offer a number of advantages—lower cost, increased efficiency, fewer workers, no absenteeism, and a solution to the at-times inadequate supply of workers needed to work at fast-food restaurants. The professor who came up with the idea for the robot that cooks hamburgers said, "Kitchens have not been looked at as factories, which they are. . . . Fast-food restaurants were the first to do that."[33] Taco Bell developed "a computer-driven machine the size of a coffee table that . . . can make and seal in a plastic bag a perfect hot taco."[34] Another company worked on an automated drink dispenser that produced a soft drink in 15 seconds: "Orders are punched in at the cash register by a clerk. A computer sends the order to the dispenser to drop a cup, fill it with ice and appropriate soda, and place a lid on top. The cup is then moved by conveyor to the customer."[35] These technologies have not yet been widely used, although Starbucks has its automated machines that grind beans and spit out espresso. When such technologies are refined and prove to be less expensive and more reliable than humans, fast-food restaurants will employ them more widely.

The 2017 acquisition of Whole Foods by Amazon, as well the existence of Amazon Go, both already discussed several times in this book, auger the replacement of human cashiers by nonhuman robot-cashiers in supermarkets and convenience stores, as well as in fast-food restaurants (and elsewhere). Being lost is human interaction as well the cashiers (and other workers) with whom we often interact and who serve the role of "important connective social tissue."[36] This represents a further step in our declining opportunities to interact with others, "especially those outside our social circles, of different races, classes or nationalities."[37]

Even managers are not immune from efforts to find nonhuman controls over them. There is a computerized system that, among other things, tells managers how many hamburgers or orders of French fries they will require at a given time (e.g., the lunch hour). The computerized system takes away the need for managers to make such judgments and decisions.[38] Thus, "Burger production has become an exact science in which everything is regimented, every distance calculated and every dollop of ketchup monitored and tracked."[39]

Education: McChild Care Centers

An even more extreme version of the emphasis on nonhuman technology appears in the child care equivalent of the fast-food restaurant. KinderCare, now part of the KinderCare Education, was founded in 1969 and currently has about 3,700 centers worldwide reaching over 300,000 students.[40] There are approximately 1,700 KinderCare learning centers in the United States.[41] About 200,000 children between the ages of 6 weeks and 12 years attend the centers.[42] Kinder-Care tends to hire short-term employees with little or no training in child care. What these employees do in the "classroom" is largely determined by an instruction book with a ready-made curriculum. Staff members open the manual to find activities spelled out in detail for each day. Clearly, a skilled, experienced, creative teacher is not the kind of person "McChild" care centers seek to hire; relatively untrained employees are more easily controlled by the nonhuman technology of the omnipresent "instruction book."

Another example of organizational control over teachers is to be found in the franchised Sylvan Learning, often thought of as the "McDonald's of Education."[43] (There are about 800 Sylvan Learning centers worldwide, and they claim to have helped 2 million students.[44]) Sylvan Learning centers are afterschool centers for remedial education. The corporation "trains staff and tailors a McDonald's type uniformity, down to the U-shaped tables at which instructors work with their charges."[45] Through their training methods, rules, and technologies, for-profit systems such as Sylvan Learning, as well as for-profit colleges in general,[46] exert great control over their "teachers."

Health Care: Who's Deciding Our Fate?

As is the case with all rationalized systems, medicine has moved away from human and toward nonhuman technologies. The two most important examples are the growing importance of bureaucratic rules and controls and the growth of modern medical machinery. For example, the prospective payment and diagnosis-related group (DRG) systems—not physicians and their medical judgment—tend to determine how long a patient can be hospitalized (see Chapter 5). Similarly, the doctor (as internist or general practitioner) operating alone out of a black bag with a few simple tools has become virtually a thing of the past. Instead, internists often serve as dispatchers, sending patients on to the appropriate machines and specialists. Computer programs can even diagnose illnesses.[47] Although it is unlikely that they will ever replace the physician, computers may one day be the initial, if not the prime, diagnostic agents. It is now even possible for people to get diagnoses, treatment, and prescriptions over the Internet without face-to-face contact with a physician.

These and other developments in modern medicine demonstrate increasing external control over the medical profession by third-party payers, employing organizations, for-profit hospitals, health maintenance organizations (HMOs), the federal government (e.g., Medicare), and "McDoctor"-like organizations. Even in its heyday, the medical profession was not free of external control, but now the nature of the control is changing, and its degree and extent are increasing dramatically. Instead of mostly autonomous doctors in private practice making decisions, doctors are more likely to conform to bureaucratic rules and regulations. In bureaucracies, employees are controlled by their superiors. Physicians' superiors are increasingly likely to be professional managers and not other doctors. Also, the existence of hugely expensive medical technologies often mandates that they be used. As the machines themselves grow more sophisticated, physicians come to understand them less and are therefore less able to control them. Instead, control shifts to the technologies as well as to the experts who create and handle them.

An excellent example of increasing external control over physicians (and other medical personnel) is called "clinical pathways."[48] A clinical pathway is a standardized series of steps prescribed for dealing with an array of medical problems. Involved are a series of "if–then" decision points—if a certain circumstance exists, the action to follow is prescribed. What physicians do in a variety of situations is determined by the pathway and not the individual physician. To put it in terms of this chapter, the pathway—a nonhuman technology—exerts external control over physicians.

Various terms have been used to describe these pathways—standardization, "cookbook" medicine, a series of recipes, a neat package tied together with a bow, and so on—and all describe the rationalization of medical practice. The point is that there are prescribed courses of action under a wide range of circumstances. While doctors need not, indeed should not, follow a pathway at all times, they do so most of the time. A physician who spearheaded the protocol movement said he grew concerned when physicians followed a pathway more than 92% of the time. While this leaves some leeway for physicians, it is clear that what they are supposed to do is predetermined in the vast majority of instances.

In the case of an asthma patient, the pathway says that, if the patient's temperature rises above 101°, a complete blood count is to be ordered. A chest X-ray is needed under certain circumstances—if it's the patient's initial wheezing episode or if there is chest pain, respiratory distress, or a fever of over 101°. And so it goes—a series of if–then steps prescribed for and controlling what physicians and other medical personnel do. While there are undoubted advantages associated with such pathways (e.g., lower likelihood of using procedures or medicines that have been shown not to work), they do tend to take decision making away from physicians. Continued reliance on such pathways is likely to adversely affect the ability of physicians to make independent decisions.

Phoneheads, Online Chats, and De-Skilled Pilots: It's Like Being in Prison

Control is exerted over the "phoneheads," or customer service representatives, who work for many companies. Those who handle reservations for the airlines (e.g., United Airlines) must log every minute spent on the job and justify each moment away from the phone. Employees have to punch a "potty button" on the phone to let management know of their intentions. Supervisors sit in an elevated "tower" in the middle of the reservations floor, "observing like [prison] guards the movements of every operator in the room." They also monitor phone calls to make sure that employees say and do what they are supposed to. This control is part of a larger process of "omnipresent supervision increasingly taking hold in so many workplaces—not just airline reservations centers but customer service departments and data-processing businesses where computers make possible an exacting level of employee scrutiny."[49] No wonder customers often deal with representatives who behave like automatons. Said one employee of United Airlines, "My body became an extension of the computer terminal that I typed the reservations into. I came to feel emptied of self."[50]

Sometimes, telephone service representatives are literally prisoners. Prison inmates are now used in many states in this way. The attractions of prisoners are obvious—they work for very little pay and can be controlled to a far higher degree than even the "phoneheads" discussed previously. Furthermore, they can be relied on to show up for work. As one manager put it, "I need people who are there every day."[51] Following this logical progression, some companies now use computer callers instead of having people solicit potential customers over the phone.[52] Computer voices are far more predictable and controllable than even the most rigidly controlled human operator, including prisoners. Indeed, in our increasingly McDonaldized society, I have had some of my most "interesting" conversations with such computer voices. More extremely, in the 2013 movie *Her,* the male hero falls in love, and has verbal sex, with a computerized feminine voice on the phone.

Increasingly, people are *not* using phones and dealing with phoneheads in order to obtain information. Instead, they are increasingly likely to rely on online chats lacking in even the minimal human interaction that occurs with phoneheads. This is also another example of the increase in prosumption because online chats require more work on the part of consumers than do phone interactions where the workers do much more of the work.

Of course, lower-level employees are not the only ones whose problem-solving skills are lost in the transition to more nonhuman technology. Already mentioned are the controls exerted over professors and doctors. In addition, pilots flying the modern, computerized airplane (such as the Boeing 787 and the Airbus A380) are being controlled and, in the process, de-skilled. Instead of flying "by the seat of their pants" or occasionally using old-fashioned autopilots for simple maneuvers, modern pilots can "push a few buttons and lean back while the plane flies to its destination and lands on a predetermined runway." Said one Federal Aviation Administration (FAA) official, "We're taking more and more of these functions out of human control and giving them to machines." These airplanes are in many ways safer and more reliable than older, less technologically advanced models. Pilots, dependent on these technologies, however, may lose the ability to be creative in handling emergency situations. The problem, said one airline manager, is that "I don't have computers that will do that [be creative]; I just don't."[53]

Digital Settings: More Elimination Than Control

Once again, because most employees have been eliminated from digital sites, control over them is largely a nonissue. Or, it could be said that the ultimate control over humans has been achieved on such sites because humans have been largely eliminated—as employees—from them. Unfortunately, it is human beings who are still accessing those sites and they are likely to be frustrated by the absence of employees on them, as well as the hurdles put in their way in their efforts to get help from a person rather than a computer.

Controlling the Process and the Product

In a McDonaldizing society, people as employees are the greatest threat to predictability. Control over employees can be enhanced by controlling processes and products, but control over processes and products also comes to be valued in itself.

Food Production: It Cooks Itself

In the fast-food industry, companies have lengthy procedure manuals that exert considerable control over processes and products. For example, as a result of such procedures, Burger King Whoppers are cooked the same way by employees at all restaurants in the chain, and the same is true for the McDonald's Quarter Pounders and their garnishes.[54] Technologies designed to reduce uncertainties are also found throughout the manufacture of food. For example, the mass manufacturing of bread is not controlled by skilled bakers who lavish love and attention on a few loaves of bread at a time. Such skilled bakers cannot produce enough bread to supply the needs of our society. Furthermore, the bread they do produce can suffer from the uncertainties involved in having humans do the work. The bread may, for example, turn out to be too brown or too doughy. To increase productivity and eliminate these unpredictabilities, mass producers of bread have developed an automated system in which, as in all automated systems,[55] humans play a minimal role because they are rigidly controlled by the technology:

> The most advanced bakeries now resemble oil refineries. Flour, water, a score of additives, and huge amounts of yeast, sugar, and water are mixed into a broth that ferments for an hour. More flour is then added, and the dough is extruded into pans, allowed to rise for an hour, then moved through a tunnel oven. The loaves emerge after eighteen minutes, to be cooled, sliced, and wrapped.[56]

In one food industry after another, production processes in which humans play little more than planning and maintenance roles have replaced those dominated by skilled craftspeople. The warehousing and shipping of food has been similarly automated.

Further along in the food production process, other nonhuman technologies have affected how food is cooked. Technologies such as ovens with temperature probes "decide" for the cook when food is done. Many ovens, coffeemakers, and other appliances can turn themselves on and off. The instructions on all kinds of packaged foods dictate precisely how to prepare and cook the food. Premixed products, such as Mrs. Dash, eliminate the need for the cook to come up with creative combinations of seasonings. Even cookbooks are designed to take creativity away from the cook and control the process of cooking.

Food Production: Of Sea Farms and Factory Farms

Some rather startling technological developments have occurred in the ways in which animals are raised for food. For instance, "aquaculture"[57] is growing dramatically, especially in China, because of the spiraling desire for seafood in an increasingly cholesterol-conscious world.[58] Instead of the old inefficient, unpredictable methods of harvesting fish—a lone angler casting a line or even boats catching tons of fish at a time in huge nets—we now have the much more predictable and efficient "farming" of seafood. More than half of the fresh salmon found in restaurants is now raised in huge sea cages off the coast of Norway. Almost all of the shrimp consumed in the United States is farmed and imported.

Sea farms offer several advantages. Most generally, aquaculture allows humans to exert far greater control over the vagaries that beset fish in their natural habitat, thus producing a more predictable supply. Various drugs and chemicals increase predictability in the amount and quality of seafood. Aquaculture also permits a more predictable and efficient harvest because the creatures are confined to a limited space. In addition, geneticists can manipulate them to produce seafood more efficiently. For example, it takes a standard halibut about 10 years to reach market size, but a new dwarf variety can reach the required size in only 3 years. Sea farms also allow for greater calculability—the greatest number of fish for the least expenditure of time, money, and energy.

Small, family-run farms for raising other animals are being rapidly replaced by "factory farms" and their employees.[59] The first animal to find its way into the factory farm was the chicken. Here is the way one observer describes a chicken "factory":

A broiler producer today gets a load of 10,000, 50,000, or even more day-old chicks from the hatcheries, and puts them straight into a long, windowless shed. . . . Inside the shed, every aspect of the birds' environment is controlled to make them grow faster on less feed. Food and water are fed automatically from hoppers suspended from the roof. The lighting is adjusted. . . . For instance, there may be bright light twenty-four hours a day for the first week or two, to encourage the chicks to gain [weight] quickly.[60]

Among their other advantages, such chicken farms allow one worker to raise more than 50,000 chickens.

Raising chickens this way ensures control over all aspects of the business. For instance, the chickens' size and weight are more predictable than that of free-ranging chickens. "Harvesting" chickens confined in this way is also more efficient than catching chickens that roam over large areas. However, confining chickens in crowded quarters creates unpredictabilities, such as violence and even cannibalism. Farmers deal with these irrational "vices" in a variety of ways, such as dimming the lights as chickens approach full size and "debeaking" chickens so they cannot harm each other.

Some chickens are allowed to mature so they can be used for egg production. However, they receive much the same treatment as chickens raised for food. Hens are viewed as little more than "converting machines" that transform raw material (feed) into a finished product (eggs). Peter Singer describes the technology employed to control egg production:

> The cages are stacked in tiers, with food and water troughs running along the rows, filled automatically from a central supply. They have sloping wire floors. The slope . . . makes it more difficult for the birds to stand comfortably, but it causes the eggs to roll to the front of the cage where they can easily be collected. . . [and], in the more modern plants, carried by conveyor belt to a packing plant. . . . The excrement drops through [the wire floor] and can be allowed to pile up for many months until it is all removed in a single operation.[61]

This system obviously imposes great control over the production of eggs, leading to greater efficiency, a more predictable supply, and more uniform quality than the old chicken coop.

Other animals—pigs, lambs, steers, and calves especially—are raised similarly. To prevent calves' muscles from developing, which toughens the veal, they are immediately confined to tiny stalls where they cannot exercise. As they grow, they may not even be able to turn around. Being kept in stalls also prevents the calves from eating grass, which would cause their meat to lose its pale color; the stalls are kept free of straw, which, if eaten by the calves, would also darken the meat. "They are fed a totally liquid diet, based on nonfat milk powder with added vitamins, minerals, and growth-promoting drugs," says Peter Singer in his book *Animal Liberation*.[62] To make sure the calves take in the maximum amount of food, they are given no water, which forces them to keep drinking their liquid food. By rigidly controlling the size of the stall and the diet, veal producers can maximize two quantifiable objectives: the production of the largest amount of meat in the shortest possible time and the creation of the tenderest, whitest, and therefore most desirable veal.

Employment of a variety of technologies obviously leads to greater control over the process by which animals produce meat, thereby increasing the efficiency, calculability, and predictability of meat production. In addition, the technologies exert control over farmworkers. Left to their own devices, ranchers might feed young steers too little or the wrong food or permit them too much exercise. In fact, in the rigidly controlled factory ranch, human ranch hands (and their unpredictabilities) are virtually eliminated.

Control of Process and Products on Digital Sites: Not Really the Most Chosen

As with much else on the Internet, control over process and products is largely taken away from human employees and built into the computerized programs that manage them. The process of getting on a site and working one's way through it appears to be managed by consumers. In reality, much of it involves selection from a range of choices and directions preset by computer programs. There is a seemingly infinite variety of products available on these sites, although, as we've seen in the case of Google, those products that head many lists are not there because they have been selected the most, but because the corporations offering them have paid Google a fee to be placed there. In contrast to appearances, they are *not* really the most chosen items, but rather paid ads for those products. The result is that consumer choice on at least some Internet sites is controlled, or at least guided, by their placement on the list. Pop-up ads are another mechanism websites use to guide consumers in the direction of certain choices.

A good example of control on digital sites is to be found on the Stitch Fix site (others like it are Trunk Club and Birchbox). Clothing is mailed to those who are on the site on the basis of algorithms derived, in part, from information they provide. Those algorithms generate five selections that are then mailed to the consumer. The consumer does have enough control over the process to return, free of charge, some or all of the clothing sent to them. However, Stitch Fix attempts to exert control over even this by offering consumers a 25% discount if they keep all five pieces of clothing.

These algorithms also control Stitch Fix employees. That is, they pick out the clothing for customers on the basis of the generated selections. Additional controls are exerted over employees. For example, they are limited in the number of steps they can take to pick out the clothing.

As is the case with consumers, great control is exercised in many different ways over workers in a number of highly diverse settings. However, because they are in the employ of organizations and are paid by them, workers can be, and are, controlled to a far higher degree than are consumers. The ultimate step in the control of workers is to eliminate them completely from jobs that involve relationships with consumers. This leaves consumers, as prosumers, on their own to do much, or even all, of the work once done by paid employees.

THE IRRATIONALITY OF RATIONALITY

Traffic Jams on Those "Happy Trails"

McDonaldization has swept across the social landscape because it offers increased efficiency, predictability, calculability, and control. Despite these advantages, as the preceding chapters have shown, McDonaldization has some serious disadvantages. Rational systems inevitably spawn irrationalities that limit, eventually compromise, and perhaps even undermine their rationality.

The irrationality of rationality is simply a label for many of the negative aspects of McDonaldization. Irrationality can be seen as the opposite of rationality. Most generally, McDonaldization can be viewed as leading to inefficiency, unpredictability, incalculability, and loss of control.[1] More specifically, the wider range of irrationalities discussed in this chapter includes inefficiency, excessively high cost, false friendliness, disenchantment, health and environmental hazards, homogenization, and dehumanization. Also discussed are the problems associated with the McJobs spawned by the process of McDonaldization. As problematic as those jobs are, perhaps even more of a problem is their loss as a result of nonhuman technologies (i.e., automation, robotization) replacing them. Most of this chapter, like Chapters 3 and 4, focuses on the irrationalities that confront consumers in McDonaldized settings. However, as in Chapters 5 and 6, we will also deal with the workers in these settings and the irrationalities associated with their occupations, especially their McJobs. Irrationality also means that rational systems are disenchanted; they have lost their magic and mystery. Most important, rational systems are unreasonable systems that deny the humanity, the human reason, of the people who work within them or are served by them. In other words, rational systems are dehumanizing. Please note, therefore, that although the terms *rationality* and *reason* are often used interchangeably, in this discussion, they are antithetical phenomena:[2] Rational systems are often unreasonable.

INEFFICIENCY: LONG LINES AT THE CHECKOUT

Rational systems certainly bring with them many new or increased efficiencies, but this should not cause us to lose sight of the inefficiencies they spawn. For example, contrary to their promise, these systems often end up being quite inefficient for consumers. For instance, in fast-food restaurants, long lines of people often form at the counters, or parades of cars idle in the drive-through lanes. What is purported to be an efficient way of obtaining a meal often turns out to be quite inefficient.

The problem of inefficiency at drive-throughs in the United States is, interestingly, among the greatest at McDonald's. While its goal is a maximum of a 90-second wait in the drive-through line, it averaged 152.5 seconds in 2004 and 167.9 seconds in 2005.[3] By 2009, the wait had increased further to 174.2 seconds. In fact, McDonald's ranked only seventh in 2009 in the average time waiting in its drive-throughs. The leader, with an average of 134 seconds per vehicle, was Wendy's.[4] Of course, to some degree, McDonald's is the victim of its own success, especially of the growth in its drive-through business. The paragon of efficiency, however, cannot hide behind its success and must deliver efficiency, even in the face of its burgeoning drive-through business. Furthermore, problems at the drive-through at McDonald's are not restricted to long waits—there are also many inaccuracies in its drive-through orders. In fact, in 2005, McDonald's ranked *last* among 25 fast-food chains in terms of accuracy. Said one customer, "McDonald's is the worst at getting things right. . . . McDonald's always gets at least one thing wrong."[5] And, it takes time to correct errors, further increasing the problem of inefficiency at McDonald's. Furthermore, time is money, and the increased time required to get an order right means higher costs and lower profits. In fact, one franchisee explicitly recognizes the irrational consequences of the rational emphasis on speed: "With continued emphasis on speed, accuracy suffers."[6] While inefficiency is a problem in the United States, it is a more serious problem elsewhere.

A Hong Kong restaurant serves about 600,000 people a year (versus 400,000 in the United States). To handle long lines, 50 or more employees move along the lines taking orders with handheld computers. The orders are transmitted wirelessly to the kitchen.[7] In the United States, a few McDonald's have been experimenting with the use of handheld tablet PCs. An employee stands outside with the tablet taking orders from cars as soon as they get in line. The orders are transmitted wirelessly to the kitchen and are ready, at least theoretically, as soon as the car reaches the pick-up window. While this should speed things up, the initial experience was that the wait was "slow and frustrating."[8]

The fast-food restaurant is far from the only aspect of a McDonaldized society that exhibits inefficiency. Even the once-vaunted Japanese industry has its inefficiencies. Take the "just-in-time" system discussed in Chapter 2. Because this system often requires that parts be delivered several times a day, the streets and highways around a factory often became cluttered with trucks. Because of the heavy traffic, people were often late for work or for business appointments, resulting in lost productivity. But the irrationalities go beyond traffic jams and missed appointments. All these trucks use a great deal of fuel, very expensive in Japan, and contribute greatly to air pollution. The situation became even worse when Japanese convenience stores, supermarkets, and department stores began to use a just-in-time system, bringing even greater numbers of delivery trucks onto the streets.[9]

Here is the way columnist Richard Cohen describes another example of inefficiency in the McDonaldized world:

> Oh Lord, with each advance of the computer age, I was told I would benefit. But with each "benefit," I wind up doing more work. This is the ATM [automated teller machine] rule of life . . . I was told—nay promised—that I could avoid lines at the bank and make deposits or withdrawals any time of the day. Now, there are lines at the ATMs, the bank seems to take a percentage of whatever I withdraw or deposit, and, of course, I'm doing what tellers (remember them?) used to do. Probably, with the new phone, I'll have to climb telephone poles in the suburbs during ice storms.[10]

Cohen underscores at least three different irrationalities: (1) Rational systems are not less expensive; (2) they force consumers to do unpaid work; and, of most importance here, (3) they are often inefficient. It might be more efficient to deal with a human teller, either in the bank or at a drive-through window, than to wait in line at an ATM.

Similarly, preparing a meal might be more efficient at home than packing the family in the car, driving to McDonald's, loading up on food, and then driving home again. Meals cooked at home from scratch might not be more efficient, but certainly microwave meals are. They may even be more efficient than full-course meals picked up at the supermarket or Boston Market. Yet many people persist in the belief, fueled by propaganda from the fast-food restaurants, that eating there is more efficient than eating at home.

Although the forces of McDonaldization trumpet greater efficiency, they never tell us for whom the system is more efficient. Is it efficient for supermarket consumers who need only a loaf of bread and a carton of milk to wend their way past thousands of items they don't need? Is it efficient for consumers to push their own food over the supermarket scanner, swipe their own credit or debit cards, and then bag their groceries? Is it efficient for people to pump their own gasoline? Is it efficient for callers to push numerous combinations of telephone numbers before they hear a human voice? Is it efficient to go through innumerable websites, and many options on each? Most often, consumers find that such systems are *not* efficient for them. Most of the gains in efficiency go to those who are pushing, and profiting from, rationalization.

Those at the top of an organization impose efficiencies not only on consumers but also on those who work at or near the bottom of the system: the assembly-line workers, the counter persons, the call-center staff. The owners, franchisees, and top managers want to control subordinates, but they want their own positions to be as free of rational constraints—as inefficient—as possible. Subordinates are to follow blindly the rules, regulations, and other structures of the rational system, while those in charge remain free to be "creative."

The digital systems to which consumers are increasingly exposed are highly efficient for the corporations that employ them and they seem to operate efficiently from the perspective of the digital consumer. For example, it is clearly much more efficient to shop online than it is to trek to a shopping mall that may or may not have what one is looking for. If it does not, a trip to other shopping sites will be necessary. However, from another angle digital sites are highly inefficient for consumers, really prosumers, who are forced to do a series of tasks that were, in other settings, performed for them by paid employees. To consumers, digital sites seem to be efficient because of the capabilities of their computerized systems. As a result, it often appears to consumers that it is more efficient for them to do the work themselves online than it is to go to a brick-and-mortar location. Supporting this view is the fact paid employees are increasingly difficult to find at those locations and many of those who work there are poorly trained and often not very helpful.

HIGH COST: BETTER OFF AT HOME

The efficiency of McDonaldization (assuming it *is* efficient) does not ordinarily save consumers money. For example, some years ago, a small soda was shown to cost one franchise owner 11 cents, but it was sold for 85 cents (a price that is laughable today).[11] A fast-food meal for a family of four might easily cost $30 (less if a few Happy Meals are in the mix) these days. Such a sum would go further if spent on ingredients for a home-cooked meal. For example, a meal for four (or even six) people, including a roast chicken, vegetables, salad, and milk, would cost about half that amount.[12] While oats, and real oatmeal, are very inexpensive, the oatmeal at McDonald's (see below) sold for $2.49 in 1992, more than twice as much as a Double Cheeseburger, and 10 times as expensive as the real thing.[13] A nutrition adviser points out that a Dollar Menu is "least economical" from the point of view of the nutrients obtained.[14]

As Cohen demonstrated with ATMs, people must often pay extra to deal with the inhumanity and inefficiency of rationalized systems. The great success of McDonaldized systems, the rush to extend them to ever-more sectors of society, and the fact that so many people want to get into such businesses indicate that these systems generate huge profits.

Bob Garfield noted the expense of McDonaldized activities in his article, "How I Spent (and Spent and Spent) My Disney Vacation."[15] Garfield took his family of four to Walt Disney World, which he found might more aptly be named "Expense World." The five-day vacation cost $1,700 in 1991; admission to Disney World alone cost $551.30 (much more costly today). And the prices keep going up. (Today, the cost of admission for only four days for a family of four is more than double that.) He calculates that, during the five days, they had less than seven hours of "fun, fun, fun. That amounts to $261 c.p.f.h. (cost per fun hour)." Because most of his time in the Magic Kingdom was spent riding buses, "queuing up and shlepping from place to place, the 17 attractions we saw thrilled us for a grand total of 44 minutes."[16] Thus, what is thought to be an inexpensive family vacation turns out to be quite expensive.

In contrast, prices and costs are often lower on digital sites, especially if the consumer uses a bot to search out the lowest price. There are additional cost savings (e.g., on gasoline) involved in not having to travel to consumption sites, but rather staying at home (or in the workplace) and ordering products online. There is a great deal of competition among online sites with many demonstrating that their prices are lower than their competitors. For example, if you are looking for a new car, there are many sites to search for the lowest price, including TrueCar,

Cars.com, and CarsDirect. In terms of travel, Trivago is a German multinational that has aggressively advertised its low prices in comparison to its online competitors. It claims that those who use its site will never need to pay full price again. In addition to offering other quantified information such as a numerical rating of a hotel, it also provides price information from, for example, hotel websites as well as from travel sites such as Expedia, Orbitz, and Priceline. Once one clicks on a hotel site, one is offered what is presumably the lowest available price for that room.

FALSE FRIENDLINESS: "HI, GEORGE" AND EMOJIS

Because fast-food restaurants greatly restrict or even eliminate genuine fraternization, what workers and customers have left is either no human relationships or "false fraternization." This is part of what Arlie Hochschild calls the "commodification of feelings" and the tendency to turn emotions into a kind of labor.[17] As labor, the expression of emotions tends to become less genuine. Worse, false emotions come to be offered in order to expedite interactions or to increase profits.

For example, Rule Number 17 for Burger King workers is "Smile at all times."[18] The Roy Rogers employees who used to say "Happy trails" to me when I paid for my food really had no interest in what happened to me "on the trail." This phenomenon has been generalized to the many workers who say "Have a nice day" as customers depart. In fact, of course, they usually have no real interest in, or concern for, how the rest of a customer's day goes. Instead, in a polite and ritualized way, they are really saying, "Get lost," or "Move on so someone else can be served."

While the practice has declined dramatically in recent years as a result of e-mail and spam, we still receive computer-generated letters, or "junk mail" (of course, much more junk is now associated with our e-mail accounts). Great pains are sometimes taken to make a message seem personal.[19] (Similarly, I still get occasional calls from telemarketers who start out by saying, "Hi, George.") In most cases, it is fairly obvious that a computer has generated the message from a database of names. These messages are full of the kind of false fraternization practiced by Roy Rogers workers. For example, callers often adopt a friendly, personal tone designed to lead people to believe that the head of some business has fretted over the fact that they haven't, for example, shopped in his or her department store or used his or her credit card in the past few months. For example, a friend of mine received a letter from a franchise, The Lube Center, a few days after he had his car lubricated (note the use of the first name and the "deep" personal concern): "Dear Ken: We want to THANK YOU for choosing The Lube Center for all of your car's fluid needs. . . . We strongly recommend that you change your oil on a regular basis. . . . We will send you a little reminder card. . . . This will help *remind* you when your car is next due to be serviced. . . . We spend the time and energy to make sure that our employees are trained properly to give you the service that you deserve" (italics added).

Several years ago, I received the following letter from a congressman from Long Island, even though I was living in Maryland. The fact that I had never met the congressman and knew nothing about him didn't prevent him from writing me a "personal" letter: "Dear George: It is hard to believe, but I am running for my NINTH term in Congress! When I think back over the 8,660 votes I've cast. . . . I realize how many battles *we've shared*. Please let me know that I can count on *you*" (italics added).

A *Washington Post* correspondent offers the following critique of false friendliness in junk mail:

> By dropping in people's names and little tidbits gleaned from databases hither and yon in their direct mail pitches, these marketing organizations are trying to create the illusion of intimacy. In reality, these technologies conspire to *corrupt and degrade intimacy*. They cheat, substituting the insertable fact for the genuine insight. These pitches end up with their own synthetic substitutes for the real thing.[20]

However false it may be, such junk mail is designed to exert control over customers by getting them to take desired courses of action.

There is some false friendliness on online sites—for example, "welcome back" messages—but in the main, signs of friendliness are virtually nonexistent online because there are no employees there to act in a friendly manner. One exception is e-cards, which are loaded with false friendliness. However, that is nothing new, material greeting cards have epitomized false friendliness since their inception. (Hallmark was founded in 1910.)

Mention should also be made in this context of the memification of everything: the reduction of human interaction to tweets of 140 characters or to fleeting images. Major examples of the latter are the wildly popular emojis, which greatly McDonaldize the expression of emotions online by reducing them to, for example, a single symbol, most notably a smiley face. Reflective of the emphasis on calculability, such symbols can appear multiple times indicating ever-stronger emotions.

DISENCHANTMENT: WHERE'S THE MAGIC?

One of Max Weber's most general theses is that, as a result of rationalization, the Western world has grown increasingly disenchanted.[21] The "magical elements of thought" that characterized less rationalized societies have been disappearing.[22] Thus, instead of a world dominated by enchantment, magic, and mystery, we have one in which everything seems clear, cut-and-dried, logical, and routine. As Schneider puts it, "Max Weber saw history as having departed a deeply enchanted past en route to a disenchanted future—a journey that would gradually strip the natural world both of its magical properties and of its capacity for meaning."[23] The process of rationalization leads, by definition, to the loss of a quality—enchantment—that was at one time very important to people.[24] Although we undoubtedly have gained much from the rationalization of society in general, and from the rationalization of consumption settings in particular, we also have lost something of great, if hard to define, value. Consider how the dimensions of McDonaldization work against enchantment.

Efficient systems have no room for anything smacking of enchantment and systematically seek to root it out. Anything that is magical, mysterious, fantastic, dreamy, and so on is considered inefficient. Enchanted systems typically involve highly convoluted means to ends, and they may well have no obvious goals at all. Efficient systems do not permit such meanderings, and their designers and implementers will do whatever is necessary to eliminate them. The elimination of meanderings and aimlessness is one of the reasons that Weber saw rationalized systems as disenchanted systems.

Enchantment has far more to do with quality than with quantity. Magic, fantasies, dreams, and the like relate more to the inherent nature of an experience and the qualitative aspects of that experience than, for example, to the number of such experiences one has or the size of the setting in which they occur. An emphasis on producing and participating in a large number of experiences tends to diminish the magical quality of each of them. Put another way, it is difficult to mass produce magic, fantasy, and dreams. Such mass production may be common in the movies, but "true" enchantment is difficult, if not impossible, to produce in settings designed to deliver large quantities of goods and services frequently and over great geographic spaces. The mass production of such things is virtually guaranteed to undermine their enchanted qualities.

No characteristic of rationalization is more inimical to enchantment than predictability. Magical, fantastic, dreamlike experiences are almost by definition unpredictable. Nothing will destroy an enchanted experience more easily than having it become predictable or having it recur in the same way time after time (see the 1993 movie *Groundhog Day,* as well as the 2017 Broadway play of the same name).

Both control and the nonhuman technologies that produce control tend to be inimical to enchantment. As a general rule, fantasy, magic, and dreams cannot be subjected to external controls; indeed, autonomy is much of what gives them their enchanted quality. Fantastic experiences can go anywhere; anything can happen. Such unpredictability clearly is not possible in a tightly controlled environment. For some people, tight and total control could be a fantasy, but for many, it would be more of a nightmare. Much the same can be said of nonhuman technologies. Cold, mechanical systems are usually the antithesis of the dream worlds associated with enchantment. Again, some people have fantasies associated with nonhuman technologies, but they, too, tend to be more nightmarish than dreamlike.

Digital consumption sites are cold, mechanical, highly McDonaldized systems. This is the case, if no other reason, because no humans are available to make them magical. I say this even though to those of my generation who came of age before computers and the Internet, digital consumption sites, indeed the Internet in general, seem quite magical. What seemed unbelievable (e.g., getting e-books instantly) became possible in the computer and Internet age. While that magic is still there to some degree, people tend to grow accustomed to it over time. The fact is that in the end the computer and the Internet offer what are perhaps the coldest, most mechanical, most McDonaldized locations in the contemporary world.

McDonaldization, then, is related to, if not inextricably intertwined with, disenchantment. A world without magic and mystery is another irrational consequence of increasing rationalization. For example, Christmas has lost much of its magic as it has been increasingly rationalized and commercialized. The magic of children's gifts may be lost because of their ability to do a Google search and find out how much (or little) they cost.

HEALTH AND ENVIRONMENTAL HAZARDS: A DAY'S CALORIES IN ONE FAST-FOOD MEAL

Progressive rationalization has threatened not only the fantasies but also the health, and perhaps the lives, of people. One example is the danger posed by the content of most fast food: a great deal of fat, cholesterol, salt, and sugar. Such meals are the last things Americans need, suffering as many of them do from obesity, high cholesterol levels, high blood pressure, and perhaps diabetes. In fact, there is much talk these days of an obesity epidemic (including children), and many observers place a lot of the blame on the fast-food industry—its foods and their contents—and its (continuing) emphasis on "supersizing" everything (even though they are now chary about using that term).[25]

The fast-food industry spends billions of dollars on advertising designed to convince people to consume its food. The processed food that it advertises has an addictive quality. According to a former Food and Drug Administration commissioner, the industry created food that was "energy-dense, highly stimulating, and went down easy. They put it on every street corner and made it mobile, and they made it socially acceptable to eat anytime and anyplace. They created a food carnival. . . [we're] used to self-stimulation every 15 minutes."[26]

The negative impact of fast food on health is not restricted to the United States. The growth of fast-food restaurants, as well as the emphasis on ever-larger portions, is helping to lead to escalating health problems (e.g., diabetes) in various parts of the world, including the Far East in general and Vietnam in particular.[27] A comparative study of 380 regions in Ontario, Canada, showed that the regions with more fast-food services were likely to have higher rates of acute coronary syndrome and a higher mortality rate from coronary disease.[28]

Fast-food restaurants contribute to the development of various health problems later in life by helping create poor eating habits in children. By targeting children, fast-food restaurants create not only lifelong devotees of fast food but also people addicted to diets high in salt, sugar, and fat.[29] An interesting study showed that the health of immigrant children deteriorates the longer they are in the United States, in large part because their diet begins to more closely resemble the junk-food diet of most American children.[30] In fact, Disney ended its long-term, cross-promotional relationship with McDonald's because of the growing concern about the link between fast food and childhood obesity.[31] A sociologist associated with the study of immigrant children stated, "The McDonaldization of the world is not necessarily progress when it comes to nutritious diets."[32]

Attacks against the fast-food industry's harmful effects on health have mounted over the years. Many of the franchises have been forced to respond by offering more and better salads, although the dressings for them are often loaded with salt and fat. They have also been forced to list nutritional information for all products in their stores and online. Still, most consumers never consult these lists and continue to order the typical McDonald's meal of a Big Mac, large fries, and a large vanilla shake, which totals 1,850 calories, with few of these calories having great nutritional value. The trend toward larger and larger portions has only increased the problem (McDonald's Big Breakfast with hotcakes and a large biscuit has 1,350 calories). Adding a 22-ounce Chocolate McCafé Shake (with 840 calories) to that McDonald's meal raises the total to more than 2,000 calories.[33] Burger King's Double Whopper alone has 900 calories (and 56 grams of fat).[34] Recommended calorie intake per day is less than 2,000 calories for women and just above 2,500 calories for men. Thus, just the typical McDonald's meal with the large shake meets the recommended daily calorie intake for women and is close to the recommended amount of daily calories for men.

McDonald's oatmeal is called a "bowl full of wholesome."[35] In itself, unadulterated oatmeal is a healthy food, but predictably McDonald's has done "everything it can to turn oatmeal into yet another bad choice."[36] One observer described the ingredients as "oats, sugar, sweetened dried fruit, cream and 11 weird ingredients you would never keep in your kitchen."[37] It contains more sugar than a Snickers candy bar. The observer wonders, why would McDonald's take a healthy food like oats "and turn it into expensive junk food? Why create a hideous concoction of 21 ingredients, many of them chemical and/or unnecessary?"[38] Although McDonald's (and others) has responded to its critics by changing its menu a bit and by offering publicly available nutritional facts about its products, it also reacted, predictably, with ad campaigns. In one ad, Ronald McDonald is seen as a "sports dude," juggling vegetables and dodging strawberries, without a burger in view. Experts, however, see such ads for what they are—propaganda—while McDonald's continues to push fatty, high-calorie foods and huge portion sizes. Given the epidemic of childhood obesity, the huge sums spent on the marketing of such foods to children have to be of particular concern.[39]

McDonaldization poses even more immediate health threats. Regina Schrambling links outbreaks of diseases such as salmonella to the rationalization of chicken production: "Salmonella proliferated in the poultry industry only after . . . Americans decided they wanted a chicken in every pot every night. But birds aren't like cars: you can't just speed up the factory line to meet demand. . . . Birds that are rushed to fryer size, then killed, gutted, and plucked at high speed in vast quantities are not going to be the cleanest food in the supermarket."[40] Schrambling also associates salmonella with the rationalized production of eggs, fruit, and vegetables.[41] Outbreaks of Escherichia coli, or E coli, infections have also been increasing in recent years, and the fast-food industry has taken note of this fact. Indeed, the first reported outbreak in the United States was traced to McDonald's in 1982. In 1997, Hudson Foods, a meatpacking company that supplied meat to McDonald's and Burger King, among others, was forced out of business because an outbreak of E. coli was traced to its frozen hamburg-ers.[42] Hamburger is a particular culprit because E. coli can be passed from steer to steer, and ultimately the hamburger from many steers, some of it infected, is mixed together. That meat is then turned into patties and frozen, and those frozen patties are distributed widely. The fast-food industry did respond to the danger of E. coli by cooking its hamburgers at a higher temperature to kill the bacterium, but E. coli is finding its way into an ever-larger number of highly McDonaldized foods (e.g., bagged salad and spinach).[43]

E. coli remains a great concern today, especially in McDonaldized foods of all types.[44] For example, Taco Bell experienced an outbreak of E. coli in 2006 that was traced to contaminated lettuce; another occurred in 2014 linked to clover sprouts eaten in several places, including Jimmy John's; then there was the health scare at Chipotle in 2016 that continues to threaten the survival of the company.[45] There is also evidence that the fast-food industry, and McDonaldization more generally, adversely affect psychological well-being. For example, calculability, especially the emphasis on speed, leads people to be impatient and to seek instant gratification. More specifically, people grow more impatient about financial mat-ters and less likely to take the time to savor their experiences.[46]

The fast-food industry has run afoul not only of nutritionists and epidemi-ologists but also of environmentalists; McDonald's and McDonaldization have produced a wide array of adverse effects on the environment. For example, the fast-food industry is directly linked to an enormous increase in meat production (projected to grow from 275 million tons in 2007 to 465 million tons in 2050)[47] and consumption. This increase in meat production is associated with a num-ber of environmental problems such as land degradation, climate change, water and air pollution, water shortage, and a decline in biodiversity.[48] Large-scale hog farms, for example, produce a huge amount of manure that ultimately finds its way into our waterways and then our drinking water; people have been made ill and women have had miscarriages as a result of drinking water contaminated in this way.[49] The dosing of factory-farmed animals with antibiotics may lead to bacteria that are resistant to antibiotics, thereby putting people at risk.[50]

Aquaculture creates a similar set of environmental problems and health risks to humans.[51] Another adverse environmental effect stems from the need to grow uni-form potatoes from which to create predictable French fries. The huge farms of the Pacific Northwest that now produce such potatoes rely on the extensive use of chemi-cals. In addition, the need to produce a perfect fry means that much of the potato is wasted, with the remnants either fed to cattle or used for fertilizer. The underground water supply in the area is now showing high levels of nitrates, which may be traceable to the fertilizer and to animal wastes.[52]

The fast-food industry produces an enormous amount of trash, some of which is nonbiodegradable. The litter from fast-food meals is a public eyesore. Innumerable square miles of forest are sacrificed to provide the paper needed each year by McDonald's alone.[53] Whole forests are being devoured by the fast-food industry. For a time, paper containers were replaced by Styrofoam and other products. However, the current trend is back to paper (and other biodegradable) products; Styrofoam, virtually indestructible, piles up in landfills, creating mountains of waste that endure there for years, if not forever. Overall, despite various efforts to deal with its worst abuses, the fast-food industry contributes to climate change (especially global warming), destruction of the ozone layer, depletion of natural resources, and destruction of natural habitats.

Of course, the above merely scratches the surface of the ecological problems associated with the McDonaldization of the fast-food industry. To take another specific example, great inefficiency and huge environmental effects are associated with the care and feeding of immense herds of cattle. That is, it would be far more efficient for us to consume the grain ourselves than it is to consume the much smaller amount of beef derived from cattle that are grain fed.

More generally, all of this is part of a fast-paced, highly mobile, and vast energy-consuming way of life that is having untold negative effects on the ecology of the world. While it is impossible to calculate exactly what this way of life contributes to the problem, there is no question that the fast-food industry and McDonaldized systems in general are significant causes of a number of potential global calamities.[54] The automobile assembly-line has been extraordinarily successful in churning out millions of cars a year. But all those cars have wreaked havoc on the environment. Their emissions pollute the air, soil, and water; an ever-expanding system of highways and roads has scarred the countryside; and we must not forget the thousands of people killed and the far greater number injured each year in traffic accidents. It was the widespread use of the automobile that helped lead to the fast-food industry, and the nature of fast-food restaurants (their locations and their drive-through windows) encourages ever-greater use of the automobile.

HOMOGENIZATION: IT'S NO DIFFERENT IN PARIS

Another irrational effect of McDonaldization is increased homogenization. Anywhere you go in the United States and, increasingly, throughout the world, you are likely to find the same products offered in the same way. The expansion of franchising across the United States means that people find little difference between regions and between cities.[55] On a global scale, travelers are finding more familiarity and less diversity. Exotic settings are increasingly likely sites for American fast-food chains and other McDonaldized settings.

Furthermore, in many nations, restaurant owners are applying the McDonald's model to native cuisine. In Paris, tourists may be shocked by the number of American fast-food restaurants but even more shocked by the incredible spread of indigenous forms, such as the fast-food croissanterie. One would have thought that the French, who seem to consider the croissant a sacred object, would resist rationalizing its manufacture and sale, but that is just what has happened.[56] The spread of such outlets throughout Paris indicates that many Parisians are willing to sacrifice quality for speed and efficiency. And, you may ask, if the Parisian croissant can be tamed and transformed into a fast-food success, what food is safe?

The spread of American and indigenous fast food causes less and less diversity from one setting to another. In the process, the human craving for new and diverse experiences is being limited, if not progressively destroyed. It is being supplanted by the desire for uniformity and predictability.

In general, McDonaldized institutions have been notably unsuccessful in creating new and different products. Please recall Ray Kroc's failures in this realm, notably the Hula Burger. Such systems excel instead at selling familiar products and services in shiny new settings or packages that can be easily replicated. For instance, the fast-food restaurant wraps that prosaic hamburger in bright packages and sells it in a carnival-like atmosphere that differs little from one locale to another. This point extends to many other manifestations of McDonaldization. For example, Jiffy Lube and its imitators sell people nothing more than the same old oil change and lube job.

Just as the franchises are leveling differences among goods and services, online consumption sites and online and mail-order catalogs are eliminating temporal and seasonal differences. When columnist Ellen Goodman received her Christmas catalog at the beginning of the fall, she offered this critique: "The creation of one national mail-order market has produced catalogues without the slightest respect for any season or region. Their holidays are now harvested, transported and chemically ripened on the way to your home. . . . I refuse to fast forward through the fall."[57] This, of course, was written before the coming of online catalogues, to say nothing of online consumption sites, where everything is available all the time.

There is unquestionably the greatest diversity of goods and services available online. However, because most of them are produced by McDonaldized firms using standardized techniques, most of them are themselves McDonaldized. Yet, the Internet is so vast and so diverse that the most unique, one-of-a-kind, non-McDonaldized goods and services can be found there. Many of these can be found on eBay, but especially on peer-to-peer sites such as Etsy, which matches sellers and buyers. On Etsy you can find handmade and vintage products, as well as unique manufactured products, that must be at least 20 years old to be listed on the site. Not long ago you could have bought, among other things, a $250,000 teapot.

This brings us to concepts of something and nothing developed in my book *The Globalization of Nothing.*[58] *Something* is defined as any social form (i.e., products, Internet sites, etc.) that is rich in distinctive content (e.g., the vintage teapot worth $250,000 mentioned above). *Nothing* is any social form that is largely devoid any distinctive content. Examples include not only a McDonald's hamburger, but also the mass-produced teapots for sale at the Dollar Store.

There is great diversity in what is for sale on Internet sites. Some of the products meet the definition of something, but the vast majority of them qualify as nothing. Furthermore, the sites themselves have grown very similar; offering the customer similar formats and similar ways of negotiating the sites (see Chapter 4). In other words, the sites themselves also increasingly meet the definition of nothing.

DEHUMANIZATION: GETTING HOSED AT "TROFF 'N' BREW"

The main reason to think of McDonaldization as irrational, and ultimately unreasonable, is that it tends to be dehumanizing. While McJobs are dehumanized, our focus in this section is the way McDonaldized systems, especially fast-food restaurants, dehumanize customers.

Fast-Food Restaurants: Like Eating From a Pig Trough

Illustrating dehumanization, by eating on a sort of assembly-line, diners are reduced to automatons rushing through a meal with little gratification derived from the dining experience or from the food itself. The best that can usually be said is that the meal is efficient and is over quickly. Typical diners at a McDonald's are described as "slouching toward a quick and forgettable meal."[59] Some customers might even feel as if they are being fed like livestock on an assembly-line. This point was made on TV a number of years ago in a *Saturday Night Live* parody of a small fast-food chain. In the skit, some young executives learn that a new fast-food restaurant called "Troff 'n' Brew" has opened, and they decide to try it for lunch. When they enter the restaurant, bibs are tied around their necks. They then discover what resembles a pig trough filled with chili and periodically refilled by a waitress scooping new supplies from a bucket. The customers bend over, stick their heads into the trough, and lap up the chili as they move along the trough, presumably making "high-level business decisions" en route. Every so often they come up for air and lap some beer from the communal "brew basin." After they have finished their "meal," they pay their bills "by the head." Since their faces are smeared with chili, they are literally "hosed off" before they leave the restaurant. The young executives are last seen being herded out of the restaurant, which is closing for a half hour so that it can be "hosed down." *Saturday Night Live* was clearly ridiculing the fact that fast-food restaurants tend to treat their customers like lower animals.

Customers (and workers) are also dehumanized by scripts and other efforts to make interactions uniform. "Uniformity is incompatible when human interactions are involved. Human interactions that are mass-produced may strike consumers as dehumanizing if the routinization is obvious or manipulative if it is not."[60] In other words, dehumanization occurs when prefabricated interactions take the place of authentic human relationships. Bob Garfield's critique of Walt Disney World provides another example of dehumanized customers: "I actually believed there was real fun and real imagination in store only to be confronted with an extruded, injection-molded, civil-engineered brand of fantasy, which is to say: no fantasy at all. . . . From the network of chutes and corrals channeling people into attractions, to *the chillingly programmed Stepford Wives demeanor of the employees,* to the compulsively litter-free grounds, to the generalized North Korean model Socialist Society sense of totalitarian order, to the utterly passive nature of the entertainment itself, Disney turns out to be the very antithesis of fantasy."[61] Thus, instead of being creative and imaginative, Disney World turns out to be an uncreative, unimaginative, and ultimately inhuman experience.

Fast-food restaurants and other McDonaldized settings also minimize contact among human beings. The relationships between employees and customers are fleeting at best. Because employees typically work part-time and stay only a few months, even regular customers rarely develop personal relationships with them. All but gone are the days when one got to know well a waitress at a diner or the short-order cook at a local "greasy spoon." There are fewer and fewer places where an employee knows who you are and knows what you are likely to order.

Fast being overwhelmed are what Ray Oldenburg calls "great good places," such as local cafés and taverns.[62] Contact time between workers and customers at the fast-food restaurant is also very short. It takes little time at the counter to order, receive the food, and pay for it. Both employees and customers are likely to feel rushed and to want to move customers on to their meal and employees to the next order.[63] There is virtually no time for customer and counter person to interact. This is even truer of the drive-through window where, thanks to the speedy service and the physical barriers, the server is even more distant.

Relationships among fast-food customers are largely curtailed as well. Although some McDonald's ads would have people believe otherwise, gone for the most part are the days when people met in the diner or cafeteria for coffee or a meal and lingered to socialize. Fast-food restaurants clearly do not encourage such socializing. The exception seems to be Starbucks, but as mentioned in Chapter 4, this is more myth than reality.

In some cases, fast-food restaurants have sought to restrict the amount of time a person can linger in the restaurant. In fact, the managers of one McDonald's in New York City called the police in early 2014 because elderly diners were spending too much time there and not buying enough food. In fact, a sign is now in place: "Please—No Loitering. 30 Minute Time Limit While Consuming Food."[64]

Family: The Kitchen as Filling Station

Fast-food restaurants also negatively affect the family, especially the so-called family meal.[65] The fast-food restaurant is not conducive to a long, leisurely, conversation-filled dinnertime. Furthermore, because of the fast-food restaurant, teens are better able to go out and eat with their friends, leaving the rest of the family to eat somewhere else or at another time. Of course, the drive-through window only serves to reduce further the possibility of a family meal. The family that gobbles its food while driving on to its next stop can hardly enjoy "quality time."

Here is the way one journalist describes what is happening to the family meal:

Do families who eat their suppers at the Colonel's, swinging on plastic seats, or however the restaurant is arranged, say grace before picking up a crispy brown chicken leg? Does dad ask junior what he did today as he remembers he forgot the piccalilli and trots through the crowds over to the counter to get some? Does mom find the atmosphere conducive to asking little Mildred about the problems she was having with third conjugation

French verbs, or would it matter since otherwise the family might have been at home chomping down precooked frozen food, warmed in the microwave oven and watching [television]?[66]

There is much talk these days about the disintegration of the family, and the fast-food restaurant may well be a crucial contributor to that disintegration. Conversely, the decline of the family creates ready-made customers for fast-food restaurants.

In fact, dinners at home may now be not much different from meals at the fast-food restaurant. Families long ago tended to stop having lunch and breakfast together. Today, the family dinner is following the same route. Even at home, the meal is probably not what it once was. Following the fast-food model, people have ever more options to "graze," "refuel," nibble on this, or snack on that rather than sit down at a formal meal. Also, because it may seem inefficient to do nothing but just eat, families are likely to watch television, play computer games, or text or tweet while they are eating; they might even split up and, plate in hand, head for their own computers.[67] The din, to say nothing of the lure, of dinnertime TV programs such as *Wheel of Fortune,* the "buzzes" and "beeps" associated with smartphones, and the distraction associated with sending and receiving text messages are likely to make it difficult for family members to interact with one another. We need to decide whether we can afford to lose the primary ritual of the communal meal: "If it is lost to us, we shall have to invent new ways to be a family. It is worth considering whether the shared joy that food can provide is worth giving up."[68]

Beyond the computer and the smartphone, a key technology in the destruction of the family meal has been the microwave oven and the vast array of microwavable foods it helped generate.[69] Some time ago, a *Wall Street Journal* poll indicated that Americans consider the microwave their favorite household product (today that would undoubtedly be replaced by the smartphone and the laptop computer). Said one consumer researcher, "It has made even fast-food restaurants not seem fast because at home you don't have to wait in line." As a general rule, consumers demand meals that take no more than 10 minutes to microwave, whereas in the past, people were more often willing to spend a half hour or even an hour cooking dinner. This emphasis on speed has, of course, brought with it lower quality, but people do not seem to mind this loss: "We're just not as critical of food as we used to be."[70] The speed of microwave cooking and the wide variety of microwavable foods make it possible for family members to eat at different times and places. With microwaveable products such as Hormel "Compleats" microwave meals and "Kid Cuisine" (the latter has similar products in frozen food), even children can "zap" their own meals. As a result, "Those qualities of the family meal, the ones that imparted feelings of security and well-being, might be lost forever when food is 'zapped' or 'nuked' instead of cooked."[71] The advances in microwave cooking continue. On some foods, plastic strips turn blue when the food is done. The industry has even promised strips that communicate cooking information directly to the microwave oven. "With cooking reduced to pushing a button, the kitchen may wind up as a sort of filling station. Family members will pull in, push a few buttons, fill up and leave. To clean up, all we need do is throw away plastic plates."[72] The family meal is not the only aspect of family life threatened by McDonaldization. For example, busy and exhausted parents are being advised that, instead of reading to their children at night, they should have them listen to audiotapes.[73]

Threats to the family meal have escalated in the computer age, especially with ever-present smartphones ringing and beeping throughout the meal. Many find it difficult not to respond, or at least peek at the identity of callers or at the content of text messages and e-mails.

Higher Education: McLectures, McColleges, and MOOCs

The modern university has, in various ways, become a highly irrational place. The impact of McDonaldization is clear, for example, in the way that students increasingly relate to professors as if they were workers in the fast-food industry. If the "service" in class is not up to their standards, students feel free to complain and even behave abusively toward their professors. Both students and faculty members are put off by schools' factory-like atmosphere. They may feel like automatons processed by the bureaucracy and computers, or feel like cattle run through a meat-processing plant. In other words, education in such settings can be a dehumanizing experience.

The "massification" of the university with hordes of students, large and impersonal dorms, and huge lecture classes make getting to know other students difficult. The large lecture classes, constrained tightly by the clock, also make it virtually impossible to know professors personally (of course, even more true online); at best, students might get to know a graduate assistant teaching a discussion section. Grades (and students are obsessed by this quantifiable measure of education) might be derived from a series of machine-graded, multiple-choice exams and posted on Blackboard. Students may feel like little more than objects into which knowledge is poured as they move along an information-providing and degree-granting educational assembly-line. Professors are less likely to be tenured and more likely to be part-time employees ("McLecturers" at "McColleges"),[74] who are apt to be treated as disposable service workers by both the university and students.

Technological advances are leading to even greater irrationalities in education. The minimal contact between teacher and student is being limited further by advances such as taking online courses on one's own,[75] distance learning, computerized instruction, and teaching machines. In taking courses online without an instructor, we have reached the ultimate step in the dehumanization of education: the elimination of a human teacher and of human interaction between teacher and student. Said one historian, "Taking a course online, by yourself, is not the same as being in a classroom with a professor who can respond to you, present different viewpoints and push you to work a problem."[76] Many believe that the future of college (and even high school) education in the United States lies in the expansion of a relatively new online education system known as "Massive Open Online Education," producing "Massive Open Online Courses" (MOOCs). MOOCs are different from most other forms of online education because a student almost anywhere in the world can watch professors (often well-known international academic "stars") lecture and there can be interaction with them, or more likely with their assistants. In most cases, there is currently no charge to students for taking a MOOC, although it is likely that there will be charges in the future, as many of the organizations involved are profit oriented. The definition of a MOOC is to be found in its four elements:

- It is designed to enroll a *massive* number of students (early courses have had 100,000-plus students).

- Even though MOOCs are, at least so far, offered by traditional, even elite, universities (e.g., Stanford), they are *open* to anyone.

- MOOCs exist only *online* and are accessible to anyone in the world with access to a computer and the Internet.

- And, of course, their main function is to *educate*.

Some of the ideas behind MOOCs are traceable to the early 1960s. The first true MOOC began in 2008, but the big breakthrough came in 2011 with three Stanford University MOOCs each enrolling more than 100,000 students in nearly every country in the world. A corporation, Coursera (which claims almost 25 million students ("learners" or "Courserians"), over 2,000 courses, and 149 university "partners" as of mid 2017,[77] emerged out of the MOOCs at Stanford. Today other companies (Udacity, edX) and many other universities are offering MOOCs. There is a widespread feeling that MOOCs are going to spread rapidly and in many ways dramatically alter higher education. A major driving force is the increasing costs of traditional higher education and the fact that MOOCs are able to reach a far greater number of students at much lower cost (one instructor can teach those 100,000-plus students). MOOCs also use advanced modern technologies rather than traditional, and rather primitive, face-to-face interaction in small classes, or the far less personal large lectures, characteristic of traditional college education.

One MOOC begun in 2012 is an introduction to sociology taught by Professor Mitch Duneier at Princeton University and offered to about 40,000 students worldwide on Coursera.[78] Like all others involved in these early courses, Professor Duneier felt his way through the various aspects of the course. As in most of the early MOOCs, less than 5% of the students who began the course completed it and took the final exam. However, there was a great deal of student involvement, and Duneier found that, "within three weeks, I had more feedback on my sociological ideas than I'd had in my whole teaching career."[79] Feedback came through global exchanges on an online discussion and a video chat room, as well as study groups that formed throughout the world (e.g., Kathmandu, Nepal). Duneier was also delighted to find that he could discuss highly sensitive sociological topics such as the lack of public restrooms for those who sold things on the street (a topic that Duneier wrote about in his famous sociological monograph, *Sidewalk*[80]). Despite these outcomes, as a result of rising criticisms—especially the low completion rate of students and objections by faculty members because of the threats posed to their jobs—MOOCs seem to have passed their peak; Duneier himself abandoned his involvement in it.

An underlying criticism of MOOCs is the fact that they serve to further McDonaldize higher education. It will be difficult, if not impossible, to avoid McDonaldization with MOOCs. In fact, there is a far higher level of McDonaldization on MOOCs than in a variety of traditional educational settings that are, themselves, increasingly highly McDonaldized. Why?

For one thing, while it is possible to invent each MOOC anew every semester, there will be a strong tendency to develop a script that can be reused, perhaps modified slightly, each year. To provide *predictability* in the evaluation of students, detailed "rubrics," or standardized scoring systems, will be created, provided to students, and used to evaluate them. The more standardized and detailed the rubric, the less room for unpredictability, and for creativity, on the part of both students and teachers. MOOCs will tend to be prepackaged systems with a series of short segments (often no more than 8 to 12 minutes of lecture), embedded questions, and immediate (albeit automatic) feedback. In addition, as MOOCs evolve, they are going to require higher and higher production values to rival those in the movies, on TV, or in Internet performances of one kind or another. Once corporations invest serious amounts of money in techniques to improve the quality of MOOCs, there will be a strong interest in using those courses over and over in order to maximize the return on investment. Furthermore, MOOCs are likely to be videotaped, or otherwise recorded, so that each class can be repeated semester after semester. Even if this were to be resisted at the major universities (e.g., Stanford) and by the academic stars (like Duneier) most likely, at least at the present, to teach these classes, the classes would still be recorded so that they could be used, probably for a charge, at lesser colleges and universities. This would be highly *predictable* with each academic setting that uses the prerecorded classes getting exactly the same content. While some interactive elements could be added to any prerecorded class, it would not even have the limited spontaneity of live MOOCs.

The *efficiency* of many McDonaldized systems, including MOOCs, is heightened by substituting nonhuman for human technology. In the case of MOOCs, this is especially clear in the need to use computer-graded exams rather than more subjective essay exams graded by instructors. Efficiency is also increased in McDonaldized systems by prosumption, in this case by "putting students (the customers) to work." In the case of education in general, and MOOCs especially, there is a strong tendency to have the "customers" in the educational system, the students, do work performed by teachers in other contexts. For example, it is impossible for MOOC instructors to respond to thousands of online comments and questions. Instead, through the use of "crowdsourcing" (a kind of prosumption), students may be allowed to vote up or down on each question and comment. Based on student voting, instructors can focus on those issues that are considered important by the crowd; rather than the instructor, the class does the work of deciding what's important.[81] After the video presentation of a lecture, much of the educational process is left to the students either on their own or through in-person or online groups and other forms of interaction. The best example of this is the grading process. In classes of 100,000 students, or more, instructors, no matter how many assistants they might have, are not going to be able to do the grading. Thus, much of the grading is left up to the students themselves (more prosumption). Each student's exam or paper might be read by, say, five other students with the student's grade being the average of the five evaluations.

The major irrationality associated with MOOCs is that they tend to limit, if not eliminate, the human processes that lie at the heart of the educational process. In his work on British education, Wilkinson argues,[82] following up on some of my ideas, that the way to do this is to focus on the everyday, face-to-face, activities of teaching rather than developing large-scale systems—like MOOCs—to create a meaningful educational experience. As Wilkinson puts it, the answer lies in finding ways of "making 'excellence' enjoyable, engaging and rewarding for both children and education workers."[83] In my view, the solution lies in focusing on everyday activities of education, making them not only the center of concern but where the true spectacle of education—excellent teachers finding new and exciting ways to educate students—is to be found. The problem with MOOCs from this perspective is that they move in exactly the opposite direction in focusing on creating a new system of education rather than working within the traditional system of everyday face-to-face education. This is where excellent teachers engage with students in collectively finding what works for a specific issue at any given moment. MOOCs lack that direct contact, and when classes are prerecorded, there is little or no possibility for creative, mutual engagement between teacher and student.

There are a variety of other irrationalities associated with MOOCs beyond the fact that such a small percentage of students complete courses. One is the difficulties involved in creating web-based courses that have the production values that students are accustomed to in movies, videos, and online content (although one instructor has figured out "how to make PowerPoint dance").[84] Another is that the requirements of being a good teacher mediated by the computer and the Internet are different from those required in the classroom (and few are trained, or have any experience, in teaching in this way). For many, it will be a difficult if not impossible transition. However, some will master this medium, and they will become teaching superstars who earn large salaries and may even be offered shares in the company.[85] Such professors will reverse the historic tendency for elite universities to reward professors for their publications and may discount their teaching prowess. Then, as pointed out above, there is the issue of evaluating the work of thousands, potentially many thousands, of students. This will overwhelm the instructor, even with many assistants and having the students evaluate themselves.

Yet to be determined is how students can earn degrees through MOOCs, as well as how colleges will be able to collect fees and tuition and earn profits from what will ultimately be an expensive undertaking.[86] In terms of the latter, venture capitalists seem to think that the money will be there because they are investing millions in MOOCs. One then needs to worry about the nature and quality of an educational system controlled by capitalists. Finally, there is the concern that MOOCs will lead to an even more stratified educational system. On the one hand, students in less developed countries, and in community colleges and lower-tier colleges and universities in the United States, will be exposed to elite educators and courses, thereby democratizing education and reducing inequality in education. For example, one Harvard professor has created a course that will be viewed by about 130,000 students enrolled in the University of Phoenix.[87] On the other hand, those in less developed countries and lower-tier educational institutions will be increasingly, if not totally, reliant on MOOCs and similar modes of delivering mass education (e.g., Udemy, which allows professors to put their own courses online). In contrast, students in developed countries, especially in their elite universities, will continue to get highly expensive and more effective face-to-face education.

Harvard Business School is seeking to have it both ways. It is seeking to retain its elite status and Master of Business Administration (MBA) program by not turning it into a MOOC. Rather, it has added a pre- MBA "HBX" program based on online courses.[88] Lesser colleges and universities without such elite programs are not as likely to be able to have it both ways, and more likely to move increasingly in the direction of MOOCs and other online offerings.

Health Care: You're Just a Number

For the physician, the process of rationalization carries with it a series of dehumanizing consequences. At or near the top of the list is the shift in control away from the physician and toward rationalized structures and institutions. In the past, private practitioners had a large degree of control over their work, with the major constraints being peer control as well as the needs and demands of patients. In rationalized medicine, external control increases and shifts to social structures and institutions. Not only is the physician more likely to be controlled by these structures and institutions, but he or she is also constrained by managers and bureaucrats who are not themselves physicians. The ability of physicians to control their own work lives is declining. As a result, many physicians are experiencing increased job dissatisfaction and alienation. Some are even turning toward unionization such as the Union of American Physicians and Dentists.[89] From the patients' viewpoint, the rationalization of medicine causes a number of irrationalities. The drive for efficiency can make people feel like products on a medical assembly-line. The effort to increase predictability will likely lead patients to lose personal relationships with physicians and other health professionals, because rules and regulations lead physicians to treat all patients in essentially the same way. This is also true in hospitals, where instead of seeing the same nurse regularly, a patient may see many different nurses. The result, of course, is that nurses never come to know their patients as individuals.

Another dehumanizing development is the advent (at least in the United States) of "hospitalists," doctors who practice exclusively in hospitals. Now instead of seeing their personal physician (if they still have such a doctor), hospitalized patients are more likely to be seen by physicians whom they probably have never seen and with whom they have no personal relationship.[90] As a result of the emphasis on calculability, the patient is more likely to feel like a number in the system rather than a person. Minimizing time and maximizing profits may lead to a decline in the quality of health care provided to patients. Like physicians, patients are apt to be controlled increasingly by large-scale structures and institutions, which will probably appear to them as distant, uncaring, and impenetrable. Finally, patients are increasingly likely to interact with technicians and impersonal technologies. In fact, because more and more technologies may be purchased at the drug store, patients can test themselves and thereby cut out human contact with both physicians and technicians.

The ultimate irrationality of this rationalization would be the unanticipated consequences of a decline in the quality of medical practice and a deterioration in the health of patients. Increasingly rational medical systems, with their focus on lowering costs and increasing profits, may reduce the quality of health care, especially for the poorest members of society. At least some people may become sicker, and perhaps even die, because of the rationalization of medicine. Health in general may even decline. These possibilities can be assessed only in the future as the health care system continues to rationalize. Because the health care system will continue to rationalize, health professionals and their patients may need to learn how to control rational structures and institutions to ameliorate their irrational consequences.

Yet to be determined is the effect of the Affordable Care Act ("Obamacare"), which took effect in 2014. As a centralized and bureaucratized system, there was great fear that it would lead to a dramatic increase in the irrationalities associated with the McDonaldization of health care. President Trump and other Republican leaders promised to do away with Obamacare. However, as of mid-2017, their efforts had failed and the Affordable Care Act remains in force. This is the case in spite of ongoing difficulties related to funding, increasing cost, and insufficient choices in many parts of the United States because of the lack of involvement of medical insurance companies or the fact that they have dropped out of the program. It remains to be seen whether, and if so how, the Affordable Care Act will be changed and what its irrationalities will prove to be.

DEHUMANIZED DEATH: DYING AMIDST MACHINES AND STRANGERS

Then, as introduced in Chapter 4, there is the dehumanization of the very human process of death. People are increasingly likely to die (as they are likely to be born) impersonally, in the presence of total strangers: "A patient is every day less a human being and more a complicated challenge in intensive care to the consulting superspecialists . . . he is a case. . . . Doctors thirty years his junior call him by his first name. Better that, than to be called by the name of the disease or the number of the bed."[91]

This dehumanization is part of the process, according to Philippe Aries, by which the modern world has "banished death."[92] Here is the way Sherwin B. Nuland describes our need to rationalize death: "In recent generations, we have . . . created the *method of modern dying* . . . in modern hospitals, where it can be hidden, cleansed of its organic blight, and finally packaged for modern burial. We can now deny the power not only of death but of nature itself."[93] Similarly, Jean Baudrillard has written of "designer deaths," paralleling "designer births": "To streamline death at all costs, to varnish it, cryogenically freeze it, or condition it, put make-up on it, 'design' it, to pursue it with the same relentlessness as grime, sex, bacteriological or radioactive waste. The makeup of death . . . 'designed' according to the purest laws of . . . international marketing."[94] Closely related to the growing power of physicians and hospitals over death, nonhuman technologies play an increasing role in the dying process. Technology has blurred the line between life and death by, for example, keeping people's hearts going even though their brains are dead. Medical personnel have also come to rely on technology to help them decide when it is acceptable to declare death. What could be more dehumanizing than dying alone amid machines rather than with loved ones?

When people are asked how they wish to die, most respond with something like this: quickly, painlessly, at home, surrounded by family and friends. Ask them how they expect to die, and the fear emerges: in the hospital, all alone, on a machine, in pain.[95] Here is the way Nuland describes dehumanized death amid a sea of nonhuman technologies:

> The beeping and squealing monitors, the hissings of respirators and pistoned mattresses, the flashing multicolored electronic signals—the whole technological panoply is background for the tactics by which we are deprived of the tranquility we have every right to hope for, and separated from those few who would not let us die alone. By such means, biotechnology created to provide hope serves actually to take it away, and to leave our survivors bereft of the unshattered final memories that rightly belong to those who sit nearby as our days draw to a close.[96]

THE IRRATIONALITIES OF McJOBS: JUST HAND THE BAG OUT

There is nothing inherently irrational about McJobs, including the fact that those in them do their work in an efficient manner. It can be quite satisfying to work efficiently. This is true not only of efficiency in general, but also of the specific aspects of efficiency discussed in Chapters 3 and 5. For example, a streamlined work process makes for fewer wasted motions. Simplified products are easier for workers to deal with than those that are highly complex. McWorkers generally like the fact that customers are put to work in McDonaldized settings because it reduces the demands placed on them (although it might cost some of them their jobs). Conversely, inefficiency can frustrate workers and make their work lives more difficult by, for example, having to handle poorly organized tasks. Inefficiency on the part of workers might well lead to difficulties dealing with angry customers frustrated by their inefficiency.

Nonetheless, there are various irrationalities associated with the emphasis on *efficiency,* especially when it is pushed to ever-higher levels. For one thing, efficiency is generally built into systems like Burger King's assembly-line. For another, greater efficiency tends to be associated with progressive increases in the pace of work (see below). McWorkers may be forced to work faster and faster with no increase in pay. This, in turn, leaves them little time to think, let alone to express their creativity on the job. This can leave McWorkers feeling unfulfilled in their work. As a result, their employers are not able to get the benefits that could be derived from their on-the-job creativity.

There is also nothing inherently wrong with an emphasis on *calculability* from the perspective of those who hold McJobs. An emphasis on things that can be quantified makes it easier for workers to know what they need to do, how close they are to accomplishing their tasks, how much more they need to do, and so on. Conversely, more ambiguous qualitative measures make such assessments more difficult. When qualitative criteria are employed, it is difficult for employees to know whether their work is good enough, whether it is done quickly enough, and so on. Many of those who hold McJobs are likely to prefer knowing how they are doing on the basis of quantitative measures to the ambiguity of qualitative criteria.

Among the irrationalities associated with an emphasis on calculability is that it, like efficiency, tends to be associated with speed and the pace of work. It tends to lead to systems where "faster is better!" We have already discussed the emphasis on how fast hamburgers can be served at McDonald's and how quickly customers can be processed at Burger King, and the need to "hustle" and "do it" at Domino's (see Chapter 5). Such emphases put great pressure on McWorkers, and such pressure tends to be associated with a decline in the quality of what they do. For example, a customer might get a Filet-O-Fish rather than a Big Mac, or a hamburger might be missing the requisite pickle slices. This not only means poorer-quality service and products for consumers, but the decline in quality as a result of the emphasis on speed can also threaten the workers who may be reprimanded and perhaps ultimately fired for poor-quality work, as well as customers being irate because of it.

As is the case with calculability, there is basically nothing wrong with *predictability* from the perspective of those who hold McJobs. Ultimately, predictability means that the workers know what is expected of them and what they are to do when they are on the job. For example, the scripts that McWorkers are expected to follow make it far easier for them to interact with customers than if they had to create new dialogue with each interaction. Similarly, engaging in the same actions, following the same steps over and over, also serves to make work easier. For example, following a prescribed series of steps for grilling a hamburger is much easier for those who work at the grill than inventing a new or different technique each time a burger is prepared. The same is true of serving a product that looks the same each time and has the same basic elements. Even wearing a uniform and adhering to rules on what can and cannot be worn is easier than needing to decide each day what outfit to wear to work. McWorkers are likely to appreciate the fact that predictability means that there is less likely to be unpleasantness and even danger on the job. Customers tend to have the same sense of predictability as do employees in McDonaldized settings. As a result, if they get what they expect, they are likely to treat employees well and to pose no threat to them. Reduced or eliminated are such things as verbal abuse of employees or even physical assaults on them.

The irrationality here from the perspective of those who hold McJobs is the sheer boredom associated with saying the same things, engaging in the same actions, and offering the same products and services hour after hour, day after day. These mind-numbing routines may be preferred, even welcomed, by some workers, but many others are led to quit in an attempt to find more interesting work. This tends to produce a high turnover rate in many McDonaldized settings, which is, in itself, an irrationality of these rational systems. Among the irrationalities of excessive employee turnover are the loss of capable employees, confusion on the job associated with a constantly changing workforce, the need to train (however minimally) new employees, and the time needed for them to learn and be comfortable with the routines associated with the job.

Much of the above, in terms of both rationality and irrationality, stems from the *control* exercised by McDonaldized organizations over their employees. It is rational for an organization to want to control its employees, especially those who occupy the lower reaches of the organization. It is also rational to use that control to increase efficiency, calculability, and predictability. That control can be exercised by other human beings in supervisory positions, by nonhuman technologies, or even by the threat to use nonhuman technologies to control, even replace, workers. However, there is a delicate balance here in that an adequate level of control can produce positive outcomes for the organization and most of its employees, but excessive control can help to create many of the irrationalities mentioned here. It can also alienate many employees and create a great deal of job dissatisfaction and resentment to management and the organization. This, in turn, can cause employees to work more slowly and less efficiently, to sabotage the work process, to organize collectively (that is to unionize), and perhaps to quit the job altogether.[97] In fact, the fast-food industry has the highest turnover rate—approximately 300% a year[98]—of any industry in the United States. That means that the average fast-food worker lasts only about four months; the entire workforce of the fast-food industry turns over approximately three times a year.

Although the simple and repetitive nature of the jobs makes it relatively easy to replace workers who leave, an excessive turnover rate is undesirable from both the organization's and the employee's perspective. From an organization's point of view, it would clearly be better to keep most (but not all) employees longer. The costs involved in turnover, such as hiring and training, greatly increase with extraordinarily high turnover rates. In addition, failure to use employees' skills in simple, repetitive jobs is irrational for the organization. If the jobs were more complex and demanding, it could obtain much more from its employees for the money (however negligible) it pays them.

Just as it is dehumanizing to be a customer in a McDonaldized system, it is also *dehumanizing* to work in such systems. For example, employees who hold McJobs can be seen as handling a series of "McTasks." One of many McTasks at McDonald's is known as HBO—"Hand Bag Out."[99] Doing such simple McTasks over and over clearly does not need the full range of human skills and abilities. Forced to make do with McTasks, many of those employed in McJobs feel, and are, dehumanized by the nature of their work.

Other characteristics of McJobs also serve to dehumanize work in fast-food restaurants. For example, just as customers are unlikely to develop relationships with employees, employees are unlikely to develop fully formed, that is fully human, relationships with customers. Other potential relationships for employees in fast-food restaurants are also limited greatly. Because they tend to remain on the job for only a few months, satisfying personal relationships among employees are unlikely to develop. More permanent employment helps foster long-term relationships on the job, and workers with more job stability are likely to get together after work hours and on weekends. Also hampering the ability of employees to develop personal relationships with other employees is the temporary and part-time character of jobs in fast-food restaurants, and other McDonaldized settings.

The automobile assembly-line is well known for the way it dehumanizes life on a day-to-day basis for those who work on it. Although Henry Ford felt, as we saw earlier (see Chapter 6), that he personally could not do the kind of repetitive work required on the assembly-line, he believed that most people, with their limited mental abilities and aspirations, could adjust to it quite well. Ford said, "I have not been able to discover that repetitive labour injures a man in any way. . . . The most thorough research has not brought out a single case of a man's mind being twisted or deadened by the work."[100] Objective evidence of the destructiveness of the assembly-line, however, is found in the high rates of absenteeism, tardiness, and turnover among employees. More generally, most people seem to find assembly-line work highly alienating. Here is the way one worker describes it: "I stand in one spot, about a two—or three—[foot] area, all night. The only time a person stops is when the line stops. We do about thirty-two jobs per car, per unit, forty-eight units an hour, eight hours a day. Thirty-two times forty-eight times eight. Figure it out, that's how many times I push that button."[101]

Another worker offers a similar view: "What's there to say? A car comes, I weld it; a car comes, I weld it; a car comes, I weld it. One hundred and one times an hour." Others get quite sarcastic about the nature of the work: "There's a lot of variety in the paint shop. . . . You clip on the color hose, bleed out the color and squirt. Clip, bleed, squirt; clip, bleed, squirt, yawn; clip, bleed, squirt, scratch your nose."[102] Another assembly-line worker sums up the dehumanization he feels: "Sometimes I felt just like a robot. You push a button and you go this way. You become a mechanical nut."[103] Alienation affects not only those who work on the automobile assembly-line but also people in the wide range of settings built, at least in part, on the principles of the assembly-line.[104] In our McDonaldized society, the assembly-line has implications for many of us and for many different settings. The demands in the meatpacking industry (which is heavily dependent on the business provided by fast-food restaurants) are responsible, at least in part, for increasing dehumanization—inhuman work in inhumane conditions. Workers are reduced to fast-moving cogs in the assembly-line killing and butchering of animals. They are forced to perform repetitive and physically demanding tasks on animals that may, at least initially, not even be dead. They are often covered in, and forced to stand in, pools of blood. They wield very sharp knives at great speed in close proximity to other workers. The result is an extraordinarily high injury (and even death) rate, although many injuries go unreported out of fear of being fired for being injured and unable to perform at peak levels. Because they are often undocumented immigrants, workers are almost totally at the whim of a management free to hire and fire them at will. Management is also able to ignore the horrid working conditions confronted by these powerless employees or able to make those conditions even more horrific.[105]

DIGITAL SITES: DEHUMANIZATION AND OTHER IRRATIONALITIES

It is clear that dehumanization reaches something of a peak on the Internet because there are, as discussed many times in this book, generally no employees there with whom consumers can communicate. Consumers are left to deal with nonhuman, impersonal sites. However, there are certainly many examples of greater dehumanization as a result of McDonaldization—the Holocaust and its concentration camps come to mind. No one dies because of the impersonal interaction with websites, but nonetheless because one is interacting with an increasing number of "dumb," nonhuman websites, interaction on the Internet is highly and increasingly dehumanized. The next logical step would be for the consumers' robots to interact with website bots and, in the process, completely dehumanize the digital world.

In addition to the dehumanization associated with dealing with nonhuman sites, the digital world has a number of other irrational consequences for human interaction. While we will focus on the irrationalities here, it is also the case that the use of, and interaction in, the digital world brings with it many advantages (e.g., breaking down barriers, increasing the breadth of interaction). Many people would be loath to give up such advantages in order to deal with these irrationalities. Among the irrationalities associated with the digital world are the following:

- People can "become so used to the ease and convenience of connecting digitally that they feel anxious, lost, and unmoored when disconnected."[106]

- The digital world can lead to a decline in "sensible" actions such as planning and paying attention to details.

- While various online activities are entertaining, there is the fear that people, especially the young, come to have the unreasonable expectation of constant and instant entertainment, that they will never to be bored.

- The ability to multitask online has many advantages, but it can lead to a decline in the attention span of those who do it routinely.

- There are a variety of stresses associated with life online such as information overload, having too many choices, and the constant fear of missing out on something important.

- While digital technologies, especially cell phones, are useful in emergencies, they can also create a situation where more and more events begin to seem like emergencies.

- Use of digital technologies can deteriorate into dependency on, and addiction to, these technologies.

- Excessive time spent online can adversely affect people both psychologically and physically.

DEALING WITH IRRATIONALITY: OF VELVET, RUBBER, OR IRON CAGES?

What can people do to deal with an increasingly McDonaldized world, especially its many irrationalities? The answer to that question depends, at least in part, on their attitudes toward McDonaldization. Many people view a McDonaldized world as a "velvet cage." To them, McDonaldization represents not a threat but nirvana. Weber's metaphor of an iron cage of rationalization communicates a sense of coldness, hardness, and great discomfort. But many people like, even crave, McDonaldization and welcome its proliferation. This is certainly a viable position and one especially likely to be adopted by those who have lived only in McDonaldized societies and who have been reared since the advent of the McDonaldized world. McDonaldized society, the only world they know, represents their standard of good taste and high quality. They can think of nothing better than a world uncluttered with too many choices and options. They like the predictability of many aspects of their lives. They relish an impersonal world in which they interact with human and nonhuman automatons. They seek to avoid, at least in the McDonaldized portions of their world, close human contact. Such people probably represent an increasingly large portion of the population.

As in many other instances, Internet sites represent in many ways and for many, especially those raised and skilled in the digital world, the ultimate velvet cage. This is especially true of the desire for an impersonal world. If one wants, one can live much of one's life on the Internet with no tiresome and inefficient human contact. Digital systems work in a highly predictable way, assuming one knows how to use them. It is true that there are infinitely more choices available to the consumer on the Internet, but the user can also choose to ignore many of them. In the political climate in the Trump era, a good example is to be found where many people opt for only those websites (and TV channels) that espouse their point of view. For consumers faced with infinite choice, a similar decision can be made to focus on one or a few sites. More likely, one can use bots to simplify the process of making one's way through a variety of sites and the nearly infinite number of choices available on them. Thus, the Internet has provided (too) many choices and options, but it has also provided McDonaldized methods of navigating one's way through them.

For many other people, McDonaldization is a "rubber cage," the bars of which can be stretched to allow adequate means for escape. Such people dislike many aspects of McDonaldization but find others quite appealing. Like those who see themselves in a velvet cage, these people may like the efficiency, speed, predictability, and impersonality of McDonaldized systems and services. Such people may be busy and therefore will appreciate obtaining a meal (or some other McDonaldized service) efficiently. However, they also recognize the costs of McDonaldization and therefore seek to escape it when they can. Its efficiencies may even enhance their ability to escape from it. That is, getting a fast meal may allow them the time to luxuriate in other, nonrationalized activities.

These people are the types who, on weekends and vacations, go into the wilderness to camp the old-fashioned way; who go mountain climbing, spelunking, fishing, hunting (without elaborate equipment), antique hunting, and museum browsing; and who search out traditional restaurants, inns, and bed-and-breakfasts. Such people try to humanize their telephone answering machines with creative messages such as "Sorry, ain't home, don't break my heart when you hear the tone."[107] Although the bars may seem like rubber, they are still there. For example, a company that sells prerecorded, humorous messages now rationalizes the escape route for those who prefer creative answering machine messages. Thus, people can buy a machine with an impressionist imitating Humphrey Bogart: "Of all the answering machines in the world, you had to call this one."[108] Similarly, for many, home baking now includes the use of bread-baking machines, which do not produce a very good loaf but "do everything but butter the bread."[109]

The Internet is clearly such a rubber cage. On the one hand it is a cage in which people spend huge amounts of time and from which they find it difficult to extricate themselves. On the other hand, there is within that cage an infinite number of choices. However, the making of those choices still takes place in the context of the rubber cage of the Internet. Of course, people possess the ability to truly stretch the rubber bars of that cage and leave the Internet any time they wish or even—heaven forbid—turn off their computers.

A third type of person believes that the McDonaldized cage is made of iron. If the impregnability of the cage has not led such a person to surrender completely, he or she is likely to be deeply offended by the process but to see few, if any, ways out. Unlike the second type of person, these individuals see escape routes (if they see them at all) that provide only temporary respites, soon to fall under the sway of McDonaldization. They share the dark and pessimistic outlook of Max Weber—and myself—viewing the future as a "polar night of icy darkness and hardness."[110] These are the severest critics of McDonaldization and the ones who see less and less place for themselves in modern society.[111]

There are those who see the Internet in this way as an iron cage from which they cannot escape. Many are increasingly hooked on, if not dependent on, the

Internet and to whom escape seems unthinkable. For example, although I worry about the enslaving nature of life on the Internet, I am able to communicate—simultaneously verbally and visually—with my children and grandchildren in Singapore via WhatsApp (Skype is another alternative) and to do so, amazingly, free of charge. The nondigital alternatives available to me are far less satisfying. Snail mail includes no audio-visual contact and is slow and comparatively expensive. A telephone call is much more expensive and offers no visual contact. So, if I want to have meaningful contact with my family in Singapore, I must do so via WhatsApp or some other Internet-based system.

CONCLUSION

Those who view McDonaldization as creating a velvet or a rubber cage are unlikely to see the need to take much, if any, action to deal with its irrationalities (and they may not even think of them as irrationalities). It is those who see it as an iron cage who are likely to be the ones most likely to be highly motivated to take such action. After all, being locked in such a cage is apt to be infuriating to most people. In previous editions of this book I dealt, at length, with actions that groups, organizations, and individuals have taken to deal with the problems associated with McDonaldization. However, I have omitted that discussion from this edition partly due to space constraints, but mainly because those actions seem to have abated dramatically. Most of the groups and organizations I wrote about in the past have declined and grown increasingly less important. There is also less and less evidence that many people are aware of the irrationalities associated with McDonaldization. There is even less individual action to deal with McDonaldization and its irrationalities. McDonaldization seems evermore entrenched and most people seem to have little interest in opposing it in any substantial way.

Yet, McDonaldization and its many irrationalities, especially those created by its iron cage character, *must* be resisted. This is the case because, if for no other reason, without some counter forces, the bars of the cage are likely to grow thicker and stronger. As a result, the problems associated with McDonaldization are likely to grow in strength and scope in the future. Faced with Max Weber's iron cage and the image of a future dominated by the polar night of icy darkness and hardness that he feared so much, I hope that, if nothing else, you will consider the words of the poet Dylan Thomas: "Do not go gentle into that good night. . . . Rage, rage against the dying of the light."[112]

NOTES

Preface

1. George Ritzer. "The McDonaldization of Society." *Journal of American Culture* 6 (1983): 100–107.
2. Deborah Lupton. *The Quantified Self: A Sociology of Self-Tracking.* Cambridge: Polity Press, 2016.
3. See, for example, George Ritzer. "Prosumer Capitalism." *Sociological Quarterly* 56 (2015): 413–445; George Ritzer and Nathan Jurgenson. "Production, Consumption, Prosumption: The Nature of Capitalism in the Age of the Digital 'Prosumer.'" *Journal of Consumer Culture* 10 (2010): 13–36.
4. George Ritzer. *The McDonaldization Thesis.* London: Sage, 1998.
5. George Ritzer. *The Globalization of Nothing.* Thousand Oaks, CA: Pine Forge Press, 2004 (2nd edition published in 2007 as *The Globalization of Nothing 2*); George Ritzer. *Globalization: A Basic Text.* Oxford: Wiley-Blackwell, 2010 (2nd ed., 2015, with Paul Dean).

Chapter 1

1. George Ritzer and Paul Dean. *Globalization: A Basic Text.* 2nd ed. Malden, MA: Wiley-Blackwell, 2015.
2. For a similar but narrower viewpoint to the one expressed here, see Benjamin R. Barber. "Jihad vs. McWorld." *The Atlantic Monthly,* March 1992, pp. 53–63; and also by Barber, *Jihad vs. McWorld.* New York: Times Books, 1995. For a more popular discussion of a similar conflict, see Thomas L. Friedman. *The Lexus and the Olive Tree: Understanding Globalization.* New York: Farrar, Straus, and Giroux, 1999.
3. Since the publication of the first edition of this book in 1993, the term *McDonaldization* has, at least to some degree, become part of the academic and public lexicon. For example, among the academic works are Dennis Hayes and Robin Wynyard, eds. *The McDonaldization of Higher Education.* Westport, CT: Bergin and Garvey, 2002; John Drane. *The McDonaldization of the Church: Consumer Culture and the Church's Future.* London: Smyth and Helwys, 2012; C. Christopher Smith, John Pattison, and Jonathan Wilson-Hartgrove. *Slow Church.* Downers Grove, IL: Inter Varsity Press, 2014; John Drane. *After McDonaldization: Mission, Ministry, and Christian Discipleship in an Age of Uncertainty.* Grand Rapids, MI: Baker Academic, 2008; Bridgette Jackson. *Drive Thru Teachers: The McDonaldization of the Classroom Teacher.* Suwanee, GA: Faith Books and More, 2012; Donna Dustin. *The McDonaldization of Social Work.* Farnham, Surrey, UK: Ashgate, 2008; Robert Dirks. *Come & Get It: McDonaldization and the Disappearance of Local Food From a Central Illinois Community.* Bloomington, IL: McLean County Historical Society, 2011; Barry Smart, ed. *Resisting McDonaldization.* London: Sage, 1999; Mark Alfino, John Caputo, and Robin Wynyard, eds.

McDonaldization Revisited. Westport, CT: Greenwood, 1998; a special issue of the Dutch journal *Sociale Wetenschappen* (vol. 4, 1996) devoted to McDonaldization; the essays in my *McDonaldization: The Reader,* 3rd ed. Thousand Oaks, CA: Sage, 2010; and a special issue (also edited by me) of the *American Behavioral Scientist* titled "McDonaldization: Chicago, America, the World" (October 2003). One also finds many mentions of McDonaldization in the popular media including, www.huffingtonpost.com/2014/04/24/mcdonalds-protest-art_n_4981799.html? utm_hp_ref=food&ir=Food

4. Alan Bryman has suggested the term *Disneyization,* which he defines in a parallel manner: "the process by which the principles of Disney theme parks are coming to dominate more and more sectors of American society as well as the rest of the world" (p. 26). See Alan Bryman. "The Disneyization of Society." *Sociological Review* 47 (February 1999): 25–47; and Alan Bryman. *The Disneyization of Society.* London: Sage, 2004.

5. Arthur Asa Berger. *Signs in Contemporary Culture: An Introduction to Semiotics,* 2nd ed. Salem, WI: Sheffield, 1999.

6. Max Weber. *Economy and Society.* Totowa, NJ: Bedminster, 1921/1968; Stephen Kalberg. "Max Weber's Types of Rationality: Cornerstones for the Analysis of Rationalization Processes in History." *American Journal of Sociology* 85 (1980): 1145–1179.

7. See Chapter 3 for a description of Uber that uses almost exactly these terms.

8. The origin of this choreography is well-illustrated in an early scene of *The Founder* where the McDonald brothers lead the workers in developing a routine for producing and serving fast food on an outline of a fast-food restaurant laid out on a tennis court.

9. Ian Mitroff and Warren Bennis. *The Unreality Industry: The Deliberate Manufacturing of Falsehood and What It Is Doing to Our Lives.* New York: Birch Lane, 1989, p. 142.

10. Melanie Warner. "McDonald's Revival Has Hidden Health Costs." *International Herald Tribune,* April 20, 2006.

11. Melanie Warner. "U.S. Restaurant Chains Find There Is No Too Much." *New York Times,* July 28, 2006.

12. Dana Boyd and Kate Crawford. "Critical Questions for Big Data." *Information, Communication and Society* 15, 2012: 662–679.

13. Martin Plimmer. "This Demi-Paradise: Martin Plimmer Finds Food in the Fast Lane Is Not to His Taste." *Independent* (London), January 3, 1998.

14. As we will see in Chapters 4 and 6, this increased control often comes from the substitution of nonhuman for human technology.

15. Robert J. Samuelson. "In Praise of McDonald's." *Washington Post,* November 1, 1989.

16. Edwin M. Reingold. "America's Hamburger Helper." *Time,* June 29, 1992.

17. I would like to thank my colleague, Stan Presser, for suggesting that I enumerate the kinds of advantages listed on these pages.

18. Alan Riding. "Only the French Elite Scorn Mickey's Debut." *New York Times,* April 13, 1992.

19. George Stauth and Bryan S. Turner. "Nostalgia, Postmodernism and the Critique of Mass Culture." *Theory, Culture and Society* 5 (1988): 509–526; Bryan S. Turner. "A Note on Nostalgia." *Theory, Culture and Society* 4 (1987): 147–156.

20. Lee Hockstader. "No Service, No Smile, Little Sauce." *Washington Post,* August 5, 1991.

21. Douglas Farah. "Cuban Fast Food Joints Are Quick Way for Government to Rally Economy." *Washington Post,* January 24, 1995.

22. In this sense, this resembles Marx's critique of capitalism. Marx was animated not by a romanticization of precapitalist society but, rather, by the desire to produce a truly human (communist) society on the base provided by capitalism. Despite this specific affinity to Marxist theory, this book is, as you will see, premised far more on the theories of Max Weber.

23. These concepts are associated with the work of social theorist Anthony Giddens. See, for example, *The Constitution of Society.* Berkeley: University of California Press, 1984.

24. Ray Kroc. *Grinding It Out.* New York: Berkeley Medallion Books, 1977; Stan Luxenberg. *Roadside Empires: How the Chains Franchised America.* New York: Viking, 1985; John F. Love. *McDonald's: Behind the Arches.* Toronto, ON: Bantam, 1986; Lisa Napoli. *Ray and Joan: The Man Who Made the McDonald's Fortune and the Woman Who Gave It Away.* New York: Dutton, 2016.

25. John F. Love. *McDonald's: Behind the Arches.* Toronto, ON: Bantam, 1986, p. 18.

26. Ibid., p. 20.

27. Thomas S. Dicke. *Franchising in America: The Development of a Business Method, 1840–1980.* Chapel Hill: University of North Carolina Press, 1992, pp. 2–3.

28. Taco Bell website: www.tacobell.com

29. Ray Kroc. *Grinding It Out.* New York: Berkeley Medallion Books, 1977, p. 8.

30. Max Boas and Steve Chain. *Big Mac: The Unauthorized Story of McDonald's.* New York: E. P. Dutton, 1976, pp. 9–10.

31. Ibid.

32. Ray Kroc. *Grinding It Out.* New York: Berkeley Medallion Books, 1977, pp. 96–97.

33. www.washingtonpost.com/lifestyle/magazine/whos-lovin-it/2011/08/12/gIQAoOVRuJ_story.html

34. John Vidal. *McLibel: Burger Culture on Trial.* New York: New Press, 1997, p. 34.

35. Wayne Huizenga played a similar role in the video business by taking over a chain developed by a Dallas entrepreneur and turning it into the Blockbuster empire. See David Altaner. "Blockbuster Video: 10 Years Running Family-Oriented Concept Has Changed Little Since 1985, When Chain Was Founded by a Dallas Businessman." *Sun-Sentinel* (Fort Lauderdale, FL), October 16, 1995.

36. John F. Love. *McDonald's: Behind the Arches.* Toronto, ON: Bantam, 1986, pp. 68–69.

37. www.aboutmcdonalds.com/mcd/corporate_careers/training_and_development/hamburger_university/our_faculty.html

38. Natalie Walters. "McDonald's Hamburger University Can Be Harder to Get Into Than Harvard and Is Even Cooler Than You'd Imagine." October 24, 2015; www.businessinsider.com/mcdonalds-hamburger-university-233.

39. Like McDonald's Hamburger University, Burger King set up its own Burger King University in 1978; see Ester Reiter. *Making Fast Food.* Montreal: McGill-Queen's University Press, 1991, p. 68.

40. John F. Love. *McDonald's: Behind the Arches.* Toronto, ON: Bantam, 1986, pp. 141–142.

41. Nancy Folbre. "The 300 Billionth Burger." *New York Times,* July 22, 2013.

42. Ibid.

43. www.aboutmcdonalds.com/content/dam/AboutMcDonalds/Investors/McDs2013Annual Report.pdf

44. McDonald's Corporation *Annual Report,* December 31, 2015.

45. Ibid.

46. Ibid.

47. www.datapointed.net/2010/10/the-farthest-place-from-mcdonalds-lower-48 -states/

48. Martin Plimmer. "This Demi-Paradise: Martin Plimmer Finds Food in the Fast Lane Is Not to His Taste." *Independent* (London), January 3, 1998.

49. Alexandra Alter. "Amazon Sets Up Shop in the Heart of the Publishing Industry." *New York Times,* May 24, 2017.

50. Nick Wingfield and Michael J. de la Merced. "Amazon to Buy Whole Foods for $13.4 Billion." *New York Times,* June 16, 2017.

51. www.statista.com/statistics/190317/

52. International Franchise Association: www.franchise.org

53. In 2008, McDonald's completed the sale of 1,571 company-owned restaurants to a developmental licensee organization. Moreover, in 2008, McDonald's refranchised 675 restaurants, with a goal of refranchising between 1,000 and 1,500 restaurants by 2010. (The rest are either company owned or affiliates; McDonald's 2008 Annual Report.) McDonald's invested in a Denver chain, Chipotle, in 1998 and became its biggest investor in 2001. At the time, Chipotle had 15 stores. By the time McDonald's divested itself of its interest in the company on October 13, 2006, there were more than 500 Chipotle restaurants. In 2008, McDonald's also divested itself from Boston Market, Pret A Manger, and Redbox.

54. Yum! Brands website: www.yum.com

55. Yum! Brands 2013 Annual Report: www.yum.com/annualreport

56. Subway website: www.world.subway.com

57. Subway press release: "Subway Restaurants Named Number One Franchise." January 2003.

58. Janet Adamy. "For Subway, Anywhere Is Possible Franchise Site." *Wall Street Journal Online,* September 1, 2006.

59. Stacy Perman. *In-N-Out Burger.* New York: Collins Business, 2009, p. 26.

60. www.pret.com/about

61. Stephanie Clifford. "Would You Like a Smile With That?" *New York Times,* August 6, 2011.

62. Alex Vadukul. "Cashing in on Halal Street-Food Cred, All the Way to the Strip Mall." *New York Times,* June 15, 2014.

63. http://finance.yahoo.com/blogs/daily-ticker/1-500-people-waited-in-a-seven-hour -line-to-get-a-shake-shack-burger-would-you

64. Glenn Collins. "A Big Mac Strategy at Porterhouse Prices." *New York Times,* August 13, 1996.

65. Ibid.

66. Ibid.

67. A similarly high-priced chain of steakhouses, Ruth's Chris, claims, perhaps a little too loudly and self-consciously, "Ours is not a McDonald's concept" (Glenn Collins. "A Big Mac Strategy at Porterhouse Prices." *New York Times,* August 13, 1996). Even if it is true (and that's doubtful), it makes it clear that all restaurants of this type must attempt to define themselves, either positively or negatively, against the standard set by McDonald's.

68. Timothy Egan. "Big Chains Are Joining Manhattan's Toy Wars." *New York Times*, December 8, 1990.
69. Stacey Burling. "Health Club . . . for Kids." *Washington Post*, November 21, 1991.
70. Andrew Adam Newman. "A Place to Camp, and Make Memories." *New York Times*, June 18.
71. Tamar Lewin. "Small Tots, Big Biz." *New York Times Magazine*, January 19, 1989.
72. www.curves.com/about-curves; Lauren L. O'Toole. "McDonald's at the Gym? A Tale of Two Curves." *Qualitative Sociology* 32 (2009): 75–91.
73. Maik Huttinger and Vincentas Rolandas Giedraitis. "Ryanization: How One European Airline Exemplifies the 'McDonaldization' Model." *Ekonomika/Economics* 89 (2010): 123–132.
74. www.aboutmcdonalds.com/content/dam/AboutMcDonalds/Investors/McDs2013AnnualReport.pdf
75. www.aboutmcdonalds.com/content/dam/AboutMcDonalds/Investors/McDs2013Annual Report.pdf
76. Mike Ives. "McDonald's Opens in Vietnam, Bringing Big Mac to Fans of Banh Mi." *New York Times*, February 8, 2014.
77. www.mcdonalds.co.jp
78. www.chinaretailnews.com/2014/04/21/7055-fast-growth-equals-more-fast-food-for-mcdonalds-in-china/; www.reuters.com/article/2013/10/28/us-china-fastfood-idUSBRE99Q0CC20131028
79. www.yum.com/brands/china.asp
80. www.bloomberg.com/news/2011-01-26/mcdonald-s-no-match-for-kfc-in-china-where-colonel-sanders-rules-fast-food.html
81. Michael Steinberger. "Can Anyone Save French Food?" *New York Times*, March 28, 2014.
82. www.mcdonalds.ru/
83. Andrew E. Kramer. "Delivering on Demand: American Fast Food Meets a Warm Reception in Russia." *New York Times*, August 4, 2011.
84. Robin Young. "Britain Is Fast-Food Capital of Europe." *Times* (London), April 25, 1997.
85. Ilene R. Prusher. "McDonaldized Israel Debates Making Sabbath 'Less Holy.'" *Christian Science Monitor*, January 30, 1998; see also Uri Ram. "Glocommodification: How the Global Consumes the Local McDonald's in Israel." *Current Sociology* 52 (2004): 11–31.
86. http://corporate.walmart.com/our-story/
87. www.timhortons.com/ca/en/about/the-story-of-tim-hortons.php; Les Whittington. "Tim Hortons: Canada Success Story." *Gazette* (Montreal), October 17, 1997.
88. www.bloomberg.com
89. Eric Margolis. "Fast Food: France Fights Back." *Toronto Sun*, January 16, 1997.
90. Stephanie Strom. "Let Them Eat Bread." *New York Times*, July 12, 2017: D1, D10.
91. Liz Alderman. "France, of all Places, Finds Itself in a Battle Against Processed Food." *New York Times*, January 30, 2014.
92. Valerie Reitman. "India Anticipates the Arrival of the Beefless Big Mac." *Wall Street Journal*, October 20, 1993.
93. www.mosburger.com.sg/global_network.php
94. Mos Food Services website: www.mos.co.jp; Mos Burger 2008 Business Report.
95. Alison Leigh Cowan. "Unlikely Spot for Fast Food." *New York Times*, April 29, 1984.

96. Thomas Erdbrink. "Iran Capitalizing on a Taste for America's Biggest Brands." *New York Times,* August 2, 2015.

97. www.campero.com/about-us.aspx; "Pollo Campero Refreshes Brand Logo Getting Ready for Expansion." *Business Wire,* June 16, 2006.

98. www.jollibee.com.ph/international/usa/store-locator

99. http://pollotropical.com/franchising/markets/; Hugh Morley. "A Hunger for the Hispanic: Combining Fast Food, Ethnic Cuisine." *The Record* (Bergen County, NJ), March 22, 2006; www.pollotropical.com

100. Jonathan Hutchison. "High Octane Burger Chain From New Zealand Aims at the U.S." *New York Times,* May 12, 2014.

101. Lauren Collins. "House Perfect: Is the IKEA Ethos Comfy or Creepy?" *New Yorker,* October 3, 2011.

102. Ibid.

103. "Stylish, Swedish, 60-ish; IKEA's a Global Phenomenon." *Western Mail,* May 20, 2003.

104. http://franchisor.ikea.com/Whoweare/Documents/Facts%20and%20Figures%202013.pdf

105. Lauren Collins. "House Perfect: Is the IKEA Ethos Comfy or Creepy?" *New Yorker,* October 3, 2011.

106. http://about.hm.com

107. http://about.hm.com; H&M 2013–2014 Three-Month Report.

108. www.inditex.com

109. Ibid.

110. Michael Arndt. "McDonald's Goes 24/7," www.msnbc.msn.com/id/16828944; McDonald's 2008 Annual Report.

111. Richard L. Papiernik. "Mac Attack?" *Financial World,* April 12, 1994.

112. Laura Shapiro. "Ready for McCatfish?" *Newsweek,* October 15, 1990; N. R. Kleinfeld. "Fast Food's Changing Landscape." *New York Times,* April 14, 1985.

113. Henry Samuel. "McDonald's Restaurants to Open at the Louvre." *Daily Telegraph.* www.telegraph.co.uk/news/worldnews/europe/france/6259044/McDonalds-restaurants-to-open-at-the-Louvre.html

114. Louis Uchitelle. "That's Funny, Those Pickles Don't Look Russian." *New York Times,* February 27, 1992.

115. Center for Defense Information website: www.cdi.org/russia (no longer available online).

116. Nicholas D. Kristof. "Billions Served (and That Was Without China)." *New York Times,* April 24, 1992.

117. Gilbert Chan. "Fast Food Chains Pump Profits at Gas Stations." *Fresno Bee,* October 10, 1994.

118. Cynthia Rigg. "McDonald's Lean Units Beef Up NY Presence." *Crain's New York Business,* October 31, 1994.

119. Anthony Flint. "City Official Balks at Placement of McDonald's at New Courthouse." *Boston Globe,* March 9, 1999.

120. Anita Kumar. "A New Food Revolution on Campus." *St. Petersburg Times,* May 11, 2003.

121. Carole Sugarman. "Dining Out on Campus." *Washington Post/Health,* February 14, 1995.

122. Edwin McDowell. "Fast Food Fills Menu for Many Hotel Chains." *New York Times,* January 9, 1992.

123. Dan Freedman. "Low Fat? The Kids Aren't Buying; Districts Struggle to Balance Mandates for Good Nutrition With Reality in the Cafeteria." *The Times Union*, September 22, 2002.

124. "Back to School: School Lunches." *Consumer Reports*, September 1998.

125. Mike Berry. "Redoing School Cafeterias to Favor Fast-Food Eateries." *Orlando Sentinel*, January 12, 1995.

126. "Pediatric Obesity: Fast-Food Restaurants Cluster Around Schools." *Obesity, Fitness and Wellness Week*, September 24, 2005.

127. "Grade 'A' Burgers." *New York Times*, April 13, 1986.

128. Jennifer Curtis. "McDonald's Attacked for Toys That Push Its Fatty Fast Food." *The West Australian* (Perth), January 16, 2007.

129. Lindsey Tanner. "Pediatric Hospitals That Serve Fast Food Raise More Alarm." *Houston Chronicle*, December 28, 2006.

130. Gloria Pitzer. *Secret Fast Food Recipes: The Fast Food Cookbook*. Marysville, MI: Author, 1995.

131. Brooks Barnes. "To Woo Young Moviegoers, AMC Thinks Like McDonald's." *New York Times* April 10: B4

132. Ibid.

133. This discussion is derived from George Ritzer, "Revolutionizing the World of Consumption." *Journal of Consumer Culture* 2 (2002): 103–118.

134. George Anders. "McDonald's Methods Come to Medicine as Chains Acquire Physicians' Practices." *Wall Street Journal*, August 24, 1993.

135. Peter Prichard. *The Making of McPaper: The Inside Story of* USA TODAY. Kansas City, MO: Andrews, McMeel and Parker, 1987.

136. Terri Deshotels, Mollie Tinney, and Craig J. Forsyth. "McSexy: Exotic Dancing and Institutional Power." *Deviant Behavior* 33 (2012): 140–148.

137. I would like to thank Lee Martin for bringing this case (and menu) to my attention.

138. Peter Prichard. *The Making of McPaper: The Inside Story of* USA TODAY. Kansas City, MO: Andrews, McMeel and Parker, 1987, pp. 232–233.

139. Howard Kurtz. "Slicing, Dicing News to Attract the Young." *Washington Post*, January 6, 1991.

140. Kathryn Hausbeck and Barbara G. Brents. "McDonaldization of the Sex Industries? The Business of Sex." In George Ritzer, ed., *McDonaldization: The Reader*, 3rd ed. Thousand Oaks, CA: Sage, 2010, pp. 102–117.

141. Martin Gottlieb. "Pornography's Plight Hits Times Square." *New York Times*, October 5, 1986.

142. Sohia Kercher. "First Comes Tinder. Then Comes Marriage?" *New York Times*, April 19, 2017.

143. http://sociologycompass.wordpress.com/2009/11/02/augmented-reality-going-the-way-of-the-dildo/

144. Jean Sonmor. "Can We Talk Sex: Phone Sex Is Hot-Wiring Metro's Lonely Hearts." *Toronto Sun*, January 29, 1995.

145. Ibid.

146. For a selection of this work, see George Ritzer, ed., *McDonaldization: The Reader*, 3rd ed. Thousand Oaks, CA: Sage, 2010.

147. Sera J. Zegre et al. "McDonaldization and Commercial Outdoor Recreation and Tourism in Alaska." *Managing Leisure* 17 (2012): 333–348.

148. Ian Heywood, "Urgent Dreams: Climbing, Rationalization, and Ambivalence." In George Ritzer, ed., *McDonaldization: The Reader*, 3rd ed. Thousand Oaks, CA: Sage, 2010, pp. 65–69.

149. Tan Zhi-wu. "McDonaldization of International Top-level Golf Professional Tournament." *Journal of Guangzhou Sport University*, 2010.

150. Sanette L.A. Ferreira and Gessina W. Van Zyl. "Catering for Large Numbers of Tourists: The McDonaldization of Casual Dining in Kruger National Park." *Bulletin of Geography* 33, September, 2016.

151. Richard Heslop. "The British Police Service: Professionalisation or 'McDonaldization'?" *International Journal of Police Science & Management* 13 (2011): 312–321.

152. David Wood. "Swift and Sure: McJustice for a Consumer Society." *Criminal Justice Matters* 91 (2013): 10–11; Matthew B. Robinson, "McDonaldization of America's Police, Courts, and Corrections." In George Ritzer, ed., *McDonaldization: The Reader*, 3rd ed. Thousand Oaks, CA: Sage, 2010, pp. 85–100.

153. Sara Raley. "McDonaldization and the Family." In George Ritzer, ed., *McDonaldization: The Reader*, 3rd ed. Thousand Oaks, CA: Sage, 2010, pp. 138–148.

154. Gary Wilkinson. "McSchools for McWorld: Mediating Global Pressures With a McDonaldizing Education Policy Response." In George Ritzer, ed., *McDonaldization: The Reader*, 3rd ed. Thousand Oaks, CA: Sage, 2010, pp. 150–157.

155. Philip G. Altbach. "Franchising: The McDonaldization of Higher Education." *Global Perspective on Higher Education* 2013: 111–113; Andrew Nadolny and Suzanne Ryan. "McUniversities Revisited: A Comparison of University and McDonald's Casual; Employee Experiences in Australia." *Studies in Higher Education*, published online July 2013.

156. Noel Carroll. "E-Learning: The McDonaldization of Education." *European Journal of Higher Education* 3 (2013): 342–356.

157. Jason Lane and Kevin Kinser. "MOOC's and the McDonaldization of Global Higher Education." *Chronicle of Higher Education*, September 28, 2012; http://chronicle.com/blogs/worldwise/moocs-mass-higher-education-and-the-mcdonaldization-of-higher-educa tion/30536

158. David L. Andrews et al. "McKinesiology." *Review of Education, Pedagogy, and Cultural Studies* 35 (2013): 335–356.

159. Justin Waring and Simon Bishop. "McDonaldization or Commercial Re-stratification: Corporatization and the Multimodal Organisation of English Doctors." *Social Science and Medicine* 82 (2013): 147–155.

160. Michael R. Montgomery. "The McDonaldization of Psychotherapy?" *Existential Analysis* 27 (2016).

161. Zafar Iqbal. "McDonaldization, Islamic Teachings, and Funerary Practices in Kuwait." *OMEGA: Journal of Death and Dying* 63 (2011): 95–112.

162. Lee F. Monaghan. "McDonaldizing Men's Bodies? Slimming, Associated (Ir) Rationalities and Resistances." In George Ritzer, ed., *McDonaldization: The Reader*, 3rd ed. Thousand Oaks, CA: Sage, 2010, pp. 119–136.

163. Andrew J. Knight. "Supersizing Farms: The McDonaldization of Agriculture." In George Ritzer, ed., *McDonaldization: The Reader*, 3rd ed. Thousand Oaks, CA: Sage, 2010, pp. 192–205.

164. John Drane. *The McDonaldization of the Church: Consumer Culture and the Church's Future.* London: Smyth and Helwys, 2012; John Drane. "From Creeds to Burgers: Religious Control, Spiritual Search, and the Future of the World." In George Ritzer, ed., *McDonaldization: The Reader,* 3rd ed. Thousand Oaks, CA: Sage, 2010, pp. 222–227.

165. Terry Hyland. "McDonaldizing Spirituality." *Journal of Transformative Education,* published online March 16, 2017.

166. Emeka W. Dumbili. "McDonaldization of Nigerian Banking Industry in the Post-Consolidated Era: An Exploration of the Unavoidable Consequences." *Mediterranean Journal of Social Sciences* 4 (2013): 343–352.

167. Jos Gamble. "Multinational Retailers in China: Proliferating 'McJobs' or Developing Skills?" In George Ritzer, ed., *McDonaldization: The Reader,* 3rd ed. Thousand Oaks, CA: Sage, 2010, pp. 172–190.

168. Bryan Turner. "McCitizens: Risk, Coolness and Irony in Contemporary Policy." In George Ritzer, ed., *McDonaldization: The Reader,* 3rd ed. Thousand Oaks, CA: Sage, 2010, pp. 229–232.

169. Marshall Fishwick, ed. *Ronald Revisited: The World of Ronald McDonald.* Bowling Green, OH: Bowling Green University Press, 1983.

170. John F. Harris. "McMilestone Restaurant Opens Doors in Dale City." *Washington Post,* April 7, 1988.

171. E. R. Shipp. "The McBurger Stand That Started It All." *New York Times,* February 27, 1985.

172. http://news.mcdonalds.com/

173. Bill Keller. "Of Famous Arches, Beeg Meks and Rubles." *New York Times,* January 28, 1990.

174. "Wedge of Americana: In Moscow, Pizza Hut Opens 2 Restaurants." *Washington Post,* September 12, 1990.

175. Jeb Blount. "Frying Down to Rio." *Washington Post/Business,* May 18, 1994.

176. Thomas L. Friedman. *The Lexus and the Olive Tree: Understanding Globalization.* New York: Farrar, Straus and Giroux, 1999, p. 235.

177. Thomas Friedman. "A Manifesto for the Fast World." *New York Times Magazine,* March 28, 1999, pp. 43–44.

178. bigmacindex.org/2013; "Cheesed Off," *The Economist,* February 16, 2009.

179. Reflective of the emergence of a newer global icon, an Australian bank has developed a similarly tongue-in-cheek idea—"the iPod index" (see http://www.smh.com.au/news/technology/ipod-index-trumps-the-bigmac-one/2007/01/18/1169095897045.html).

180. Thomas Friedman. "A Manifesto for the Fast World." *New York Times Magazine,* March 28, 1999, p. 84.

181. Conrad Kottak. "Rituals at McDonald's." In Marshall Fishwick, ed., *Ronald Revisited: The World of Ronald McDonald.* Bowling Green, OH: Bowling Green University Press, 1983.

182. Bill Keller. "Of Famous Arches, Beeg Meks and Rubles." *New York Times,* January 28, 1990.

183. William Severini Kowinski. *The Malling of America: An Inside Look at the Great Consumer Paradise.* New York: William Morrow, 1985, p. 218.

184. Stephen M. Fjellman. *Vinyl Leaves: Walt Disney World and America.* Boulder, CO: Westview, 1992.
185. Bob Garfield. "How I Spent (and Spent and Spent) My Disney Vacation." *Washington Post/Outlook*, July 7, 1991. See also Margaret J. King. "Empires of Popular Culture: McDonald's and Disney." In Marshall Fishwick, ed., *Ronald Revisited: The World of Ronald McDonald.* Bowling Green, OH: Bowling Green University Press, 1983, pp. 106–119.
186. Steven Greenhouse. "The Rise and Rise of McDonald's." *New York Times*, June 8, 1986.

Chapter 2

1. Katie Benner. "Airbnb Tries to Behave More Like a Hotel." *New York Times*, June 18, 2017.
2. Nick Wingfield. "Amid Brick-and-Mortar Travails, a Tipping Point for Amazon in Apparel." *New York Times*, April 30, 2017.
3. Zygmunt Bauman. *Liquid Modernity.* Cambridge, U.K.: Polity Press, 2000; see also, George Ritzer and P. J. Rey. "From 'Solid' Producers and Consumers to 'Liquid' Prosumers." In Mark Davis, ed. *Liquid Sociology.* New York: Routledge, 2013, pp. 157–176; George Ritzer and Jim Murphy. "Solidity in a World of Liquidity: The Persistence of Modernity in an Increasingly Postmodern World." In Matthias Junge Kron, eds., *Zygmunt Bauman.* Stuttgart: Leske and Budrich, 2002, pp. 51–79 (in German).
4. For a very different, far less rationalized view of the Holocaust, see David Cesarini. *Final Solution: The Fate of the Jews 1933–1949.* New York: St. Martin's Press, 2016.
5. Zygmunt Bauman. *Modernity and the Holocaust.* Ithaca, NY: Cornell University Press, 1989.
6. Zygmunt Bauman. *Liquid Life.* Cambridge, UK: Polity Press, 2005, p. 9.
7. Fleura Bardhi and Giana M. Eckhardt. "Liquid Consumption." *Journal of Consumer Research*, forthcoming. While this article deals with consumers and the consumption process, the focus in this book is on liquid vs. solid sites of consumption.
8. Nick Wingfield. "Amazon Apparel Plan: Try Before You Buy, Send Back the Rest." *New York Times*, June 21, 2017.
9. Michael Ruhlman. "Grocery: The Buying and Selling of Food in America. New York: Abrams, 2017.
10. Julia Moskin. "Is the Supermarket Done For?" *New York Times*, May 17, 2017, p. D7.
11. Nathan Jurgenson. "When Atoms Meet Bits: Social Media, the Mobile Web, and Augmented Revolution." *Future Internet* (41): 83–91.
12. Mike Isaac. "New Gamble By Facebook: Augmented Reality Apps." *New York Times*, April 19, 2017, p. B1.
13. Elizabeth Paton. "A Glimpse of Our Shopping Future." *New York Times*, April 13, 2017, p. D2.
14. Lindsey Rittenhouse. "Amazon Should be Terrified by This New Service Walmart is Testing in China." *The Street Video*, May 21, 2017.
15. www.finance.yahoo.com/news/wal-mart-offers-discounts-online-040809027.html
16. Susan Berfield. "Delivering a $9 Billion Empire." *Bloomberg Businessweek*, March 20-29, 2017, no pp. indicated.

17. Michael de la Merced. "Walmart to Buy Bonobos, Men's Wear Company, for $310 Million." *New York Times*, June 16, 2017.
18. John Taggart and Kevin Granville. "From 'Zombie Malls' to Bonobos: America's Retail Transformation." *New York Times*, April 15, 2017.
19. www.amazon.com
20. Deep learning is a type of machine learning. In this case it is an automated system using algorithms to analyze masses of (big) data, learn more about that data, calculate the relative importance of various factors, and make predictions about consumer choices and their impact on, for example, what products the Amazon Go needs to (re-)stock or drop from the shelves because of lack of demand.
21. Farhad Manjoo. "In Whole Foods, Bezos Gets a Sustainably Source Guinea Pig." *New York Times*, June 17, 2017.
22. Lina M. Khan. "Amazon's Growing Monopoly Bite." *New York Times*, June 21, 2017.
23. Elizabeth Paton. "A Glimpse of Our Shopping Future." *New York Times*, April 13, 2017, p. D2.
24. Ibid.
25. Michael Corkery. "Is American Retail at a Historic Tipping Point?" *New York Times* April 15, 2017.
26. Kai-fu Lee. "The Real Threat of Artificial Intelligence." *New York Times*, June 25, 2017, p. 4.
27. Nick Wingfield."Amazon's Ambitions Unboxed: Stores for Furniture, Appliances and More." *New York Times*, March 25, 2017, p. 7.
28. Nicholas K. Geranios. "Fearing Lack of Labor: Growers Look to Robots." *Sarasota Herald Tribune*, April 29, 2017, D2; italics added.
29. Ursula Huws. "Where Did Online Platforms Come From? The Virtualization of Work Organization and the New Policy Challenges It Raises." In Pamela Meil and Vssil Kirov, eds., *Policy Implications of Virtual Work*, 2017: 29–48.
30. Arne L. Kalleberg and Michael Dunn. "Good Jobs, Bad Jobs in the Gig Economy." *Perspectives on Work*, 2016: 10–19; 74.
31. Nathan Heller. "The Gig Is Up." *The New Yorker*, May 15, 2017, p. 52ff.
32. Antonio Casilli. "Venture Labor, Media Work, and the Communicative Construction of Economic Value: Agendas for the Field and Critical Commentary: How Venture Labor Sheds Light on the Digital Platform Economy." *International Journal of Communication* 11 (2017): 2067–2070.
33. Ibid.
34. Guy Standing. *The Precariat: The New Dangerous Class.* Bloomsbury, 2011.
35. Nathan Heller. "The Gig Is Up." *The New Yorker*, May 15, 2017, p. 63.
36. Claire Cain Miller. "Amazon's Move Signals End of Line for Many Cashiers." *New York Times*, June 17, 2017.
37. Julia La Roche. "McDonald's Is Hiring a New Kind of Employee." Yahoo Finance, April 27, 2017; www.financeyahoo.com
38. Dyer Gunn. "The Long and Painful Decline of the Retail Store." psmag.com/the-long-and-painful-decline-of-the-retail-store-2440e58fa57f
39. Although the precursors discussed in this chapter do not exhaust the rationalized institutions that predate McDonald's, they are the most important for understanding McDonald's and McDonaldization.

40. Zygmunt Bauman. *Modernity and the Holocaust.* Ithaca, NY: Cornell University Press, 1989, p. 149.

41. Ibid., p. 8.

42. However, in contemporary Rwanda, an estimated 800,000 people were killed in 100 days (three times the rate of Jewish dead during the Holocaust) in warfare between the Hutus and Tutsis. The methods employed—largely machete—were decidedly not rationalized. See Philip Gourevitch. *We Wish to Inform You That Tomorrow We Will Be Killed With Our Families: Stories From Rwanda.* New York: Farrar, Straus and Giroux, 1998.

43. As you will see in Chapter 3, the fast-food restaurants enhance their efficiency by getting customers to perform (without pay) a variety of their tasks.

44. Zygmunt Bauman. *Modernity and the Holocaust.* Ithaca, NY: Cornell University Press, 1989, p. 103.

45. Ibid., p. 89.

46. Ibid., p. 8.

47. Ibid., p. 102.

48. Feingold, cited in Zygmunt Bauman. *Modernity and the Holocaust.* Ithaca, NY: Cornell University Press, 1989, p. 136.

49. Frederick W. Taylor. *The Principles of Scientific Management.* New York: Harper & Row, 1947; Robert Kanigel. *One Best Way: Frederick Winslow Taylor and the Enigma of Efficiency.* New York: Viking, 1997.

50. Frederick W. Taylor. *The Principles of Scientific Management.* New York: Harper & Row, 1947, pp. 6–7.

51. Ibid., p. 11.

52. Henry Ford. *My Life and Work.* Garden City, NY: Doubleday, 1922; James T. Flink. *The Automobile Age.* Cambridge: MIT Press, 1988.

53. Henry Ford. *My Life and Work.* Garden City, NY: Doubleday, 1922, p. 80.

54. McKinsey Global Institute. *A Future That Works: Automation, Employment, and Productivity.* San Francisco: Author, January, 2017.

55. Jerry Newman. *My Secret Life on the McJob.* New York: McGraw-Hill, 2007, pp. 168–169.

56. Bruce A. Lohof. "Hamburger Stand Industrialization and the Fast-Food Phenomenon." In Marshall Fishwick, ed., *Ronald Revisited: The World of Ronald McDonald.* Bowling Green, OH: Bowling Green University Press, 1983, p. 30; see also Ester Reiter. *Making Fast Food.* Montreal: McGill-Queen's University Press, 1991, p. 75.

57. Justine Griffin. "Sushi to Be Served Differently in Mall." *Sarasota Herald Tribune,* June 12, 2014.

58. Nick Wingfield and Kelly Couturier. "Detailing Amazon's Custom-Clothing Patent." *New York Times,* May 1, 2017.

59. Marshall Fishwick. "Cloning Clowns: Some Final Thoughts." In Marshall Fishwick, ed., *Ronald Revisited: The World of Ronald McDonald.* Bowling Green, OH: Bowling Green University Press, 1983, pp. 148–151. For more on the relationship described in the same paragraph between the automobile and the growth of the tourist industry, see James T. Flink. *The Automobile Age.* Cambridge: MIT Press, 1988.

60. General Motors, especially Alfred Sloan, further rationalized the automobile industry's bureaucratic structure. Sloan is famous for GM's multidivisional system,

in which the central office handled long-range decisions while the divisions made the day-to-day decisions. This innovation proved so successful in its day that the other automobile companies as well as many other corporations adopted it. See James T. Flink. *The Automobile Age.* Cambridge: MIT Press, 1988; Alfred P. Sloan Jr. *My Years at General Motors.* Garden City, NY: Doubleday, 1964.

61. "Levitt's Progress." *Fortune,* October 1952.
62. Richard Perez-Pena. "William Levitt, 86, Suburb Maker, Dies." *New York Times,* January 29, 1994.
63. "The Most House for the Money." *Fortune,* October 1952.
64. Ibid., p. 153.
65. Herbert Gans. *The Levittowners: Ways of Life and Politics in a New Suburban Community.* New York: Pantheon, 1967, p. 13.
66. Patricia Dane Rogers. "Building . . ." *Washington Post/Home,* February 2, 1995; Rebecca Lowell. "Modular Homes Move Up." *Wall Street Journal,* October 23, 1998.
67. Richard E. Gordon, Katherine K. Gordon, and Max Gunther. *The Split-Level Trap.* New York: Gilbert Geis Associates, 1960.
68. Georgia Dullea. "The Tract House as Landmark." *New York Times,* October 17, 1991.
69. Herbert Gans. *The Levittowners: Ways of Life and Politics in a New Suburban Community.* New York: Pantheon, 1967, p. 432.
70. William Severini Kowinski. *The Malling of America: An Inside Look at the Great Consumer Paradise.* New York: William Morrow, 1985.
71. www.bloomingtonmn.org/page/1/mall-of-america.jsp
72. http://theseoultimes.com/ST/db/read.php?idx=1962
73. Janice L. Kaplan. "The Mall Outlet for Cabin Fever." *Washington Post/Weekend,* February 10, 1995.
74. William Severini Kowinski. *The Malling of America: An Inside Look at the Great Consumer Paradise.* New York: William Morrow, 1985, p. 25. For a discussion of the significance of the mall in the history of consumption, see Lizabeth Cohen. *Consumer's Republic: The Politics of Mass Consumption in Postwar America.* New York: Knopf, 2003, especially Chapter 6.
75. Steven Kurutz. "An Ode to Shopping Malls." *New York Times,* July 27, 2017, p. D1, D8.
76. John Taggart and Kevin Granville. "From 'Zombie Malls' to Bonobos: America's Retail Transformation." *New York Times,* April 15, 2017.
77. Ibid.
78. David Montgomery. "Deep in the Malls of Texas, a Vision of Shopping's Future." *New York Times,* June 21, 2017, p. B6.
79. Anne D'Innocenzio. "Clothing Retailers Feel the Brunt of Change." *Sarasota Herald-Tribune,* March 24, 2017, p. D3.
80. John Taggart and Kevin Granville. "From 'Zombie Malls' to Bonobos: America's Retail Transformation." *New York Times,* April 15, 2017.
81. Michael Corkery. "Is American Retail at a Historic Tipping Point?" *New York Times,* April 15, 2017.
82. Ibid.
83. George Ritzer. "The McDonaldization of Society," *Journal of American Culture* 6, Spring, 1983: 100–107.
84. However, there is much more to the Internet than consumption sites that compete with brick-and-mortar retail locales.

85. Harriet Edleson. "Putting the Front Desk in the Hotel Guest's Pocket." *New York Times,* April 24, 2017.

86. Jeff Sommer. "Amazon's Mind-Boggling Ascent." *New York Times,* July 30, 2017, p. 4.

87. Ravi Gandhi. "Amazon Almost Crushed Me, and I'm Not Even a Retailer: CEO OP-ed." *CNBC,* May 17, 2017.

88. Nicole Sinclair. "Walmart's online business is booming." *Yahoo Finance* May 18, 107.

89. Christina Farr. "Amazon Is Hiring People to Break Into the Multibillion-Dollar Pharmacy Market." *CNBC* May 16, 2017.

90. Daisuke Wakabayashi. "People Who Train Robots (to Do Their Jobs)." *New York Times,* April 30, 2017.

91. Nick Srnicek. *Platform Capitalism.* Cambridge, UK: Polity Press, p. 43.

92. John Herman. "Platforms Might Soon Consume Huge Swaths of Our Economy—But What Do They Want With Their Power? *New York Times Magazine,* March 26, 2017, pp. 16–20.

93. Mark Scott. "A Legal Opinion Is a Blow for Uber in Its Fight to Conquer Europe." *New York Times,* May 12, 2017, p. B4.

94. Michael J. de la Merced and Katie Benner. "As Department Stores Close, Stitch Fix Expands Online." *New York Times,* May 10, 2017.

95. Nick Wingfield. "Amid Brick-and-Mortar Travails, a Tipping Point for Amazon in Apparel." *New York Times,* April 30, 2017.

Chapter 3

1. John Herrman. "Platform Companies are Becoming More Powerful, but What Exactly Do They Want?" *New York Times,* March 21, 2017.

2. Jeff Bercovici. "Amazon vs. Book Publishers, By the Numbers." *Forbes,* February 10, 2014.

3. Jeremy Rifkin. *The Zero Marginal Cost Society: The Internet of Things, The Collaborative Commons, and the Collapse of Capitalism.* New York: Palgrave Macmillan, 2014; George Ritzer and Nathan Jurgenson. "Production, Consumption, Prosumption: The Nature of Capitalism in the Age of the Digital Prosumer." *Journal of Consumer Culture* 10 (2010): 13–36; George Ritzer. "Prosumption: Evolution, Revolution or Eternal Return of the Same?" *Journal of Consumer Culture* 14 (2014): 3–24.

4. Herbert Simon. *Administrative Behavior,* 2nd ed. New York: Free Press, 1957.

5. Jack Ewing. "Robocalypse No? Bankers Ask, Will Automation Kill Jobs?" *New York Times,* June 29, 2017, p. B4.

6. Arthur Kroker, Marilouise Kroker, and David Cook. *Panic Encyclopedia: The Definitive Guide to the Postmodern Scene.* New York: St. Martin's, 1989, p. 119.

7. Michael Lev. "Raising Fast Food's Speed Limit." *Washington Post,* August 7, 1991.

8. www.cnet.com/news/mcdonalds-hires-7000-touch-screen-cashiers/

9. Mark Kurlansky. *Birdseye: The Adventures of a Curious Man.* New York: Anchor Books, 2012.

10. Jim Kershner. "Trays of Our Lives: Fifty Years After Swanson Unveiled the First TV Dinner, Meals-in-a-Box Have Never Been Bigger." *Spokesman Review,* March 19, 2003.

11. "The Microwave Cooks Up a New Way of Life." *Wall Street Journal,* September 19, 1989; "Microwavable Foods: Industry's Response to Consumer Demands for Convenience." *Food Technology* 41 (1987): 52–63.

12. "Microwavable Foods: Industry's Response to Consumer Demands for Convenience." *Food Technology* 41 (1987): 54.

13. Eben Shapiro. "A Page From Fast Food's Menu." *New York Times,* October 14, 1991.

14. Sarah Halzack. "Why This Start-Up Wants to Put Vegetables You've Never Heard of on Your Dinner Table." *Washington Post,* June 15, 2016.

15. Prosumers also provide Blue Apron with the "big data" (see subsequent discussion in this chapter) on, for example, recipes they like and dislike, needed to further rationalize what it does.

16. Sarah Halzack. "Why This Start-Up Wants to Put Vegetables You've Never Heard of on Your Dinner Table." *Washington Post,* June 15, 2016.

17. Amanda Cohen. "You Don't Need a Meal in a Box." *New York Times,* June 30, 2017, p. A27.

18. Ibid.

19. I would like to thank Dora Giemza for the insights into Nutrisystem. See also "Big People, Big Business: The Overweight Numbers Rising, Try NutriSystem." *Washington Post/Health,* October 10, 1989.

20. Lisa Schnirring. "What's Behind the Women-Only Fitness Center Boom?" *Physician and Sports Medicine* 30 (November 2002): 15.

21. William Severini Kowinski. *The Malling of America: An Inside Look at the Great Consumer Paradise.* New York: William Morrow, 1985, p. 61.

22. Wendy Tanaka. "Catalogs Deck Halls to Tune of Billions: Mail Order Called 'Necessity' for Consumers." *Arizona Republic,* December 9, 1997.

23. http://corp.7-eleven.com/aboutus/funfacts/tabid/77/default.aspx

24. Clyde W. Barrow. "The Rationality Crisis in U.S. Higher Education." *New Political Science* 32 (2010): 317–344.

25. Dennis Hayes and Robin Wynyard, eds. *The McDonaldization of Higher Education.* Westport, CT: Bergin & Garvey, 2002; Martin Parker and David Jary. "The McUniversity: Organization, Management and Academic Subjectivity." *Organization* 2 (1995): 1–19.

26. See, for example, www.12000papers.com or http://myessayservices.com/research_paper_for_sale

27. www.exclusivepapers.com/essays/Informative/mcdonaldization-of-society

28. See www.turnitin.com

29. www.drwalkin.com/home

30. http://minuteclinic.com/en/USA/; www.forbes.com/sites/greatspeculations/2014/07/11/cvs-continues-to-expand-its-minuteclinic-footprint/

31. Mark Potts. "Blockbuster Struggles With Merger Script." *Washington Post/Washington Business,* December 9, 1991; Eben Shapiro. "Market Place: A Mixed Outlook for Blockbuster." *New York Times,* February 21, 1992.

32. Stephen Fjellman. *Vinyl Leaves: Walt Disney World and America.* Boulder, CO: Westview, 1992.

33. https://disneyworld.disney.go.com/plan/my-disney-experience/fastpass-plus/

34. Michael Harrington. "To the Disney Station." *Harper's,* January 1979, pp. 35–39.

35. Lynn Darling. "On the Inside at Parks à la Disney." *Washington Post,* August 28, 1978; italics added.

36. www.amazon.com/gp/help/customer/display.html/ref=help_search_1-5? ie=UTF8 &nodeId=14101911&qid=1258841029&sr=1-5

37. http://phx.corporate-ir.net/phoenix.zhtml? ID=1565581&c=176060&p=irol-newsArticle

38. George Packer. "Cheap Words." *New Yorker,* February 17, 24, 2014; Jeff Bercovici. "Amazon vs. Book Publishers, By the Numbers." *Forbes,* February 10, 2014.

39. Ben Sisario. "Streaming Drives Up Music Sales in U.S., but Hold the Celebrations." *New York Times,* March 31, 2017, p. B2.

40. Robin Herman. "Drugstore on the Net." *Washington Post/Health,* May 4, 1999.

41. Doris Hajewski. "Employees Save Time by Shopping Online at Work." *Milwaukee Journal Sentinel,* December 16, 1998.

42. Bruno Giussani. "This Development Is One for the Books." *Chicago Tribune,* September 22, 1998.

43. Leslie Walker. "Google Turns Its Gaze on Online Shopping." *Washington Post,* December 15, 2002.

44. Nick Wingfield. "Amazon-Whole Foods Deal Clears Last Two Major Hurdles." *New York Times,* August 23, 2017.

45. This is very close to the definition of *efficiency* offered in Chapter 1; see Mike Issac. "Uber's Tallies the Costs of Its Leader's Drive to Win at Any Price." *New York Times,* April 24, 2017, p. A16; italics added.

46. www.eHarmony.com; www.match.com

47. www.adultfriendfinder.com; http://sfbay.craigslist.org/i/personals? category=cas

48. They have already McDonaldized the process of breeding, raising, and slaughtering chickens (see Chapter 6).

49. Janet Adamy. "For McDonald's, It's a Wrap." *Wall Street Journal,* January 30, 2007.

50. Stephanie Strom. "All-Day Breakfast Helps McDonald's Post Higher Earnings." *New York Times,* January 26, 2016.

51. Leslie Patton. "McDonald's Cuts Wraps from Menus After Millennials Don't Bite." *Bloomberg,* April 14, 2016.

52. Henry Ford. *My Life and Work.* Garden City, NY: Doubleday, 1922, p. 72.

53. Farhad Manjoo. "The Soylent Revolution Will Not Be Pleasurable." *New York Times,* May 28, 2014; http://nyti.ms/1msOjv3

54. Annie Correal. "The Secret Life of the New York Banana." *New York Times,* August 6, 2017, p. 23.

55. www.hrblock.com/company/index.html

56. George Ritzer and Nathan Jurgenson. "Production, Consumption, Prosumption: The Nature of Capitalism in the Age of the Digital 'Prosumer.'" *Journal of Consumer Culture* 10 (2010): 13–36; George Ritzer, Paul Dean, and Nathan Jurgenson. "The Coming of Age of Prosumption and the Prosumer" (Special double issue). *American Behavioral Scientist* 56 (April 2012); George Ritzer. "Prosumption: Evolution, Revolution or Eternal Return of the Same?" *Journal of Consumer Culture* 14 (2014): 3–24; Daniel Bell. *The Coming of Post-Industrial Society: A Venture in Social Forecasting.* New York: Basic Books, 1973.

57. Kirsten Rieder and G. Gunter Voss. "The Working Customer: An Emerging New Type of Consumer." *Journal Psychologie des Alltagshandelns / Psychology of Everyday Activity* 3, no. 2 (2010): 2–10.

58. Marie-Anne Dujarier. "The Three Sociological Types of Consumer Work." *Journal of Consumer Culture,* published online April 2014.

59. Thomas R. Ide and Arthur J. Cordell. "Automating Work." *Society* 31 (1994): 68.

60. www.steaknshakefranchise.com

61. www.worldwidepartners.com/newsletter? newsletter=21305

62. www.sweettomatoes.com/ourcompany

63. www.souplantation.com/pressroom/companyfacts.asp

64. See www.supermarketguru.com/page.cfm/25603

65. Candice Choi. "Golden Arches to the Future." *Sarasota Herald Tribune* July 14, 2017, pp. D1, D3.

66. www.nextepsystems.com/Home/tabid/36/Default.aspx

67. Brooks Barnes. "To Woo Young Moviegoers. AMC Thinks Like McDonald's." *New York Times*, April 10, 2017, p. B4.

68. Eric Palmer. "Scan-Do Attitude: Self-Service Technology Speeds Up Grocery Shopping." *Kansas City Star*, April 8, 1998.

69. Retail Banking Research news release regarding the "Global EPOS and Self-Checkout 2009."

70. Eben Shapiro. "Ready, Set, Scan That Melon." *New York Times*, June 14, 1990.

71. Ibid.

72. Chris Woodyard. "Grocery Shoppers Can Be Own Cashiers." *USA TODAY*, March 9, 1998.

73. Robert Kisabeth, Anne C. Pontius, Bernard E. Statland, and Charlotte Galper. "Promises and Pitfalls of Home Test Devices." *Patient Care* 31 (October 15, 1997): 125ff.

74. Barry Meier. "Need a Teller? Chicago Bank Plans a Fee." *Washington Post*, April 27, 1995.

75. James Barron. "Please Press 2 for Service; Press? for an Actual Human." *New York Times*, February 17, 1989.

76. Michael Schrage. "Calling the Technology of Voice Mail Into Question." *Washington Post*, October 19, 1990, p. F3.

77. www.census.gov/2010census/news/releases/operations/new-interactive-maps -showing -participation-rates.html; http://usatoday30.usatoday.com/news/nation/ census/census -participation.htm

78. Personal communication between Mike Ryan (my assistant) and Rose Cowan at the Bureau of the Census.

79. Just as quality is equated with quantity, quality is also equated with other aspects of McDonaldization, such as "standardization and predictability." See Ester Reiter. *Making Fast Food*. Montreal: McGill-Queen's University Press, 1991, p. 107.

80. Bruce Horovitz. "Fast-Food Chains Bank on Bigger-Is-Better Mentality." *USA TODAY*, September 12, 1997.

81. Protests against these garish signs helped lead to their virtual disappearance.

82. "Taco Bell Delivers Even Greater Value to Its Customers by Introducing Big Fill Menu." *Business Wire*, November 2, 1994.

83. Melanie Warner. "U.S. Restaurant Chains Find There Is No Too Much." *New York Times*, July 28, 2006.

84. Ibid.

85. Philip Elmer-DeWitt. "Fat Times." *Time*, January 16, 1995.

86. Jane Wells. "Supersizing It: McDonald's Tests Bigger Burger." *CNBC*, March 23, 2007; www.msnbc.msn.com/id/17757931/fromET

87. Barbara W. Tuchman. "The Decline of Quality." *New York Times magazine*, November 2, 1980. For example, United Airlines does not tell people anything about the quality of its numerous flights, such as the likelihood that its planes will be on time.

88. Marion Clark. "Arches of Triumph." *Washington Post/Book World,* June 5, 1977.

89. A. A. Berger. "Berger vs. Burger: A Personal Encounter." In Marshall Fishwick, ed., *Ronald Revisited: The World of Ronald McDonald.* Bowling Green, OH: Bowling Green University Press, 1983, p. 126.

90. Max Boas and Steven Chain. *Big Mac: The Unauthorized Story of McDonald's.* New York: Dutton, 1976, p. 121.

91. Ibid., p. 117.

92. A. C. Stevens. "Family Meals: Olive Garden Defines Mediocrity." *Boston Herald,* March 2, 1997.

93. "The Cheesecake Factory Restaurants Celebrate 25th Anniversary." *Business Wire,* February 25, 2003.

94. Michael D. Shear. "Colleges Rattled as Obama Presses Rating System." *New York Times,* May 26, 2014.

95. Dennis Hayes. "Beyond the McDonaldization of Higher Education." In Dennis Hayes, ed. *Beyond McDonaldization: Visions of Higher Education:* London: Routledge, 2017, p. 8.

96. "Weekly Prompts From a Mentor." *New York Times,* August 21, 2011.

97. "A Way to Speed the Pace." *New York Times,* August 21, 2011.

98. Susan Gervasi. "The Credentials Epidemic." *Washington Post,* April 30, 1990.

99. Shoshana Zuboff. *In the Age of the Smart Machine: The Future of Work and Power.* New York: Basic Books, 1988.

100. Natasha Singer. "How Google Took Over the Classroom." *New York Times,* May 13, 2017.

101. dana boyd and Kate Crawford. "Critical Questions for Big Data." *Information, Communication and Society* 15 (2012): 662–679.

102. Andrew McAfee and Eric Brynjollfson. "Big Data: The Management Revolution." *Harvard Business Review,* October, 2012, pp. 60–69; Victor Mayer-Schonberger and Kenneth Cukier. *Big Data: A Revolution that Will Transform How We Live, Work and Think.* Boston: Mariner Books, 2013.

103. Deborah Lupton. *The Quantified Self: A Sociology of Self-Tracking.* Cambridge: Polity Press, 2016.

104. Michael Lewis. *Moneyball: The Art of Winning an Unfair Game.* New York: W.W. Norton, 2004.

105. Benjamin Baumer and Andrew Zimbalist. *The Sabermetric Revolution: Assessing the Growth of Analytics in Baseball.* Philadelphia: University of Pennsylvania Press, 2014.

106. David Lazer and Jason Radford. "Deux ex Machina: Introduction to Big Data." *Annual Review of Sociology* 43 (2017): 7–21.

107. Nick Srnicek. *Platform Capitalism.* Cambridge, UK: Verso, 2016, p. 52.

108. James Cook. "Uber's Internal Charts Show How Its Driver-rating System Actually Works." *Tech Insider.* February 11, 2015.

109. Nick Srnicek. *Platform Capitalism.* Cambridge: Verso, 2016, pp. 84–85.

110. See the journal *Big Data and Society;* Viktor Mayer-Schonberger and Kenneth Cukier. *Big Data: A Revolution that Will Transform How We Live, Work and Think.* Boston: Mariner Books, 2013.

111. Samuel Greengard. *The Internet of Things.* Cambridge, MA: MIT Press, 2015.

112. Peter Sondergaard and Gartner, Inc. "Big Data Fades to the Algorithm Economy." *Forbes* April 14, 2015.

113. Adam Liptak. "Sent to Prison by a Software Program's Secret Algorithm." *New York Times* May 2, 2017: A22.
114. Mike Isaac and Steve Lohr. "Service Faces a Backlash for Selling Personal Data." *New York Times*, April 25, 2017.
115. Tim Cook. "Jean Liu: China's Ride-Sharing Innovator." *Time*, May 1-8, 2017.
116. George Packer. "Cheap Words." *New Yorker*, February 17; 24, 2014.
117. Alexandra Alter. "Amazon Sets Up Shop in the Heart of the Publishing Industry." *New York Times* May 24, 2017.
118. Ibid.

Chapter 4

1. W. Baldamus. "Tedium and Traction in Industrial Work." In David Weir, ed., *Men and Work in Modern Britain*. London: Fontana, 1973, pp. 78–84.
2. www.bestwestern.com/newsroom/factsheet_countrydetail.asp
3. InterContinental Hotels Group website: www.ihgplc.com/files/pdf/factsheets/ihg_at_a_glance.pdf
4. http://hotelfranchise.wyndhamworldwide.com/portfolio/howard_johnson/ (see also www.timesunion.com/local/article/Restaurants-served-a-slice-of-Americana-3694523.php).
5. Entrepreneur website: www.entrepreneur.com
6. Lauren Lyons Cole. "Homes Away From Home." *Consumer Reports*, June, 2017, pp. 22–29.
7. Liz Moyer. "Hotels, Feeling the Pinch of Airbnb, Promote Local Experiences." *New York Times*, May 29, 2017.
8. Lauren Lyons Cole. "Homes Away From Home." *Consumer Reports* June, 2017, p. 29.
9. Ibid., p. 26.
10. Katie Benner. "Airbnb Tries to Behave More Like a Hotel." *New York Times*, June 18, 2017.
11. Ibid; italics added.
12. Ibid.
13. Robin Leidner. *Fast Food, Fast Talk: Service Work and the Routinization of Everyday Life.* Berkeley: University of California Press, 1993, pp. 45–47, 54.
14. Cited in Ibid., p. 82.
15. Margaret King. "McDonald's and the New American Landscape." *USA TODAY*, January 1980; italics added.
16. www.haircuttery.com/about-us/history.html
17. Duke Helfand. "A Super-Sized Way to Worship; California Has More Megachurches Than Any Other State, With the Majority in Suburbs Between Los Angeles and San Diego." *Los Angeles Times*, October 11, 2009.
18. http://hirr.hartsem.edu/cgi-bin/mega/db.pl?db=default&uid=default&view_records=1&ID=*&sb=3&so=descend
19. Jacqueline L. Salmon and Hamil R. Harris. "Reaching Out With the Word—And Technology." *Washington Post*, February 4, 2007.
20. From the song "Little Boxes." Words and music by Malvina Reynolds. Copyright 1962, Schroder Music Co. (ASCAP). Renewed 1990. Used by permission. All rights reserved.

21. Marcus Palliser. "For Suburbia Read Fantasia: Disney Has Created the American Dream Town in Sunny Florida." *Daily Telegraph,* November 27, 1996.
22. Robin Leidner. *Fast Food, Fast Talk: Service Work and the Routinization of Everyday Life.* Berkeley: University of California Press, 1993, p. 58.
23. Henry Mitchell. "Wonder Bread, Any Way You Slice It." *Washington Post,* March 22, 1991.
24. William Serrin. "Let Them Eat Junk." *Saturday Review,* February 2, 1980.
25. Matthew Gilbert. "In McMovieworld, Franchises Taste Sweetest." *Commercial Appeal* (Memphis), May 30, 1997.
26. John Powers. "Tales of Hoffman." *Washington Post,* Sunday Arts, March 5, 1995.
27. Matthew Gilbert. "TV's Cookie-Cutter Comedies." *Boston Globe,* October 19, 1997.
28. Ibid.
29. Ibid.
30. Similarly, Busch Gardens offers European attractions, such as a German-style beer hall, without having its clientele leave the predictable confines of the United States and the even more predictable surroundings of the modern amusement park.
31. At the opening of the Istanbul Hilton, Conrad Hilton said, "Each of our hotels . . . is a 'little America.'" This quotation is from Daniel J. Boorstin. *The Image: A Guide to Pseudo-Events in America.* New York: Harper Colophon, 1961, p. 98.
32. John Urry. *The Tourist Gaze: Leisure and Travel in Contemporary Societies.* London: Sage, 1990.
33. William Severini Kowinski. *The Malling of America: An Inside Look at the Great Consumer Paradise.* New York: William Morrow, 1985, p. 27.
34. Iver Peterson. "Urban Dangers Send Children Indoors to Play: A Chain of Commercial Playgrounds Is One Answer for Worried Parents." *New York Times,* January 1, 1995.
35. Jan Vertefeuille. "Fun Factory: Kids Pay to Play at the Discovery Zone and While That's Just Fine With Many Parents, It Has Some Experts Worried." *Roanoke Times & World News,* December 8, 1994.
36. Cited in Stephen J. Fjellman. *Vinyl Leaves: Walt Disney World and America.* Boulder, CO: Westview, 1992, p. 226; italics added.
37. Dirk Johnson. "Vacationing at Campgrounds Is Now Hardly Roughing It." *New York Times,* August 28, 1986.
38. http://koa.com/find-a-koa/; "CountryClub Campgrounds." *Newsweek,* September 24, 1984.
39. Andrew Adam Newman. "A Place to Camp, And Make Memories." *New York Times,* June 18, 2014.
40. Dirk Johnson. "Vacationing at Campgrounds Is Now Hardly Roughing It." *New York Times,* August 28, 1986.
41. Kristin Downey Grimsley. "Risk of Homicide Is Higher in Retail Jobs: Half of Workplace Killings Sales-Related." *Washington Post,* July 13, 1997.
42. McKinley, Jr., James C. "Ashanti, R&B Singer, Is Cross-Examined by Her Convicted Stalker." *New York Times.* December 16.
43. Mark Scott and Nick Wingfield. "Clock Ticking, Security Experts Scramble to Defuse Cyberattack." *New York Times,* May 14, 2017.
44. Gerry Mullany and Paul Mozur. "China Hit Hard by Hacking Attack as Asia Assesses Damage." *New York Times,* May 15, 2017.

45. Dan Bilefsky. "British Patients Reel as Hospitals Rush to Revive Computer Systems." *New York Times* May 14, 2017.

46. Robin Leidner. *Fast Food, Fast Talk: Service Work and the Routinization of Everyday Life.* Berkeley: University of California Press, 1993.

47. L. B. Diehl and M. Hardart. *The Automat: The History, Recipes, and Allure of Horn and Hardart's Masterpiece.* New York: Clarkson Potter, 2002.

48. Javier C. Hernandez. "China's Homeless Find Shelter Beneath the Golden Arches." *New York Times,* January 2, 2016.

49. Kim Barker. "A Manhattan McDonald's With Many Off-the-Menu Sales." *New York Times,* July 19, 2015.

50. Stacy Torres. "Old McDonald's." *New York Times,* January 21, 2014.

51. Stan Luxenberg. *Roadside Empires: How the Chains Franchised America.* New York: Viking, 1985.

52. Martin Plimmer. "This Demi-Paradise: Martin Plimmer Finds Food in the Fast Lane Is Not to His Taste." *Independent* (London), January 3, 1998.

53. Harold Gracey. "Learning the Student Role: Kindergarten as Academic Boot Camp." In Dennis Wrong and Harold Gracey, eds., *Readings in Introductory Sociology.* New York: Macmillan, 1967, pp. 243–254.

54. Charles E. Silberman. *Crisis in the Classroom: The Remaking of American Education.* New York: Random House, 1970, p. 122.

55. Ibid., p. 137.

56. Ibid., p. 125.

57. William Severini Kowinski. *The Malling of America: An Inside Look at the Great Consumer Paradise.* New York: William Morrow, 1985, p. 359.

58. Lenore Tiefer. "The Medicalization of Impotence: Normalizing Phallocentrism." *Gender & Society* 8 (1994): 363–377.

59. Cheryl Jackson. "Impotence Clinic Grows Into Chain." *Tampa Tribune—Business and Finance,* February 18, 1995.

60. Laura Mamo and Jennifer R. Fishman. "Potency in All the Right Places: Viagra as a Technology of the Gendered Body." *Body & Society* 7 (2001): 13. As has been made clear, Viagra serves in many ways to McDonaldize sex. Its use has become a phenomenon, and a subject of concern (and some humor), not only in the United States but elsewhere in the world. In Spain, there have been robberies focusing on stealing Viagra from pharmacies. It has become a recreational drug there, demanded even by young people, which has led to enormous sales even at high retail prices ($104 for a box of eight) and to illegal sales (at discos, for example), with one pill going for as much as $80. Why this great demand in a society noted for its macho culture? According to a spokesperson for Pfizer, the maker of Viagra, it is linked to McDonaldization: "We used to have a siesta, to sleep all afternoon. . . . But now we have *become a fast-food nation* where everyone is stressed out, and this is not good for male sexual performance" (italics added). Dan Bilefsky. "Spain Says Adios Siesta and Hola Viagra." *New York Times,* February 11, 2007.

61. Annette Baran and Reuben Pannor. *Lethal Secrets: The Shocking Consequences and Unresolved Problems of Artificial Insemination.* New York: Warner, 1989.

62. Paula Mergenbagen DeWitt. "In Pursuit of Pregnancy." *American Demographics,* May 1993.

63. Eric Adler. "The Brave New World: It's Here Now, Where In Vitro Fertilization Is Routine and Infertility Technology Pushes Back All the Old Limitations." *Kansas City Star,* October 25, 1998.

64. Clear Passage website: www.clearpassage.com/about_infertility_therapy.htm.

65. *Drug Week,* October 24, 2008.

66. "No Price for Little Ones." *Financial Times,* September 28, 1998.

67. Diederika Pretorius. *Surrogate Motherhood: A Worldwide View of the Issues.* Springfield, IL: Charles C Thomas, 1994.

68. Korky Vann. "With In-Vitro Fertilization, Late-Life Motherhood Becoming More Common." *Hartford Courant,* July 7, 1997.

69. http://news.bbc.co.uk/2/hi/europe/4199839.stm; www.nbcnews.com/id/28112285/ns/health-pregnancy/t/another—year-old-india-has-ivf-baby/

70. Angela Cain. "Home Test Kits Fill an Expanding Health Niche." *Times Union-Life and Leisure,* February 12, 1995.

71. Neil Bennett, ed. *Sex Selection of Children.* New York: Academic Press, 1983.

72. www.microsort.com/?page_id=453

73. Janet Daley. "Is Birth Ever Natural?" *The Times* (London), March 16, 1994; italics added.

74. Matt Ridley. "A Boy or a Girl: Is It Possible to Load the Dice?" *Smithsonian* 24 (June 1993): 123.

75. Roger Gosden. *Designing Babies: The Brave New World of Reproductive Technology.* New York: W. H. Freeman, 1999, p. 243.

76. Rayna Rapp. "The Power of 'Positive' Diagnosis: Medical and Maternal Discourses on Amniocentesis." In Donna Bassin, Margaret Honey, and Meryle Mahrer Kaplan, eds., *Representations of Motherhood.* New Haven, CT: Yale University Press, 1994, pp. 204–219.

77. Aliza Kolker and B. Meredith Burke. *Prenatal Testing: A Sociological Perspective.* Westport, CT: Bergin & Garvey, 1994, p. 158.

78. Jeffrey A. Kuller and Steven A. Laifer. "Contemporary Approaches to Prenatal Diagnosis." *American Family Physician* 52 (December 1996): 2277ff.

79. Aliza Kolker and B. Meredith Burke. *Prenatal Testing: A Sociological Perspective.* Westport, CT: Bergin & Garvey, 1994; Ellen Domke and Al Podgorski. "Testing the Unborn: Genetic Test Pinpoints Defects, but Are There Risks?" *Chicago Sun-Times,* April 17, 1994.

80. However, some parents do resist the rationalization introduced by fetal testing. See Shirley A. Hill. "Motherhood and the Obfuscation of Medical Knowledge." *Gender & Society* 8 (1994): 29–47.

81. Mike Chinoy. CNN, February 8, 1994.

82. Joan H. Marks. "The Human Genome Project: A Challenge in Biological Technology." In Gretchen Bender and Timothy Druckery, eds., *Culture on the Brink: Ideologies of Technology.* Seattle, WA: Bay Press, 1994, pp. 99–106; R. C. Lewontin. "The Dream of the Human Genome." In Gretchen Bender and Timothy Druckery, eds., *Culture on the Brink: Ideologies of Technology.* Seattle, WA: Bay Press, 1994, pp. 107–127.

83. "Genome Research: International Consortium Completes Human Genome Project." *Genomics & Genetics Weekly,* May 9, 2003.

84. Matt Ridley. "A Boy or a Girl: Is It Possible to Load the Dice?" *Smithsonian* 24 (June 1993): 123.

85. Jessica Mitford. *The American Way of Birth.* New York: Plume, 1993.

86. For a critique of midwifery from the perspective of rationalization, see Charles Krauthammer. "Pursuit of a Hallmark Moment Costs a Baby's Life." *Tampa Tribune,* May 27, 1996.
87. American College of Nurse-Midwives, 2008 Report; Judy Foreman. "The Midwives' Time Has Come—Again." *Boston Globe,* November 2, 1998.
88. www.midwife.org/Essential-facts-about-Midwives
89. www.allnursingschools.com/faqs/cnm.php
90. Jessica Mitford. *The American Way of Birth.* New York: Plume, 1993, p. 13.
91. Catherine Kohler Riessman. "Women and Medicalization: A New Perspective." In P. Brown, ed., *Perspectives in Medical Sociology.* Prospect Heights, IL: Waveland, 1989, pp. 190–220.
92. Michelle Harrison. *A Woman in Residence.* New York: Random House, 1982, p. 91.
93. Judith Walzer Leavitt. *Brought to Bed: Childbearing in America, 1750–1950.* New York: Oxford University Press, 1986, p. 190.
94. Ibid.
95. Paula A. Treichler. "Feminism, Medicine, and the Meaning of Childbirth." In Mary Jacobus, Evelyn Fox Keller, and Sally Shuttleworth, eds., *Body Politics: Women and the Discourses of Science.* New York: Routledge, 1990, pp. 113–138.
96. Jessica Mitford. *The American Way of Birth.* New York: Plume, 1993, p. 59.
97. An episiotomy is an incision from the vagina toward the anus to enlarge the opening needed for a baby to pass.
98. A later method, Ventouse, involves the use of a vacuum to extract the baby if the process has not proceeded as expected.
99. Jessica Mitford. *The American Way of Birth.* New York: Plume, 1993, p. 61; italics added.
100. Ibid., p. 143.
101. Michelle Harrison. *A Woman in Residence.* New York: Random House, 1982, p. 86.
102. www.ncbi.nlm.nih.gov/pmc/articles/PMC420176/
103. Michelle Harrison. *A Woman in Residence.* New York: Random House, 1982, p. 113.
104. Jeanne Guillemin. "Babies by Cesarean: Who Chooses, Who Controls?" In P. Brown, ed., *Perspectives in Medical Sociology.* Prospect Heights, IL: Waveland, 1989, pp. 549–558.
105. L. Silver and S. M. Wolfe. *Unnecessary Cesarean Sections: How to Cure a National Epidemic.* Washington, DC: Public Citizen Health Research Group, 1989.
106. Joane Kabak. "C Sections." *Newsday,* November 11, 1996.
107. www.cdc.gov/nchs/fastats/delivery.htm; www.cdc.gov/nchs/data/databriefs/db35.pdf; Denise Grady. "Caesarean Births Are at a High in U.S." *New York Times,* March 23, 2010; www.cdc.gov/fastats/delivery.htm.
108. Susan Brink. "Too Posh to Push?" *U.S. News & World Report,* August 5, 2002.
109. Randall S. Stafford. "Alternative Strategies for Controlling Rising Cesarean Section Rates." *JAMA* 263 (1990): 683–687.
110. Jeffrey B. Gould, Becky Davey, and Randall S. Stafford. "Socioeconomic Differences in Rates of Cesarean Sections." *New England Journal of Medicine* 321 (1989): 233–239; F. C. Barros, J. P. Vaughan, C. G. Victora, and S. R. Huttly. "Epidemic of Caesarean Sections in Brazil." *The Lancet* 338 (1991): 167–169.
111. Randall S. Stafford. "Alternative Strategies for Controlling Rising Cesarean Section Rates." *JAMA* 263 (1990): 683–687.

112. Although, more recently, insurance and hospital practices have led to more deaths in nursing homes or even at home.
113. Sherwin B. Nuland. *How We Die: Reflections on Life's Final Chapter.* New York: Knopf, 1994; National Center for Health Statistics. *Vital Statistics of the United States, 1992–1993, Vol. 2, Mortality, Part A.* Hyattsville, MD: Public Health Service, 1995; www.cdc.gov/nchs/data/databriefs/db118.htm; www.ncbi.nlm.nih.gov/pubmed/18043014; www.nhpco.org/sites/default/files/public/Statistics_Research/2012_Facts_Figures.pdf
114. Derek Humphry. *Final Exit: The Practicalities of Self-Deliverance and Assisted Suicide for the Dying,* 3rd ed. New York: Delta, 2002.
115. Richard A. Knox. "Doctors Accepting of Euthanasia, Poll Finds: Many Would Aid in Suicide Were It Legal." *Boston Globe,* April 23, 1998.
116. Andrea Gruneir, Vincent Mor, Sherry H. Weitzen, Rachael Truchil, Joan Teno, and Jason Roy. "Where People Die: A Multilevel Approach to Understanding Influences on Site of Death in America." *Medical Care Research and Review* 64 (2007): 351; Katie Zezima. "Home Burials Offering an Intimate Alternative, at a Lower Cost." *New York Times,* July 21, 2009.
117. Ellen Goodman. "Kevorkian Isn't Helping 'Gentle Death.'" *Newsday,* August 4, 1992.
118. Lance Morrow. "Time for the Ice Floe, Pop: In the Name of Rationality, Kevorkian Makes Dying—and Killing—Too Easy." *Time,* December 7, 1998.

Chapter 5

1. Linda Ann Treiber. "McJobs and Pieces of Flair: Linking McDonaldization to Alienating Work." *Teaching Sociology* 41 (2013): 370–376.
2. Amitai Etzioni. "McJobs Are Bad for Kids." *Washington Post,* August 1986.
3. Jerry Newman. *My Secret Life on the McJob: Lessons From Behind the Counter Guaranteed to Supersize Any Management Style.* New York: McGraw-Hill, 2007.
4. George Ritzer. "McJobs." In Rich Feller and Garry Walz, eds., *Optimizing Life Transitions in Turbulent Times: Exploring Work, Learning and Careers.* Greensboro, NC: ERIC/CASS Publications, 1996; "McJobs: McDonaldization and Its Relationship to the Labor Process." In George Ritzer, ed., *The McDonaldization Thesis.* London: Sage, 1998; there is even a scholarly book in Italian on McJobs: Filippo Di Nardo. *McJob: Il Lavoro da McDonald's Italia.* Rubbettino, 2011.
5. Dharma Raju Bathini. "Fastfood Work: McJobs in India." 3rd Biennial Conference of the Indian Academy of Management, December 2013; Pan Iianshu. "An Ethnographic Interpretation of 'McJobs' in Urban Shanghai: Insights From the Field." *Chinese Journal of Sociology* 5 (2011).
6. Anthony M. Gould. "Working at McDonald's. Some Redeeming Features of McJobs." *Work, Employment and Society* 24 (2010): 780–802.
7. Jerry Newman. *My Secret Life on the McJob: Lessons From Behind the Counter Guaranteed to Supersize Any Management Style.* New York: McGraw-Hill, 2006, p. 53.
8. Jill Lawrence. "80 Pizzas per Hour." *Washington Post,* June 9, 1996.
9. Linda Perlstein. "Software's Essay Test: Should It Be Grading?" *Washington Post,* October 13, 1998.
10. Molly Werthen. "U Can't Talk to Ur Professor Like This." *New York Times-Sunday Review,* May 14, 2017, p. 4.

11. Julia Wallace. "Dr. Denton Cooley: Star of 'The Heart Surgery Factory.'" *Washington Post*, July 19, 1980.

12. www.ng.cvz.ru

13. "Moving Right Along." *Time*, July 1, 1985, p. 44.

14. www.teleroboticsurgeons.com/davinci.htm

15. David Streitfelt. "Inside Amazon's Very Hot Warehouse." *New York Times*, September 19, 2011.

16. Spencer Soper. "Inside Amazon's Warehouse." *The Morning Call*, September 18, 2011.

17. Ester Reiter. *Making Fast Food*. Montreal: McGill-Queen's University Press, 1991, p. 85.

18. Jill Lawrence. "80 Pizzas Per Hour." *Washington Post*, June 9, 1996.

19. Susan Berfield. "Delivering a $9 Billion Empire." *Bloomberg Business Week*, March 20–26, 2017.

20. Stan Luxenberg. *Roadside Empires: How the Chains Franchised America*. New York: Viking, 1985, pp. 73–74.

21. www.washingtonpost.com/lifestyle/magazine/whos-lovin-it/2011/08/12/gIQAoOVRuJ_story.html

22. Ibid.

23. Stan Luxenberg. *Roadside Empires: How the Chains Franchised America*. New York: Viking, 1985, p. 80.

24. Ibid., pp. 84–85.

25. Robin Leidner. *Fast Food, Fast Talk: Service Work and the Routinization of Everyday Life*. Berkeley: University of California Press, 1993, p. 60.

26. Stuart Flexner. *I Hear America Talking*. New York: Simon & Schuster, 1976, p. 142.

27. Frederick W. Taylor. *The Principles of Scientific Management*. New York: Harper & Row, 1947, p. 42.

28. Ibid., p. 138.

29. Iver Peterson. "Let That Be a Lesson: Rutgers Bumps a Well-Liked but Little-Published Professor." *New York Times*, May 9, 1995.

30. http://docear.org/papers/Google%20Scholar's%20Ranking%20Algorithm%20—%20An%20Introductory%20Overview%20—%20preprint.pdf

31. http://code.google.com/p/citations-gadget/

32. Ibid.

33. Kenneth Cooper. "Stanford President Sets Initiative on Teaching." *Washington Post*, March 3, 1991, p. A12.

34. Ibid.

35. Dennis Hayes and Robin Wynyard. "Introduction." In Dennis Hayes and Robin Wynyard, eds., *The McDonaldization of Higher Education*. Westport, CT: Bergin & Garvey, 2002, p. 11.

36. An example of hundreds of DRGs is DRG 236, "Fractures of Hip and Pelvis." A set amount is reimbursed by Medicare for medical procedures included under that heading and all other DRGs.

37. Dan Colburn. "Unionizing Doctors: Physicians Begin Banding Together to Fight for Autonomy and Control Over Medical Care." *Washington Post/Health*, June 19, 1985.

38. Sports are not alone in this; the political parties have shortened and streamlined their conventions to accommodate the needs and demands of television.

39. Scott Cacciola. "Democracy. It Turns Out, Suits the Warriors Just Fine." *New York Times*, May 22, 2017.

40. Allen Guttman. *From Ritual to Record: The Nature of Modern Sports*. New York: Cambridge University Press, 1978, p. 47.

41. Ibid., p. 51.

42. www.basketbalprospectus.com

43. Michael Powell. "The Home Run Explosion Is Not Exactly Beyond Suspicion." *New York Times*, September 22, 2017, pp. B8, B11.

44. For those unfamiliar with baseball, a designated hitter is one of a team's starting players and takes a regular turn at bat throughout a game. A pinch hitter comes in during a game and bats for one of the players in the game. Pinch hitters almost always get only that one turn at bat during the game.

45. However, specialization in baseball has more than compensated for this, and it is undoubtedly the case that people now see more rather than less use of relief pitchers. Indeed, there are now very specialized relief roles—the "long reliever" who comes in early in the game, the "closer" who finishes off a game in which his team is ahead, and relievers who specialize in getting out left- or right-handed batters.

46. Filip Bondy. "Tape-Measure Blasts, but Forget the Tape." *New York Times* June 25, 2017.

47. Ibid, p. SP3.

48. www.cbc.ca/archives/categories/sports/exploits/extreme-sports-faster-riskier-more-outra geous/topic—extreme-sports-faster-riskier-more-outrageous.html

49. Carl Schoettler. "Examining the Pull of the Poll." *Sun* (Baltimore), October 11, 1998.

50. Kathleen Jamieson. *Eloquence in an Electronic Age: The Transformation of Political Speechmaking*. New York: Oxford University Press, 1988, p. 11.

51. Ibid.; see also Marvin Kalb. "TV, Election Spoiler." *New York Times*, November 28, 1988.

52. www.youtube.com/profile? user=BarackObamadotcom#g/u

Chapter 6

1. Leidner reports that employees are encouraged to vary the process in order to reduce the customers' feelings of depersonalization. But at the franchise in which she worked, limits were placed on even this.

2. Robin Leidner. *Fast Food, Fast Talk: Service Work and the Routinization of Everyday Life*. Berkeley: University of California Press, 1993, p. 25.

3. Ibid.

4. Harrison M. Trice and Janice M. Beyer. *The Cultures of Work Organizations*. Englewood Cliffs, NJ: Prentice Hall, 1993.

5. Mary-Angie Salva-Ramirez. "McDonald's: A Prime Example of Corporate Culture." *Public Relations Quarterly*, December 22, 1995.

6. www.washingtonpost.com/lifestyle/magazine/whos-lovin-it/2011/08/12/gIQAoOVRuJ_story.html

7. Robin Leidner. *Fast Food, Fast Talk: Service Work and the Routinization of Everyday Life*. Berkeley: University of California Press, 1993, p. 82.

8. Ibid.

9.   Ibid., pp. 220, 230.

10. Ibid.

11. I will have more to say about this aspect of McDonaldization in Chapter 7.

12. www.aboutmcdonalds.com/mcd/corporate_careers/training_and_development/ hamburger_university/our_faculty.html; Dick Schaaf. "Inside Hamburger University." *Training*, December 1994, pp. 18–24.

13. Robin Leidner. *Fast Food, Fast Talk: Service Work and the Routinization of Everyday Life.* Berkeley: University of California Press, 1993, p. 58.

14. Ibid., pp. 107, 108.

15. Elspeth Probyn. "McIdentities: Food and the Familial Citizen." *Theory, Culture and Society* 15 (1998): 155–173.

16. Robin Leidner. *Fast Food, Fast Talk: Service Work and the Routinization of Everyday Life.* Berkeley: University of California Press, 1993, p. 10.

17. http://wdw.disneycareers.com/en/working-here/the-disney-look

18. Lynn Darling. "On the Inside at Parks à la Disney." *Washington Post*, August 28, 1978.

19. Ibid.

20. Andrew Beyer. "Lukas Has a Franchise on Almighty Dollar." *Washington Post,* August 8, 1990; italics added.

21. Richard Edwards. *Contested Terrain: The Transformation of the Workplace in the Twentieth Century.* New York: Basic Books, 1979.

22. Erik Brynjolfsson and Andrew McAfee. *Race Against the Machine: How the Digital Revolution Is Accelerating Innovation, Driving Productivity, and Irreversibly Transforming Employment and the Economy.* Kindle Books, 2011.

23. Frederick W. Taylor. *The Principles of Scientific Management.* New York: Harper & Row, 1947, p. 59.

24. Henry Ford. *My Life and Work.* Garden City, NY: Doubleday, 1922, p. 103.

25. Robin Leidner. *Fast Food, Fast Talk: Service Work and the Routinization of Everyday Life.* Berkeley: University of California Press, 1993, p. 105.

26. Richard Edwards. *Contested Terrain: The Transformation of the Workplace in the Twentieth Century.* New York: Basic Books, 1979.

27. Jerry Newman. *My Secret Life on the McJob: Lessons From Behind the Counter Guaranteed to Supersize Any Management Style.* New York: McGraw-Hill, 2007, p. 52.

28. http://wearemjr.com/2011/06/06/the-burger-that-ate-britain/

29. Michael Lev. "Raising Fast Food's Speed Limit." *Washington Post,* August 7, 1991.

30. Ray Kroc. *Grinding It Out.* New York: Berkeley Medallion, 1977, pp. 131–132.

31. Eric A. Taub. "The Burger Industry Takes a Big Helping of Technology." *New York Times,* October 8, 1998.

32. William R. Greer. "Robot Chef's New Dish: Hamburgers." *New York Times,* May 27, 1987.

33. Ibid.

34. Michael Lev. "Taco Bell Finds Price of Success (59 cents)." *New York Times,* December 17, 1990.

35. Calvin Sims. "Robots to Make Fast Food Chains Still Faster." *New York Times,* August 24, 1988.

36. Stacy Torres. "Save America's Cashiers." *New York Times* June 23, 2017, p. A25.

37. Ibid.

38. Chuck Murray. "Robots Roll From Plant to Kitchen." *Chicago Tribune–Business,* October 17, 1993.

39. Eric A. Taub. "The Burger Industry Takes a Big Helping of Technology." *New York Times,* October 8, 1998.

40. www.kueducation.com/us

41. Ibid.

42. www.kindercare.com/about

43. "The McDonald's of Teaching." *Newsweek,* January 7, 1985.

44. http://www.sylvanlearning.com/locations

45. "The McDonald's of Teaching." *Newsweek,* January 7, 1985.

46. Tressie McMillan-Cottom. *Lower Ed: The Troubling Rise of For-Profit College in the New Economy.* New York: New Press, 2017.

47. William Stockton. "Computers That Think." *New York Times Magazine,* December 14, 1980.

48. Bernard Wysocki Jr. "Follow the Recipe: Children's Hospital in San Diego Has Taken the Standardization of Medical Care to an Extreme." *Wall Street Journal,* April 22, 2003.

49. Virginia A. Welch. "Big Brother Flies United." *Washington Post–Outlook,* March 5, 1995.

50. Ibid.

51. www.stopjunkcalls.com/convict.htm

52. Gary Langer. "Computers Reach Out, Respond to Human Voice." *Washington Post,* February 11, 1990.

53. Carl H. Lavin. "Automated Planes Raising Concerns." *New York Times,* August 12, 1989.

54. Jerry Newman. *My Secret Life on the McJob: Lessons From Behind the Counter Guaranteed to Supersize Any Management Style.* New York: McGraw-Hill, 2007, p. 21. However, Newman found that there was much greater variation from store to store on personnel procedures (e.g., the hiring, training, and motivating of employees).

55. Aaron Bobrow-Strain. *White Bread: A Social History of the Store-Bought Loaf.* Boston: Beacon Press, 2012.

56. William Serrin. "Let Them Eat Junk." *Saturday Review,* February 2, 1980.

57. www.fishfarming.com

58. Juliet Eilperin. "Farm-Fresh Fish—With a Catch; Acquaculture Boom Raises Concerns." *Washington Post,* September 20, 2009; Cornelia Dean, "Rules Guiding Fish Farming in the Gulf Are Readied." *New York Times,* September 4, 2009; Martha Duffy. "The Fish Tank on the Farm." *Time,* December 3, 1990.

59. Peter Singer. *Animal Liberation: A New Ethic for Our Treatment of Animals.* New York: Avon, 1975.

60. Ibid., pp. 96–97.

61. Ibid., pp. 105–106.

62. Ibid., p. 123.

Chapter 7

1. Negative effects other than the ones discussed here, such as racism and sexism, cannot be explained by this process. See Ester Reiter. *Making Fast Food.* Montreal: McGill-Queen's University Press, 1991, p. 145.

2. As they are to the critical theorists. See, for example, Martin Jay. *The Dialectical Imagination.* Boston: Little, Brown, 1973.

3. Julie Jargon. "McD's Service Stalls at Drive-Thru." *Crain's Chicago Business,* January 2, 2006.

4. www.qsrmagazine.com/reports/drive-thru-performance-study

5. Julie Jargon. "McD's Service Stalls at Drive-Thru." *Crain's Chicago Business,* January 2, 2006.

6. Ibid.

7. Mike Comerford. "The Forbidden Kitchen Technology and Testing Help: McDonald's Grow Around the Globe." *Chicago Daily Herald-Business,* December 11, 2006.

8. http://nerdynerdnerdz.com/2228/mcdonalds-restaraunts-launch-new-drive-thru-tablets/

9. Michael Schrage. "The Pursuit of Efficiency Can Be an Illusion." *Washington Post,* March 20, 1992.

10. Richard Cohen. "Take a Message—Please!" *Washington Post Magazine,* August 5, 1990, p. 5.

11. Peter Perl. "Fast Is Beautiful." *Washington Post Magazine,* May 24, 1992.

12. Mark Bittman. "Is Junk Food Really Cheaper?" *New York Times Sunday Review,* September 25, 2011.

13. http://opinionator.blogs.nytimes.com/2011/02/22/how-to-make-oatmeal-wrong/?emc=etal

14. Melanie Warner. "Salads or No: Cheap Burgers Revive McDonald's." *New York Times,* April 19, 2006.

15. Bob Garfield. "How I Spent (and Spent and Spent) My Disney Vacation." *Washington Post/Outlook,* July 7, 1991.

16. Ibid.

17. Arlie Russell Hochschild. *The Managed Heart.* Berkeley, CA: University of California Press, 1983.

18. Ester Reiter. *Making Fast Food.* Montreal: McGill-Queen's University Press, 1991, p. 95.

19. Jill Smolowe. "Read This!!!!" *Time,* November 26, 1990.

20. Michael Schrage. "Personalized Publishing: Confusing Information With Intimacy." *Washington Post,* November 23, 1990.

21. Mark A. Schneider. *Culture and Enchantment.* Chicago: University of Chicago Press, 1993, p. ix. Weber derived this notion from Friedrich Schiller.

22. Hans Gerth and C. Wright Mills. "Introduction." In Hans Gerth and C. Wright Mills, eds., *From Max Weber.* New York: Oxford University Press, 1958, p. 51.

23. Mark A. Schneider. *Culture and Disenchantment.* Chicago: University of Chicago Press, 1993, p. ix.

24. For an argument against this thesis, one that sees this disenchantment as a myth, see, Jason A. Josephson-Storm. *The Myth of Disenchantment: Magic, Modernity, and the Birth of the Human Sciences.* Chicago: University of Chicago Press, 2017.

25. Virginia Stagg Elliott. "Fast-Food Sellers Under Fire for Helping Supersize People." *American Medical News,* April 21, 2003.

26. Mark Bittman. "Is Junk Food Really Cheaper?" *New York Times Sunday Review,* September 25, 2011.

27. Jeremy Laurance. "Slow Killer on the March." *Toronto Star,* March 4, 2006.

28. David A. Alter and Karen Eny. "The Relationship Between the Supply of Fast-Food Chains and Cardiovascular Outcomes." *Canadian Journal of Public Health* 96 (May 2001):

173–177; Sharon Kirkey. "Nutrition: New Study Links Fast-Food Spots, Death Rates." *National Post,* May 12, 2005.

29. Maryellen Spencer. "Can Mama Mac Get Them to Eat Spinach?" In Marshall Fishwick, ed., *Ronald Revisited: The World of Ronald McDonald.* Bowling Green, OH: Bowling Green University Press, 1983, pp. 85–93.

30. Donald J. Hernandez and Evan Charney, eds. *From Generation to Generation: The Health and Well-Being of Children in Immigrant Families.* Washington, DC: National Academy Press, 1998.

31. Rachel Abramowitz. "Disney Loses Its Appetite for Happy Meal Tie-Ins." *Los Angeles Times,* May 8, 2006. However, McDonald's restaurants will remain open in Disney parks, and there is the possibility of adult cross-promotions in the future.

32. Patty Lanoue Stearns. "Double-Sized Fast Foods Means Double the Trouble." *Pittsburgh Post-Gazette,* October 10, 1996.

33. www.mcdonalds.com/us/en/full_menu_explorer.html

34. http://www.bk.com/cms/en/us/cms_out/digital_assets/files/pages/Nutrition%20MARCH%202014.pdf

35. http://opinionator.blogs.nytimes.com/2011/02/22/how-to-make-oatmeal-wrong/?emc=etal

36. Ibid.

37. Ibid.

38. Ibid.

39. "At 42, Ronald McDonald Reborn as Fitness Fanatic." *Charleston Daily Mail,* June 10, 2005.

40. Regina Schrambling. "The Curse of Culinary Convenience." *New York Times,* September 10, 1991.

41. Ibid.

42. "*E. coli* Outbreak Forces Closure of Meat Plant." *Independent* (London), August 22, 1997.

43. Erin Allday. "Technology, Eating Habits Help to Spread *E. coli*." *San Francisco Chronicle,* September 23, 2006.

44. http://abcnews.go.com/GMA/HealthyLiving/coli-spinach-salad-safe/story?id=9034833

45. www.awkolaw.com/poisoning/taco-bell/; www.nytimes.com/2006/12/05/nyregion/05coli.html?pagewanted=all; www.foodsafetynews.com/2014/05/raw-clover-sprouts-linked-to-e-coli-illness-outbreak-in-washington-and-idaho/; www.kirotv.com/news/news/e-coli-outbreak-linked-raw-clover-sprouts-served-j/nf476/

46. Sanford E. DeVoe. "Big Mac, Thin Wallet." *New York Times Sunday Review,* June 1, 2014; Chen Bo-Zhong and Sanford E. DeVoe. "You Are How You Eat: Fast Food and Impatience." *Psychological Science* 21 (2010): 619–622.

47. www.worldwatch.org/node/5443

48. Arthur Beesley. "China's Diet Revolution Threatens the Environment." *Irish Times,* December 28, 2006.

49. Bill Bell Jr. "Environmental Groups Seeking Moratorium on New or Expanded 'Animal Factories.'" *St. Louis Post-Dispatch,* December 4, 1998.

50. Tim O'Brien. "Farming: Poison Pens." *Guardian* (London), April 29, 1998.

51. Olivia Wu. "Raising Questions: Environmentalists Voice Concerns Over Booming Aquaculture Industry." *Chicago Tribune,* September 9, 1998; Colin Woodard. "Fish Farms Get Fried for Fouling." *Christian Science Monitor,* September 9, 1998.
52. Timothy Egan. "In Land of French Fry, Study Finds Problems." *New York Times,* February 7, 1994.
53. Max Boas and Steve Chain. *Big Mac: The Unauthorized Story of McDonald's.* New York: E. P. Dutton, 1976.
54. Al Gore. *An Inconvenient Truth: The Planetary Emergency of Global Warming and What We Can Do About It.* New York: Rodale Press, 2006.
55. In many areas, there has been a simultaneous increase in reasonably authentic ethnic restaurants.
56. "The Grand Illusion." *The Economist,* June 5, 1999.
57. Ellen Goodman. "Fast-Forwarding Through Fall." *Washington Post,* October 5, 1991. There is another irrationality here. Those who buy things through catalogs find that their deliveries are often late or they never arrive at all. Said the president of the Better Business Bureau of Metropolitan New York, "With mail order, the biggest problem is delivery and delay in delivery." See Leonard Sloane. "Buying by Catalogue Is Easy: Timely Delivery May Not Be." *New York Times,* April 25, 1992.
58. George Ritzer. *The Globalization of Nothing,* 2nd ed. Thousand Oaks, CA: Sage, 2007.
59. www.washingtonpost.com/lifestyle/magazine/whos-lovin-it/2011/08/12/gIQAoOVRuJ_story.html
60. Robin Leidner. *Fast Food, Fast Talk: Service Work and the Routinization of Everyday Life.* Berkeley: University of California Press, 1993, p. 30.
61. Bob Garfield. "How I Spent (and Spent and Spent) My Disney Vacation." *Washington Post/Outlook,* July 7, 1991; italics added.
62. Ray Oldenburg. *The Great Good Place.* New York: Paragon, 1987.
63. One exception to the general rule that diners do not linger is the tendency for retirees to use McDonald's as a social center, especially over breakfast or coffee. Some McDonald's restaurants even allow seniors to conduct bingo games.
64. Sarah Maslin Nir. "The Food May Be Fast, but These Customers Won't Be Rushed." *New York Times,* January 28, 2014.
65. William R. Mattox Jr. "The Decline of Dinnertime." *Ottawa Citizen,* April 30, 1997.
66. Nicholas von Hoffman. "The Fast-Disappearing Family Meal." *Washington Post,* November 23, 1978, p. C4.
67. www.nytimes.com/2009/05/27/dining/27text.html? pagewanted=all; www.dailymail.co.uk/news/article-2049255/Switch-TVs-computers-improve-family-life-say-experts.html
68. Margaret Visser. "A Meditation on the Microwave." *Psychology Today* 23 (December 1989): 38–42.
69. Ibid., p. 38.
70. "The Microwave Cooks Up a New Way of Life." *Wall Street Journal,* September 19, 1989.
71. Margaret Visser. "A Meditation on the Microwave." *Psychology Today* 23 (December 1989): 38–42.
72. Ibid., p. 42.

73. Peggy Gisler and Marge Eberts. "Reader Disagrees With Advice for Mom Too Tired to Read." *Star Tribune* (Minneapolis), July 3, 1995.

74. Doug Mann. "Will You Have Fries With Your Metaphysics? The McDonaldization of Higher Learning May Make People Feel Good, but It Is Death to Education." *London Free Press* (Ontario), February 19, 2005; Dennis Hayes. "Diploma? Is That With Fries?" *The Times Educational Supplement,* June 10, 2005.

75. Tamar Lewin. "Online Enterprises Gain Foothold as Path to a College Degree." *New York Times,* August 25, 2011.

76. Ibid., p. A18.

77. http//about.coursera.org

78. Tamar Lewin. "College of Future Could be Come One, Come All." *New York Times,* November 19, 2012.

79. Ibid.

80. Mitchell Duneier. *Sidewalk.* New York: Farrar, Straus and Giroux, 2000.

81. Tamar Lewin. "College of the Future Could Be Come One, Come All." *New York Times,* November 19, 2012.

82. Gary Wilkinson. "McSchools for McWorld? Mediating Global Pressures With a McDonaldizing Education Policy Response." In George Ritzer, ed., *McDonaldization: The Reader,* 3rd ed. Thousand Oaks, CA: Sage, 2010: 149–157.

83. Ibid, p. 157.

84. Tamar Lewin. "Students Rush to Web Classes, But Profits May Be Much Later." *New York Times,* January 7, 2013.

85. Ibid.

86. Ibid.

87. Ibid.

88. Jerry Useem. "B-School, Disrupted." *New York Times: Sunday Business,* June 1, 2014.

89. www.uapd.com

90. Kris Hundley. "The Inpatient Physician." *St. Petersburg Times,* July 26, 1998.

91. Sherwin B. Nuland. *How We Die: Reflections on Life's Final Chapter.* New York: Knopf, 1994, p. 149.

92. Philippe Aries. *The Hour of Our Death.* New York: Knopf, 1981.

93. Sherwin B. Nuland. *How We Die: Reflections on Life's Final Chapter.* New York: Knopf, 1994, p. xv; italics added.

94. Jean Baudrillard. *Symbolic Exchange and Death.* London: Sage, 1976/1993, p. 180.

95. Nancy Gibbs. "Rx for Death." *Time,* May 31, 1993.

96. Sherwin B. Nuland. *How We Die: Reflections on Life's Final Chapter.* New York: Knopf, 1994, p. 254.

97. Leidner disagrees with this, arguing that McDonald's "workers expressed relatively little dissatisfaction with the extreme routinization." See Robin Leidner. *Fast Food, Fast Talk: Service Work and the Routinization of Everyday Life.* Berkeley: University of California Press, 1993, p. 134. One could ask, however, whether this indicates a McDonaldizing society in which people, accustomed to the process, simply accept it as an inevitable part of their work.

98. Another estimate puts such turnover between 200% and 250%; see Jerry Newman. *My Secret Life on the McJob: Lessons From Behind the Counter Guaranteed to Supersize Any Management Style.* New York: McGraw-Hill, 2007, p. 167.

99. www.washingtonpost.com/lifestyle/magazine/whos-lovin-it/2011/08/12/gIQAoOVRuJ_story.html

100. Henry Ford. *My Life and Work.* Garden City, NY: Doubleday Page, 1922, pp. 105, 106.

101. Studs Terkel. *Working.* New York: Pantheon, 1974, p. 159.

102. Barbara Garson. *All the Livelong Day.* Harmondsworth, UK: Penguin, 1977, p. 88.

103. Studs Terkel. *Working.* New York: Pantheon, 1974, p. 175.

104. For a review of the literature on this issue, see George Ritzer and David Walczak. *Working: Conflict and Change,* 3rd ed. Englewood Cliffs, NJ: Prentice Hall, 1986, pp. 328–372.

105. Eric Schlosser. *Fast Food Nation: The Dark Side of the All-American Meal.* Boston: Houghton Mifflin, 2001.

106. Mary Chayko. *Superconnected: The Internet, Digital Media & Techno-Social Life.* Thousand Oaks, CA: Sage, 2017, p. 178.

107. Vic Sussman. "The Machine We Love to Hate." *Washington Post Magazine,* June 14, 1987.

108. Ibid.

109. Tanya Wenman Steel. "Have Time to Bake? What a Luxury!" *New York Times,* February 8, 1995.

110. Weber, cited in Hans Gerth and C. Wright Mills, eds. *From Max Weber.* New York: Oxford University Press, 1958, p. 128.

111. The threefold typology presented here is not exhaustive. McDonaldized systems can also be seen as sets of "monkey bars." From this perspective, the iron cage is nothing more than a playground apparatus that can become anything the people involved with it want it to be. Thus, people can make it a velvet, rubber, or iron cage, if they so desire. While there is merit to this view, it probably overestimates the power of human beings. Cages, whether they are velvet, rubber, or iron, are structures, and therefore they (and those who support them) are often resistant to efforts to modify them. See Jay Klagge. "Approaches to the Iron Cage: Reconstructing the Bars of Weber's Metaphor." *Administration & Society* 29 (1997): 63–77.

112. "Do Not Go Gentle Into That Good Night" (excerpt). By Dylan Thomas, from *The Poems of Dylan Thomas,* copyright © 1952 by Dylan Thomas. Reprinted by permission of New Directions Publishing Corp.

BIBLIOGRAPHY

Rather than repeating the citations listed in the endnotes, I would like to use this section to cite some of the major (largely) academic works that served as resources for this book. There are three categories of such resources. The first is the work of Max Weber, especially that dealing with rationalization. The second is the work of various neo-Weberians who have modified and expanded on Weber's original ideas. Finally, there is a series of works that focus on specific aspects of our McDonaldizing society.

Works by Max Weber

Economy and Society: An Outline of Interpretive Sociology, edited by Guenther Roth and Claus Wittich, translated by Ephraim Fischoff et al. Berkeley: University of California Press, 1978.

General Economic History, translated by Frank H. Knight. Mineola, NY: Dover, 1927/2003.

The Protestant Ethic and the Spirit of Capitalism, new introduction and translation by Stephen Kalberg, 3rd Roxbury ed. Los Angeles: Roxbury, 2002.

The Rational and Social Foundations of Music. Carbondale: Southern Illinois University Press, 1921/1958.

The Religion of China: Confucianism and Taoism. New York: Macmillan, 1916/1964.

The Religion of India: The Sociology of Hinduism and Buddhism. Glencoe, IL: Free Press, 1916–1917/1958.

"Religious Rejections of the World and Their Directions." In H. H. Gerth and C. W. Mills, eds., *From Max Weber: Essays in Sociology.* New York: Oxford University Press, 1915/1958, pp. 323–359.

"The Social Psychology of the World Religions." In H. H. Gerth and C. W. Mills, eds., *From Max Weber: Essays in Sociology.* New York: Oxford University Press, 1915/1958, pp. 267–301.

Works by Neo-Weberians

Rogers Brubaker. *The Limits of Rationality: An Essay on the Social and Moral Thought of Max Weber.* London: Allen & Unwin, 1984.

Randall Collins. *Weberian Sociological Theory.* Cambridge, UK: Cambridge University Press, 1985.

Randall Collins. "Weber's Last Theory of Capitalism: A Systematization." *American Sociological Review* 45 (1980): 925–942.

Arnold Eisen. "The Meanings and Confusions of Weberian 'Rationality.'" *British Journal of Sociology* 29 (1978): 57–70.

Harvey Greisman. "Disenchantment of the World." *British Journal of Sociology* 27 (1976): 497–506.

Harvey Greisman and George Ritzer. "Max Weber, Critical Theory and the Administered World." *Qualitative Sociology* 4 (1981): 34–55.

Jurgen Habermas. *The Theory of Communicative Action.* Vol. 1, *Reason and the Rationalization of Society.* Boston: Beacon, 1984.

Jason A. Josephson-Storm. *The Myth of Disenchantment: Magic Modernity and the Birth of the Human Sciences.* Chicago: University of Chicago Press, 2017.

Stephen Kalberg. "Max Weber." In George Ritzer, ed., *The Blackwell Companion to Major Social Theorists.* Oxford, UK: Blackwell, 2000, pp. 144–204.

Stephen Kalberg. *Max Weber's Comparative Historical Sociology.* Chicago: University of Chicago Press, 1994.

Stephen Kalberg. "Max Weber's Types of Rationality: Cornerstones for the Analysis of Rationalization Processes in History." *American Journal of Sociology* 85 (1980): 1145–1179.

Stephen Kalberg. "The Rationalization of Action in Max Weber's Sociology of Religion." *Sociological Theory* 8 (1990): 58–84.

Donald Levine. "Rationality and Freedom: Weber and Beyond." *Sociological Inquiry* 51 (1981): 5–25.

Arthur Mitzman. *The Iron Cage: An Historical Interpretation of Max Weber,* with a new introduction by the author, preface by Lewis A. Coser. New Brunswick, NJ: Transaction Books, 1985.

Wolfgang Mommsen. *The Age of Bureaucracy.* New York: Harper & Row, 1974.

George Ritzer. "Professionalization, Bureaucratization and Rationalization: The Views of Max Weber." *Social Forces* 53 (1975): 627–634.

George Ritzer and Terri LeMoyne. "Hyperrationality." In George Ritzer, ed., *Metatheorizing in Sociology.* Lexington, MA: Lexington Books, 1991, pp. 93–115.

George Ritzer and David Walczak. "Rationalization and the Deprofessionalization of Physicians." *Social Forces* 67 (1988): 1–22.

Guenther Roth and Reinhard Bendix, eds. *Scholarship and Partisanship: Essays on Max Weber.* Berkeley: University of California Press, 1971.

Lawrence Scaff. *Fleeing the Iron Cage: Culture, Politics, and Modernity in the Thought of Max Weber.* Berkeley: University of California Press, 1989.

Wolfgang Schluchter. *The Rise of Western Rationalism: Max Weber's Developmental History*, translated, with an introduction, by Guenther Roth. Berkeley: University of California Press, 1981.

Mark A. Schneider. *Culture and Enchantment.* Chicago: University of Chicago Press, 1993.

Alan Sica. *Weber, Irrationality and Social Order.* Berkeley: University of California Press, 1988.

Ronald Takaki. *Iron Cages: Race and Culture in 19th-Century America*, rev. ed. New York: Oxford University Press, 2000.

Works on Various Aspects of a McDonaldizing Society

Mark Alfino, John Caputo, and Robin Wynyard, eds. *McDonaldization Revisited.* Westport, CT: Greenwood, 1998.

Benjamin Barber. *Consumed: How Markets Corrupt Children, Infantilize Adults, and Swallow Citizens Whole.* New York: Norton, 2007.

Benjamin Barber. *Jihad vs. McWorld.* New York: Times Books, 1995.

Zygmunt Bauman. *Modernity and the Holocaust.* Ithaca, NY: Cornell University Press, 1989.

Daniel Bell. *The Coming of Post-industrial Society: A Venture in Social Forecasting*, special anniversary edition, with a new foreword by the author. New York: Basic Books, 1999.

Max Boas and Steve Chain. *Big Mac: The Unauthorized Story of McDonald's.* New York: E. P. Dutton, 1976.

Aaron Bobrow-Strain. *White Bread: A Social History of the Store-Bought Loaf.* Boston: Beacon Press, 2012.

Daniel J. Boorstin. *The Image: A Guide to Pseudo-Events in America*, with a new foreword by the author and an afterword by George F. Will, 25th anniversary edition. New York: Atheneum, 1987.

Pierre Bourdieu. *Distinction: A Social Critique of the Judgment of Taste.* Cambridge, MA: Harvard University Press, 1984.

Alan Bryman. *Disney and His Worlds.* London: Routledge, 1995.

Alan Bryman. "The Disneyization of Society." *Sociological Review* 47 (1999): 25–47.

Alan Bryman. *The Disneyization of Society.* London: Sage, 2004.

Deborah Cameron. *Good to Talk? Living in a Communication Culture.* London: Sage, 2000.

Mary Chayko. *Superconnected: The Internet, Digital Media and Techno-Social Life.* Thousand Oaks, CA: Sage, 2017.

Simon Clarke. "The Crisis of Fordism or the Crisis of Social Democracy?" *Telos* 83 (1990): 71–98.

Ben Cohen, Jerry Greenfield, and Meredith Mann. *Ben & Jerry's Double-Dip: How to Run a Values-Led Business and Make Money, Too.* New York: Fireside, 1998.

Stanley Cohen and Laurie Taylor. *Escape Attempts: The Theory and Practice of Resistance to Everyday Life,* 2nd ed. London: Routledge, 1992.

Greg Critser. *Fat Land.* Boston: Houghton Mifflin, 2004.

Thomas S. Dicke. *Franchising in America: The Development of a Business Method, 1840–1980.* Chapel Hill: University of North Carolina Press, 1992.

Robert Dirks. *Come & Get It: McDonaldization and the Disappearance of Local Food From a Central Illinois Community.* Bloomington, IL: McLean County Historical Society, 2011.

John Drane. *After McDonaldization: Mission, Ministry, and Christian Discipleship in an Age of Uncertainty.* Grand Rapids, MI: Baker Academic, 2008.

John Drane. *The McDonaldization of the Church.* London: Darton, Longman, and Todd, 2001 (a 2008 edition was published by Smyth & Helwys, Macon, GA).

John Drane. *The McDonaldization of the Church: Consumer Culture and the Church's Future.* London: Smyth and Helwys Publishers Inc., 2012.

Donna Dustin. *The McDonaldization of Social Work.* Farnham, Surrey, UK: Ashgate, 2008.

Richard Edwards. *Contested Terrain: The Transformation of the Workplace in the Twentieth Century.* New York: Basic Books, 1979.

Morten G. Ender. *American Soldiers in Iraq: McSoldiers or Innovative Professionals?* New York: Routledge, 2009.

Charles Fishman. *The Wal-Mart Effect: How the World's Most Powerful Company Really Works—And How It's Transforming the American Economy.* New York: Penguin, 2006.

Marshall Fishwick, ed. *Ronald Revisited: The World of Ronald McDonald.* Bowling Green, OH: Bowling Green University Press, 1983.

Stephen M. Fjellman. *Vinyl Leaves: Walt Disney World and America.* Boulder, CO: Westview, 1992.

James T. Flink. *The Automobile Age.* Cambridge, MA: MIT Press, 1988.

Henry Ford. *My Life and Work.* Garden City, NY: Doubleday, Page, 1922.

Thomas L. Friedman. *The Lexus and the Olive Tree,* rev. ed. New York: Farrar, Straus, Giroux, 2000.

Thomas L. Friedman. *The World Is Flat: A Brief History of the 21st Century.* New York: Farrar, Strauss, Giroux, 2005.

Herbert J. Gans. *The Levittowners: Ways of Life and Politics in a New Suburban Community,* with a new preface by the author. New York: Columbia University Press, 1967/1982.

Barbara Garson. *All the Livelong Day: The Meaning and Demeaning of Routine Work,* rev. and updated ed. New York: Penguin, 1994.

Steven L. Goldman, Roger N. Nagel, and Kenneth Preiss. *Agile Competitors and Virtual Organizations: Strategies for Enriching the Customer.* New York: Van Nostrand Reinhold, 1995.

Richard E. Gordon, Katharine K. Gordon, and Max Gunther. *The Split-Level Trap.* New York: Gilbert Geis, 1960.

Roger Gosden. *Designing Babies: The Brave New World of Reproductive Technology.* New York: Freeman, 1999.

Harold Gracey. "Learning the Student Role: Kindergarten as Academic Boot Camp." In Dennis Wrong and Harold Gracey, eds., *Readings in Introductory Sociology.* New York: Macmillan, 1967.

Allen Guttmann. *From Ritual to Record: The Nature of Modern Sports.* New York: Cambridge University Press, 1978.

Jeffrey Hadden and Charles E. Swann. *Prime Time Preachers: The Rising Power of Televangelism.* Reading, MA: Addison-Wesley, 1981.

Jerald Hage and Charles H. Powers. *Post-Industrial Lives: Roles and Relationships in the 21st Century.* Newbury Park, CA: Sage, 1992.

David Harvey. *The Condition of Postmodernity: An Enquiry Into the Origins of Cultural Change.* Oxford, UK: Basil Blackwell, 1989.

Dennis Hayes and Robin Wynyard, eds. *The McDonaldization of Higher Education.* Westport, CT: Bergin & Garvey, 2002.

Dennis Hayes, ed. *Beyond McDonaldization: Visions of Higher Education.* London: Routledge, 2017.

Elif Izberk-Bilgin and Aaron Ahuvia. "eBayization." In George Ritzer, ed., *McDonaldization: The Reader,* 3rd ed. Thousand Oaks, CA: Sage, 2010.

Bridgett Jackson. *Drive Thru Teachers: The McDonaldization of the Classroom Teacher.* Suwanee, GA: Faith Books and More, 2012.

Kathleen Jamieson. *Eloquence in an Electronic Age: The Transformation of Political Speechmaking.* New York: Oxford University Press, 1988.

Robert Kanigel. *One Best Way: Frederick Winslow Taylor and the Enigma of Efficiency.* New York: Viking, 1997.

Joe L. Kincheloe. *The Sign of the Burger: McDonald's and the Culture of Power.* Philadelphia: Temple University Press, 2002.

Aliza Kolker and B. Meredith Burke. *Prenatal Testing: A Sociological Perspective.* Westport, CT: Bergin & Garvey, 1994.

William Severini Kowinski. *The Malling of America: An Inside Look at the Great Consumer Paradise.* New York: William Morrow, 1985.

Jon Krakauer. *Into Thin Air.* New York: Anchor, 1997.

Ray Kroc. *Grinding It Out.* New York: Berkeley Medallion Books, 1977.

Corby Kummer. *The Pleasures of Slow Food: Celebrating Authentic Traditions, Flavors, and Recipes.* San Francisco: Chronicle Books, 2002.

Raymond Kurzweil. *The Age of Intelligent Machines.* Cambridge, MA: MIT Press, 1990.

Fred "Chico" Lager. *Ben & Jerry's: The Inside Scoop.* New York: Crown, 1994.

Frank Lechner and John Boli, eds. *The Globalization Reader,* 2nd ed. Oxford, UK: Blackwell, 2004.

Robin Leidner. *Fast Food, Fast Talk: Service Work and the Routinization of Everyday Life.* Berkeley: University of California Press, 1993.

John F. Love. *McDonald's: Behind the Arches,* rev. ed. New York: Bantam Books, 1995.

Stan Luxenberg. *Roadside Empires: How the Chains Franchised America.* New York: Viking, 1985.

Jean-François Lyotard. *The Postmodern Condition: A Report on Knowledge.* Minneapolis: University of Minnesota Press, 1984.

Frank Mankiewicz and Joel Swerdlow. *Remote Control: Television and the Manipulation of American Life.* New York: Time Books, 1978.

Joseph A. Micheli. *The Starbucks Experience: 5 Principles for Turning Ordinary Into Extraordinary.* New York: McGraw-Hill, 2007.

Jessica Mitford. *The American Way of Birth.* New York: Plume, 1993.

Ian I. Mitroff and Warren Bennis. *The Unreality Industry: The Deliberate Manufacturing of Falsehood and What It Is Doing to Our Lives.* New York: Oxford University Press, 1993.

Lisa Napoli. *Ray and Joan: The Man Who Made the McDonald's Fortune and the Woman Who Gave It Away.* New York: Dutton, 2016.

Jerry Newman. *My Secret Life on the McJob: Lessons From Behind the Counter Guaranteed to Supersize Any Management Style.* New York: McGraw-Hill, 2007.

Sherwin B. Nuland. *How We Die: Reflections on Life's Final Chapter.* New York: Knopf, 1994.

Lauren L. O'Toole. "McDonald's at the Gym? A Tale of Two Curves." *Qualitative Sociology* 32 (2009): 75–91.

Martin Parker and David Jary. "The McUniversity: Organization, Management and Academic Subjectivity." *Organization* 2 (1995): 319–337.

Stacy Perman. *In-N-Out Burger.* New York: Collins Business, 2009.

Thomas J. Peters and Robert H. Waterman. *In Search of Excellence: Lessons From America's Best-Run Companies.* New York: Harper & Row, 1982.

Neil Postman. *Amusing Ourselves to Death: Public Discourse in the Age of Show Business.* New York: Viking, 1985.

Neil Postman. *Technopoly: The Surrender of Culture to Technology.* New York: Knopf, 1992.

Peter Prichard. *The Making of McPaper: The Inside Story of* USA TODAY. Kansas City, MO: Andrews, McMeel and Parker, 1987.

Stanley Joel Reiser. *Medicine and the Reign of Technology.* Cambridge, UK: Cambridge University Press, 1978.

Ester Reiter. *Making Fast Food: From the Frying Pan Into the Fryer,* 2nd ed. Montreal: McGill-Queen's University Press, 1997.

George Ritzer. "The McDonaldization of Society." *Journal of American Culture* 6 (1983): 100–107.

George Ritzer. *Expressing America: A Critique of the Global Credit Card Society.* Newbury Park, CA: Sage, 1995.

George Ritzer. *The McDonaldization Thesis.* London: Sage, 1998.

George Ritzer. "McDonaldization: Chicago, America, the World" (Special issue). *American Behavioral Scientist* 47 (October 2003).

George Ritzer. *The Globalization of Nothing,* 2nd ed. Thousand Oaks, CA: Sage, 2007.

George Ritzer. *Enchanting a Disenchanted World: Revolutionizing the Means of Consumption,* 3rd ed. Thousand Oaks, CA: Sage, 2010.

George Ritzer, ed. *McDonaldization: The Reader,* 3rd ed. Thousand Oaks, CA: Sage, 2010.

George Ritzer. "Prosumption: Evolution, Revolution or Eternal Return of the Same?" *Journal of Consumer Culture* (2014): 3–24.

George Ritzer. "Prosumer Capitalism." *Sociological Quarterly* 56 (2015): 413–445.

George Ritzer and Nathan Jurgenson. "Production, Consumption, Prosumption: The Nature of Capitalism in the Age of the Digital 'Prosumer.'" *Journal of Consumer Culture* 10, no. 1 (2010): 13–36.

George Ritzer, Paul Dean, and Nathan Jurgenson. "The Coming of Age of the Prosumer" (Special issue). *American Behavioral Scientist* 56, no. 4 (2012): 379–398.

George Ritzer and David Walczak. "The Changing Nature of American Medicine." *Journal of American Culture* 9 (1987): 43–51.

Roland Robertson. *Globalization: Social Theory and Global Culture.* London: Sage, 1992.

Chris Rojek. *Ways of Escape: Modern Transformations in Leisure and Travel.* London: Routledge, 1993.

Michael Ruhlman. *Grocery: The Buying and Selling of Food in America.* New York: Abrams, 2017.

Eric Schlosser. *Chew on This: Everything You Don't Want to Know About Fast Food.* Boston: Houghton Mifflin, 2007.

Eric Schlosser. *Fast Food Nation.* Boston: Houghton Mifflin, 2001.

Howard Schulz. *Pour Your Heart Into It: How Starbucks Built a Company One Cup at a Time.* New York: Hyperion, 1997.

Charles E. Silberman. *Crisis in the Classroom: The Remaking of American Education.* New York: Random House, 1970.

John Simmons. *My Sister's a Barista: How They Made Starbucks a Home Away From Home.* London: Cyan Books, 2005.

Bryant Simon. *Everything but the Coffee: Learning About America From Starbucks.* Berkeley: University of California Press, 2009.

Peter Singer. *Animal Liberation,* 2nd ed. New York: New York Review of Books, 1990.

Alfred P. Sloan Jr. *My Years at General Motors.* Garden City, NY: Doubleday, 1964.

Barry Smart, ed. *Resisting McDonaldization.* London: Sage, 1999.

C. Christopher Smith, John Pattison and Jonathan Wilson-Hartgrove, *Slow Church.* Downers Grove, IL: Inter Varsity Press, 2014.

Morgan Spurlock. *Don't Eat This Book: Fast Food and the Supersizing of America.* New York: Putnam, 2005.

Brad Stone. *The Upstarts: How Uber, Airbnb, and the Killer Companies of the New Silicon Valley Are Changing the World.* New York: Hachette, 2017.

Frederick W. Taylor. *The Principles of Scientific Management.* New York: Harper & Row, 1947.

John Vidal. *McLibel: Burger Culture on Trial.* New York: New Press, 1997.

James L. Watson, ed. *Golden Arches East: McDonald's in East Asia.* Stanford, CA: Stanford University Press, 1997.

David Wood. "Swift and Sure: McJustice for a Consumer Society." *Criminal Justice Matters* 91 (2013): 10–11.

Shoshana Zuboff. *In the Age of the Smart Machine: The Future of Work and Power.* New York: Basic Books, 1988.

INDEX

ABOUT THE AUTHOR

George Ritzer is Distinguished University Professor at the University of Maryland, where he has also been a Distinguished Scholar-Teacher and won a Teaching Excellence Award. He was awarded the Distinguished Contributions to Teaching Award by the American Sociological Association, an honorary doctorate from LaTrobe University in Australia, and the Robin Williams Lectureship from the Eastern Sociological Society. His best-known work, *The McDonaldization of Society,* has been read by hundreds of thousands of students over two decades and translated into more than a dozen languages. Ritzer is also the editor of *McDonaldization: The Reader;* and author of other works of critical sociology related to the McDonaldization thesis, including *Enchanting a Disenchanted World, The Globalization of Nothing, Expressing America: A Critique of the Global Credit Card Society,* as well as a series of best-selling social theory textbooks and *Globalization: A Basic Text.* He is the editor of the *Encyclopedia of Social Theory* (2 vols.), the *Encyclopedia of Sociology* (11 vols.; 2nd edition forthcoming), and the *Encyclopedia of Globalization* (5 vols.), and is *Founding Editor* of the *Journal of Consumer Culture.*